Praise for

THE RAVINE

"Lower [re-creates] the details of that day in Miropol . . . she succeeds with a vengeance . . . I read [the final] chapter of Lower's book — entitled 'Justice' — with deep and unshakable satisfaction."
— *New York Times Book Review*

"Every element in the photo serves as source material for Lower, [whose] investigation into an act of mass murder of individuals in the tiny Ukrainian town of Miropol in 1941 is a book of such breathtaking research, so well constructed and written, that I read its 178 pages in two sittings — and, had I started early enough, I would have done so in one."
— *Jewish Currents*

"Lower spent the better part of [a] decade researching the image's story . . . she set out to hold the perpetrators accountable while restoring the deceased's dignity and humanity — a feat she accomplished."
— *Smithsonian*

"The book is an act of calculated justice — turning the 'mass' in mass murder into the families, the people who suffered. Giving them something, however small. For me, that is its power."
— *Times* (UK)

"One photograph. That was what it took to start Wendy Lower on an incredible journey of discovery. Using her meticulous historical skills and her gift for shoe-leather investigation, she uncovers and tells a riveting story with implications for the the past and the present. *The Ravine* is a compelling read that is micro- and macrohistory at its very best."

— Deborah Lipstadt, author of National Jewish Book Award winner *History on Trial: My Day in Court with a Holocaust Denier* and *Antisemitism: Here and Now*

"*The Ravine* reads like a compelling detective novel."

— *Times Literary Supplement*

"An elegantly structured book . . . looks at a photograph that many refuse to face."

— *Tablet*

"Through her international investigation into a single photograph of the shooting of a Jewish family, Wendy Lower presents the Holocaust on the level of personal crime, uncovering the identities and stories of the victims, including the Jewish child, the killers, the neighbors, and the photographer. Seventy years after the crime, Lower, a historian dedicated to unveiling truths, solves what would otherwise have remained a 'cold case.' Her story is breathtaking."

— Father Patrick Desbois, author of National Jewish Book Award winner *The Holocaust by Bullets: A Priest's Journey to Uncover the Truth Behind the Murder of 1.5 Million Jews*

THE RAVINE

THE RAVINE

A Family, a Photograph,
a Holocaust Massacre Revealed

WENDY LOWER

MARINER BOOKS

Boston   New York

First Mariner Books edition 2022

marinerbooks.com

Library of Congress Cataloging-in-Publication Data has been applied for.
ISBN 978-0-358-62793-7 (pbk.)
ISBN 978-0-544-82871-1 (e-book)
ISBN 978-0-358-60512-6 (audiobook)

1 2021

4500844651

Illustration credits appear on page 245.

The letters of Lubomir Škrovina are reproduced courtesy of the Škrovina family.

For my parents,
James and Suzanne Lower

CONTENTS

THE RAVINE

I

THE PHOTOGRAPH

IN AUGUST 2009 I was in the archives of the United States
Holocaust Memorial Museum, searching for Nazi documentation that might lead to the prosecution of the most prominent
SS officer known to be alive in Germany at that time. This "last
Nazi" was Bernhard Frank, the former commandant of Adolf Hitler's Berghof compound in the Alps. Frank was a protégé of the SS
commander in chief, Heinrich Himmler, who was responsible for
carrying out the genocide of European Jews. In the early days of the
"Holocaust by bullets," Frank had certified orders for the first mass

shootings to include Jewish women and ensured that the details of those operations were accurately recorded. Between July and October 1941, Frank recorded the murder of more than fifty thousand Jewish men, women, and children in the fields, swamps, and ravines of Ukraine and Belarus.

As I was reading microfilmed SS police reports, Vadim Altskan, the museum's expert on Ukraine, interrupted me and asked if I had time to take a look at something. He introduced me to two young journalists from Prague who wanted to show me a photograph. According to the documentation they provided, it was taken on October 13, 1941, in Miropol, Ukraine.

At first glance, I could see from certain details that the image originated in the Holocaust: the Nazi uniforms, the wartime-era clothing of European civilians, the long-barreled wooden rifles, and a woman and a boy — relatives, perhaps a mother and son — being shot by Germans and local collaborators at the edge of a ravine. In my decades of researching the Holocaust, I had seen thousands of photographs and closely studied hundreds, looking for images that captured the killers in the act. Too many (like Bernhard Frank, who died in 2011) had gotten away with murder and lying about it under oath. If the perpetrators shown in a photograph could be identified, it could serve as incontrovertible evidence of their participation in murder. These were my impressions and thoughts within seconds of first seeing the photograph.

Although the documentary and photographic record of the Holocaust is greater than that of any other genocide, incriminating photographs like this that catch the killers in the act are rare. In fact, there are so few that I can list them here: an SS man aiming his rifle at a Jewish family fleeing in the fields of Ivanograd, Ukraine; naked Jewish men and boys being tormented in the forest near Sniatyn, Ukraine, before their execution on May 11, 1943; Jewish women and children, at the moment of death, falling into the sand dunes of Liepāja, Latvia; an execution squad firing in Tiraspol, Moldova; naked Jewish women and girls being "finished off" by local militia in Mizoch; one photograph from Ukraine with the caption "the last living seconds of the Jews (Dubno)," showing men being shot execution-style against a brick wall; another, also from Ukraine, captioned "the last Jew in Vinnytsia," showing a man kneeling before a pit with a pistol to the back of his head; Jews in Kovno (Kaunas) being bludgeoned to death by Lithuanian pogromists; and a few more without captions, apparently taken in the Baltic states or Belarus and depicting the Holocaust by bullets. Most of these images have been blown up and displayed in museum exhibitions; many are retrievable on the internet. They are few but represent the murder of millions. These iconic snapshots of the Holocaust give the false impression that such images are numerous, yet they number not many more than a dozen, and we know little, if anything, about who is in them, and even less about who took them.

What does one do upon discovering a photograph that documents a murder? Imagine, by way of comparison, that you are rummaging around in a flea market, an antique store, or the attic in your new home, and you find a photograph that shows a person being killed, with the perpetrator in full view. If the crime seems recent, occurring in your own lifetime, you would probably bring the photograph to a police station and file a report to start an investigation. But what if the crime depicted was a lynching from a century ago? Or a shooting in 1941? *The Ravine* tells the story of one photograph and its power to hold our attention, reveal a wealth of information about the Holocaust, and demand action.

I asked the journalists about the history of the photograph. Where did they find it? They explained that this photograph from Miropol had been locked in the stacks of Prague's Security Service headquarters, a former KGB-like authority in Soviet-controlled Czechoslovakia. It took the collapse of the Soviet Union in 1991 to bring to light this image of mass murder — living victims being killed together, as a family. It is astonishing evidence, clearly showing local militia shooting side by side with Germans in wartime Ukraine, where more than a million Jews were murdered in broad daylight. And, the journalists revealed, the photographer testified about this event in the 1950s, stating emphatically that the local killers were Ukrainians who knew some of the victims.

The Holocaust was a German-led attack against the Jews of Europe, and beyond. In recent decades, the vast and deep involvement of non-Germans has come into sharper relief and made *collaboration* a word as dirty as the mud and blood soiling the killers' uniforms and shoes. The collaborators pictured here were not prominent quislings, the treasonous fascist leaders in various countries who sided with Hitler. These were instead local militia who committed murder against their neighbors. Today, more than seventy years later, eastern European scholars who research and publish information about such local killers in Ukraine, Poland, Hungary, and elsewhere are often silenced, threatened, and even criminalized for dredging up the dark past of European anti-Semitism, greed, opportunism, and collective violence. The whitewashing of this historical stain can be seen in revisionist narratives, in state-controlled media, and in security classifications that lock records away in secret archives. But the evidence of local collaboration seen in this vivid crime photograph is as undeniable as the bones of murdered Jews lying in mass graves just below the surface of these eastern European countries.

As soon as I saw the photograph and held it in my hand, I wanted to break the frame around the crime scene, which kept the victims frozen in that awful moment. The photograph captures an event locked in time, but I knew it was part of a fluid situation. What preceded that moment of death, what followed, and what happened to each person visible there? Perhaps in finding the answers, I could unmask the killers and restore some kind of life and dignity to the victims.

Four men are clustered together — an armed gang in loose formation. In the background, we see the two German commanders, and in the foreground and to the right, two Ukrainian auxiliaries crowding the victims. One German, in a pressed jacket and jodhpurs, and the Ukrainian behind him, in a heavy woolen Red Army coat, have just pulled their triggers.

The victims of this massacre were brought to the edge of the pit and shot so quickly, one after another, that the multiple muzzle blasts have produced halos of smoke that are still hovering in the atmosphere. The Ukrainian's rifle is inches from the head of the woman, which is obscured in the smoke.

She is bending forward, in her polka-dot housedress, dark stockings, and Mary Jane–style leather shoes. She is holding the hand of a barefoot boy, dressed in a little tailored coat and pants, who is falling to his knees. In the foreground of the photograph a pair of men's leather booties is positioned as if someone had just taken them off, as if he used the tip of the right shoe to pry off the heel of the left one. Next to the shoes is an empty coat lying on its side, like the shell of a man's torso at rest. Fired cartridge casings, the litter of the mass murder, are scattered on the ground.

The victims are at the edge of a ravine. The woman is dying from the bullet wound to the head, pulling the boy — who is still alive — down with her into the grave. According to common Nazi protocol, bullets were not to be wasted on Jewish children. They were instead left to be crushed by the weight of their kin and suffocated in blood and the soil heaped over the bodies.

It must have been mid-morning. Rays of light entered the camera's aperture when this candid was taken, and in the developed print the contrasts are sharp: the boy's neatly cut dark hair and his stark white face; the shiny leather of a German policeman's visor, with silver insignias stamped on the cap; the polka dots that pop in the dark folds of the woman's dress. The forest backdrop looks like a canvas curtain painted with dark vertical tree trunks and blotchy branches.

This is an action shot. There is motion in the moment, in the explosion, in the tense postures and grimaces of the killers, in the cloud of smoke around the woman's head, and in the kneeling boy holding her hand. A civilian onlooker in a wool cap stands alert, ready to assist.

Mass murder requires a division of labor among a multitude of perpetrators, and in the Holocaust that combined effort cut across ethno-cultural lines. I was to learn that the photographer was a Slovakian security soldier, mobilized for the invasion and occupation of the Soviet Union in 1941 and stationed in Nazi-occupied Ukraine. Like millions of other soldiers, he got swept up in the camera craze of the 1920s and '30s, and when he was drafted, he packed his new Zeiss Ikon Contax to document historic events and foreign terrain. His biography — as I would learn after years of researching this photograph, studying his private collection (examining his camera), and meeting his family — is among the most surprising discoveries presented in this book.

The photographer stands about twenty feet from the executioners (his camera did not have zoom or telephoto lenses), while the helper (possibly an interpreter, gravedigger, or confiscator) walks or stands near him without any expression of alarm; he does not look at the camera. It seems that the photographer is permitted to be there, perhaps as part of the cordon of guards, and is openly snapping pictures at eye level or waist level. The photographer knows what he's doing—the image is clear and composed. It even follows photography's basic "rule of thirds" in the positioning of the main panels: the ravine, the dying victims, and the killers. If this photograph had been taken in a clandestine manner (or snapped by an amateur), it might be off-kilter or unfocused, perhaps showing an obstruction such as the seam of a coat pocket or a part of the photographer's hand.

Looking at this picture, we take on the photographer's view of the event as he stands among the perpetrators, collaborators, and other onlookers, probably including more Jewish victims waiting to be killed. We see what this close-up observer wished to capture. He opened the lens, adjusted the dial to set the aperture, pointed the camera, and pressed the button. The photograph encapsulates the sensory and the documentary, the aesthetic and the evidentiary —elements elucidated by cultural critics of photography. One might even argue that it includes the pornographic, as the camera is aimed, like the German and Ukrainian guns, at the woman and child.

The photographer, along with the Germans and Ukrainians, partakes in the disturbing intimacy of the violence. Perpetrators stand shoulder to shoulder, close to the victims. They touch the woman with their hands and the ends of their guns. Here we see genocide at its extreme: the final moment when uniformed gangs of men like this one annihilate women and children.

At the center of the image is what is left of a Jewish family and community in Miropol, a historical Jewish shtetl west of Kiev (now Kyiv). Perhaps the photograph is intended to document the end of the future of Jewry as a matrilineal "race" in Europe. The victims are clothed and will be buried en masse, a violation of Jewish religious rites. They are killed in small family groups and therefore see and feel the suffering of loved ones, including parents viewing the destruction of their own children. This is perhaps the most extreme assault that the genocidaire inflicts. What thoughts ran through this mother's mind as she was forced to march to this site with her child? Did the boy try to run away, shocked and confused? Was the father killed first, before their eyes?

This remnant of a family was among the millions who were wiped off the map of Europe during the Holocaust, most of them within an eighteen-month period, from the summer of 1941 to the end of 1942. During the war, the black earth of Ukraine, the historical heartland of Jewish life in the Russian Empire, was scorched to a smoking moonscape. Every fourth Jewish victim murdered in the Holocaust was from Ukraine (based on today's borders). According to the Central Database of Shoah Victims' Names kept by Yad Vashem, the Holocaust remembrance center in Jerusalem, about 50 percent of the Jews who were mostly gunned down in the ravines, marshes, forests, ghettos, and open fields of Ukraine have not been identified. Perhaps the image that had come into my hand was the only trace remaining of these particular persons' existence and what happened to them. What does one do with an image of the missing missing, whose lives and fates have not been registered by anyone?

The dominant scholarly and popular ways of accounting for and memorializing the Jewish victims are based on different scales: individual lives (names) and the larger aggregate (six million). As an example of the former, upon entering the United States Holocaust Memorial Museum, visitors receive an identity card giving the biographical details of one victim. Also, each year, individual names are read aloud on Yom HaShoah, the Days of Remembrance of Victims of the Holocaust. By contrast, national commemorations treat the victims as much larger entities — whole population figures, such as Poland's three million and Kiev's 33,771 who were shot in the ravine at Babi Yar on September 29–30, 1941.

But what about the loss of a family? It was the most intimate social unit holding communities together. Was not the murder of an entire family another dimension of the horror and destruction that define genocide?

The photographic documentation of the Holocaust is especially rich because the events coincided with the mass production and consumption of the small handheld camera. No longer confined to an indoor studio and prearranged sittings, photography became a widespread cultural and social practice, a new means of mass communication that ushered in today's visual age. Older stationary cameras had to be secured on a tripod or other support and required a five- to twenty-second exposure for each photograph — and patience on the part of the subject, who had to pose motionless. By contrast, the new portable cameras captured people in action. The Leica camera was patented in 1925, and the Zeiss Ikon Contax (the brand owned by the Miropol photographer) was introduced in 1933. Across Europe, Jews became skilled photographers and developed commercial studios, which flourished particularly during the mass emigration of Jews from tsarist Russia, after the pogroms of the late nineteenth century. The popular carte de visite (a calling card with the subject's image printed on one side) could be kept as a visual memento of those who had emigrated or be mailed to relatives abroad. Like many former shtetls in eastern Europe, Miropol had a local studio run by a Jewish family who specialized in family portraits.

Hobby photography was popular, and photojournalism was coming into its own as a profession. In the interwar era, the boom in photography transformed many realms of public life — advertising, political campaigns, books and other print media, museum exhibitions, ethnographic research and publications, and avant-garde movements in art, such as socialist realism and expressionism. Flash-bulbing journalists became a fixture at red-carpet events, and placards pasted on street corners and in mass transit systems featured images captured by the camera. Photography also adorned private homes in the form of personal albums and framed images of loved ones. All of this public and private imagery revolutionized how ordinary people viewed themselves, their family, their nation, and the world. Suddenly this small device, the camera, could record reality and secure one's place in it as someone who had existed (or not: a person could be cropped or airbrushed out of existence, as was common practice in Stalin's Russia). By 1939, 10 percent of the German population owned cameras. During the war, Hitler's propaganda minister, Joseph Goebbels, embedded fifteen thousand photojournalists in all theaters of the conflict, producing more than 3.5 million images.

The pocket snapshot was a common item in the soldier's knapsack. Agfa, Zeiss, and other film and camera manufacturers advertised to soldiers of the Wehrmacht (Germany's armed forces) and the SS (a racist security, policing, and military organization) that the experience of war could be captured best with the camera, especially a durable one like Voigtländer's "optical panzer." A Zeiss-Tessar campaign touted the eagle eye of the lens, "always ready to take in life's true moments." As German soldiers seized and occupied territories formerly held by the Soviet Union in 1941 and 1942, they photographed what they encountered. Perhaps they wished to document what they believed would be a military triumph over their enemies. Images of dead Jews and Soviet prisoners of war mirrored the anti-Jewish, anti-Bolshevik propaganda at home. World War II was not only the most destructive armed conflict ever; it was also the most photographed.

These years were also the peak period of Nazi mass-murder operations. When the mass killings began, in the summer of 1941, Nazi leaders forbade soldiers to take pictures of these specific events, fearing their explosive potential as counter-propaganda that could stoke resistance. The commander of the Sixth Army stationed near Miropol (in Zhytomyr, a city and the administrative center of a district of the same name) implored soldiers not to take photographs of the mass murder occurring there in August 1941. Similar bans were reissued at least five times: in September and December 1941, April 1942, and again in June and July 1944. These repeated prohibitions point to the fact that Nazi leaders were unable to control the photographing of atrocities. The orders were simply not followed. Heinrich Himmler, the Reich Leader of the SS and police, went so far as to deploy agents to confiscate negatives and prints.

In fact, the only known instance when Himmler put one of his SS officers on trial in connection with the killing of Jews had to do with such images. The verdict of the SS and police court in Munich stated in 1943 that this particular commander of the Waffen-SS (the military branch of the SS) "shall not be punished because of the actions against the Jews as such. The Jews have to be exterminated and none of the Jews that were killed is any great loss." Rather, Second Lieutenant Max Täubner was found guilty of excessive barbarism unworthy of a man in uniform; his actions included "taking tasteless and shameless pictures" (including one of a naked Jewish woman) and openly bragging about them to his wife and friends back in Germany: "By taking photographs of the incidents or having photographs taken, by having these developed in photographic shops and showing them to his wife and friends, the accused is guilty of disobedience. Such pictures could pose the gravest risks to the security of the Reich if they fell into the wrong hands [. . .]" Again, Täubner's crime was not murdering Jews, since the court affirmed their extermination. Rather, he was charged for his "barbarism" in producing and displaying atrocity photographs. His breaches of discipline and state security earned him a ten-year prison sentence. This is the only known German wartime trial of this kind.

Patriotism, anti-Semitism, lurid fascination with cruelty and death, moral outrage at witnessing genocide, and myriad other motives caused ordinary soldiers to document the spectacles of violence inflicted on Jews, Soviet POWs, resistance fighters, forced laborers, and Slavic "subhumans." The Holocaust of the Jews consisted of six million acts of murder, and the global archive of visual documentation reflects both individual victims and the scale of the genocide. It shows individuals, families, and communities in the years, months, days, and moments leading up to their deaths, and afterward as piles of corpses. We see the culmination of Nazi antiSemitic policies that forced Jews to endure conditions that necessarily caused death. Yet the act of killing is rarely portrayed. Nazi leaders suppressed images that depicted it, confiscating the most incriminating ones while employing euphemisms, such as the "Final Solution" and "Special Treatment," to allude to the brutal truth.

Photographs, if we choose to study them, open up questions and lead us down paths of discovery. There are details in the Miropol photograph that we were not supposed to witness. Some postwar theorists of photography would urge us not to look at, let alone scrutinize, the suffering of others. In 1988, when scholars and museologists deliberated over the visual content of the United States Holocaust Memorial Museum's exhibits, they explored the "question of explicit imagery including the 'pornography of murder, nudity and violence in a museum.'" The museum's creators were clear that to avoid all graphic visuals — images that elicit shock and outrage — would be to forsake the truth of Nazi evil. They did not want to display victims in a way that would further humiliate them or embarrass their families and descendants, or encourage voyeurism. They feared that images of sexual violence and nude corpses might excite erotic fantasies. Depictions of death "precisely because its meaning eludes us and because it is universal and ineluctable tit illate, fascinate, and compel attention." Viewers should not "lose sight of the fact that each of the corpses in a pile was a single, complex, multi-faceted human being with parents, families, loved ones, personal dreams and expectations and thwarted aspirations."

The cultural critic Susan Sontag argued that the shock of atrocity photography "wears off with repeated viewings." I disagree. The risk of desensitization to such images exists when we have no knowledge of their history and content. The more I learned, the more the Miropol image came to life.

One such moment occurred in October 2014. I had asked the technical support services staff at my college to create high-resolution images of the Miropol photograph. We created cutouts from it, like five puzzle pieces, each one containing a feature of the story. One showed the Germans' faces, one showed the Germans shoulder to shoulder with the Ukrainians, one showed the landscape, one the victims, and one the empty shoes. I enlarged the cutouts and printed them to study them more closely. I was looking for clues, things to place alongside postwar witness statements about the Miropol massacre in order to put these statements to the tests of veracity, probability, and logic. I focused on each piece. Did the shadows indicate the time of day? Did the clothes, such as the heavy overcoats, suggest a season? What insignia could I identify on the Germans' uniforms? Were more onlookers hidden behind the figures in the foreground or among the trees? Were the items on the ground papers or leaves? Were the victims holding anything, such as a Bible, or wearing anything of importance, such as a wedding ring?

My eyes were always drawn back to the center, to the crouching woman, and I began to wonder why she was bent over in a perpendicular angle, not buckling under or kneeling forward. And then I saw something resting on the woman's lap or being held in her right arm. It was a hazy, curved form; light was not passing through what should have been an empty space. I could make out a pair of bent knees and the translucent fabric of a dress. I started to see the faint lines of an elbow and a small head covered in a scarf. Suddenly into my view came the existence of another person, a child. I had found another soul about to be extinguished, another nameless victim of the Holocaust who was meant to be lost to us. These faint contours were the only trace of this child.

Most Holocaust photographs taken by Germans and their collaborators triumphantly document victory over Judeo-Bolshevism. These images show the victims on their way to death — waiting at deportation sites, sitting or standing solemnly among piles of clothes, being selected at the arrival ramp at Birkenau. The photographers leer sadistically at women undressing or standing in the nude. But, as the scholar Ulrich Baer astutely argues, we should not remain locked in the gaze of the onlookers. Rather, we must try our best to restore the victims as subjects, not objects, of history. In the same way, we should interrogate the motive of the photographer, the grimaces of the killers, and the forces of anti-Semitic hate that are being expelled from the ends of their guns and pistols. These things need to be investigated, exposed, and explained.

Only after the collapse of the Soviet Union was it possible to situate this Miropol image within the tens of thousands of pages of investigative material about the mass shooting and to gather dozens of accounts from those in Miropol who had access to the view we see here. They included the villagers who dug the pits, the police officers who drove this family to the edge of the pit, the perpetrators who pulled the triggers, the laborers who covered the mass grave, the forensic investigators who exhumed it in 1986, and the photographer who was haunted by this image until his death, in 2005.

In this postmodern era of research, with its millions of cataloged and digitized documents and the accessibility of sites related to historical events, I was able to draw on every extant remnant of evidence — the written, the visual, and the artifactual records of the perpetrators and their regime; the environmental and architectural landscape of the places where the victims lived and were murdered; and the generations of storytellers from Miropol and around the globe whose family trees contain severed branches dating from the Holocaust. This single photograph of the murdering of a family took me to archives, museums, living rooms, peasant huts, fields, and parks in Europe, America, and Israel.

This book is about the potential of discovery that exists if we dare look closer. It is also about the voids that exist in the history of genocide. Its perpetrators not only kill but also seek to erase the victims from written records, and even from memory. When we find one trace, we must pursue it, to prevent the intended extinction by countering it with research, education, and memorialization.

2

MIROPOL

IN THE PHOTOGRAPH Miropol is the crime scene. But to the Ukrainian men and the Jewish woman and children pictured in it, Miropol was home, a picturesque, isolated townlet located along the Sluch River. Miropol (literally, "center of the world") is not a singular place in eastern Europe. There are at least three towns by this name in Ukraine, and probably more in Russia and in Belarus. The location's layered history of Polish, Russian, and Ukrainian rule means that the town's name appears historically in different forms, in at least four languages with varying diacritics: Myropol,

Miropol, Myropil', and Miropolye. In a situation like this, the odds of pinpointing the right place in an archival search are slim. If what you are seeking does not pop up on the screen, in an index or finding aid, it can seem as if it does not exist.

Were it not for the photograph, I would have passed over Miropol in my research on Ukraine. I may have noticed the place as a spot on the map in Volhynia, a region that at one time marked the border between Polish- and Soviet-controlled Ukraine, and for over a century (1791–1917) lay at the heart of the Jewish Pale of Settlement, a restrictive area established by the Russian empress Catherine the Great in 1791. Polish nobles ruled Miropol for a longer period than the Russians or Soviets did, a fact that many have forgotten today.

In 2014, I traveled to Miropol to see if I could find the precise location shown in the photograph — it looked like a ravine — and to try to interview wartime witnesses. Nearly seventy-three years had passed since the killings in the Miropol Park. When I landed at Boryspil' airport, Kiev was once again trying to solidify its borders and stem Moscow's imperial ambitions. In the early 1990s, field research in Ukraine had been challenged mostly by the fallout from economic crises — runaway inflation, empty store shelves, a broken barter system, fuel shortages, rolling blackouts, unpredictable access to archives, and a lack of toner and paper for making copies. In 2014, I quickly realized the situation was even more dire. At the airport I was greeted by my driver, Anatoly, a refugee from Luhansk. Earlier that year he had fled the city, which had been overrun by Russian and Ukrainian separatists. Thugs had snatched him on the eve of his departure to the west. They declared him a traitor, brought him to the basement of an empty building, punched his face, and broke his ribs. He managed to escape westward with his wife and small child, looking for work, and landed in a town near Miropol. He now presented himself as an experienced chauffeur. Which he was not. We needed a screwdriver to open the car window, and I braced myself (there were no seat belts) when he turned left into a rotary and drove directly into oncoming traffic. Anatoly could not find Miropol on the map of the region where he now resided. But he needed paid work, and I needed a driver, so we continued on our journey, accompanied by my interpreter, Felix. Anatoly wanted to create common allegiance with a westerner, and he became determined to help me find the crime scene in Miropol, a peculiar assignment that perhaps distracted him from thoughts of his parents, whom he had left behind in Luhansk, and his own uncertain future.

When we arrived in Miropol with the photograph in hand, we first stopped in the central square. It was summertime and the vacant space offered no protection from the blinding sun and dust. The marketplace was not as depicted in a turn-of-the-century postcard I'd seen; over a hundred years ago it had been bustling with traders. That fin-de-siècle postcard of Miropol's center shows the commerce and architectural beauty of a bygone era: two-story stone buildings with ornamental facades, picture windows fronted by busy sidewalks.

A mid-seventeenth-century map of market towns managed by Polish nobles indicates a Jewish community had been established in Miropol. The Polish ruling class introduced the *arendia* system of landed monopolies, which combined the market town and the manorial system into a prosperous agricultural economy. The Jews were critical to the development and profitability of this system, which continued to grow for two hundred years.

A larger population of Jews migrated to Miropol in the eighteenth century, at the invitation of the Polish noble who purchased the town and was determined to make it profitable. Jews acquired the right to settle there by agreeing to many of the noble's demands. Among them was the organization of weekly bazaars and monthly fairs. Each Friday peasants streamed into the town, their carts loaded with produce and with horses and cows to sell. There were women strolling, children darting underfoot, elders in dusty caftans and black hats gesticulating, and babushkas in head scarves, clustered beside their carts and crates of apples, cucumbers, and beets. All were eager to sell and barter, and they took pride in their wares. There were bursts of laughter and rancor, handshakes and fistfights. Each week Jews and Ukrainians, as well as a minority of Poles and Russians, engaged in a lively trade in life's necessities, cultural objects, official news, and gossip.

Ukrainians and Jews had coexisted for centuries, mostly in peace, but the ties were tenuous. Despite the exchanges in the open-air marketplace and taverns, tensions existed between Jews and non-Jews. Towns like Miropol were islands in a sea of Ukrainian farmland and scattered peasant huts, but only a minuscule percentage of Jews farmed. Their religious literacy and their occupations were not valued by non-Jews as virtuous pursuits. The *dorfsgeyer* (literally, "the one who goes to the village") was the Jew who ventured out with his services and wares by foot or with a horse-drawn cart, working as tailor, carpenter, cobbler, peddler, or the dreaded tax collector.

There were too many tailors in the Pale, and most were impoverished. From the Jewish point of view, the Ukrainian majority posed a threat because of a history that could not be ignored. This Christian society could sometimes turn hostile to Jews, branding them all as Christ-killers, repressive tax collectors, greedy moneylenders, and suspicious agents of the elite Poles or Russians. Miropol had been among the towns struck by pogromists during the mid-seventeenth-century peasant rebellions and warfare among Bogdan Khmelnitsky's Cossacks, the Russians, and the Polish-Lithuanian kingdom. It is not known how much damage the town suffered in the rampages. Across the region, about fourteen thousand Jews were killed in the pogroms and warfare; some of those captured were "sold at the slave markets in Istanbul."

The decline of the shtetl coincided with the destruction of the Polish manorial system. The partitions of Poland in the late eighteenth century placed this region of Ukraine within Russian territory. With its fertile black soil, the area was at the time the most economically advanced in the tsar's expanding kingdom. The imperial government established the Jewish Pale of Settlement, restricting Jews to a swath of territory that stretched from Lithuania southward across Ukraine; the tsarina and her successors imposed an economy of extraction, draining resources from the region. A program of Russification promoted Russian culture, language, and the Orthodox Christian faith.

The accelerating decline of Jewish culture during the nineteenth and early twentieth centuries, whether through the forces of Russification, anti-Semitism, nationalism, Zionism, urbanization, or the immigration of Jews to Palestine, western Europe, and the New

World, did not go unnoticed by contemporary observers. Among them was S. Ansky, an ethnographer and the author of one of the most famous plays in Yiddish, *The Dybbuk* (1914), also known as *Between Two Worlds*. The play was adapted as a cinematic masterpiece released in 1937, and to this day it is staged around the world in Jewish communities. Remarkably, the setting for the play is Miropol. Ansky visited the town in 1912 during his mission to document and photograph a disappearing civilization, to create what he called a "portrait of the people." Ansky's research materials and the play give a rare window onto Jewish life and the spiritual, mystical world of the shtetl before the Holocaust. Jews called Miropol their holy town, in deference to G-d, the communal leaders (*kehil*), and the rhythm of life, which followed the seasons and the Jewish calendar. Time was marked by the weekly lighting of the Sabbath candles, the sharing of meals, the bazaar on Sundays, and the holy days of Yom Kippur and Passover. The diasporas of western Europe and America had not touched Miropol. Here Jews lived among Jews with relative freedom as a majority in town. Communal institutions, such as prayer houses, baths, schools, and hospitals, thrived. Ansky captures the black-and-white fabric of Jewish life among the rich and the poor, in scenes of celebratory weddings and dank cobbler's huts, although his rendering of Miropol ends in tragedy. The Dybbuk is a demon, a restless spirit that descends on the town, cleaves to the soul of a dead yeshiva student, and then possesses the student's beloved, who joins her love in death.

I had no reason to be especially nostalgic or melancholy about the vanishing shtetl as popularized by Ansky's play (also, notably, by the Yiddish author and playwright Sholem Aleichem's rendering of Avantar, and by Roman Vishniac's photographic essays). And yet, surveying Miropol's town square in 2014, I found it impossible not to feel the presence of a gutted civilization. Genocidaires think that removing a population through expulsion and mass murder will bring forth a new era of progress, even a pure utopia, for the majority. But the murderous actions of the Reich and the twentieth-century Soviet Communist experiment in the years following had failed. All I saw was poverty. Today a solitary monument, a slab of engraved granite commemorating all who died in the Great Patriotic War, stands silently in the center of the town square with few structures left to enclose it.

I had listened to and read transcripts of the videotaped testimony of Ludmilla Blekhman, the only known Jewish survivor of the Miropol massacres. She wrote of her hometown, and of this marketplace, where she first saw German soldiers in July 1941. They openly urinated in the square, because, as she recalled, "they didn't think of us as people." When I visited, the only signs of life were the plastic flowers placed at the war monument, cigarette butts, and empty vodka bottles. I looked around for any recognizable buildings. The *aptheka* (pharmacy) was still there. Behind that was the former Jewish school, closed in 1969. It had been turned into a bank and now is just an ATM. I could hear the clatter of dishes from the back kitchen of the only café remaining open in town.

From the central square, Anatoly, Felix, and I headed toward the river, drove over a small bridge, and ascended toward the forest. At a fork in the road leading to the killing site shown in the photograph, we spotted an abandoned one-story brick house, with smashed glass and bent bars on the basement windows. It looked like the former police station. Not far from this building was an abandoned Soviet military compound, standing on the hill where the Polish fortress had been located. This fortress used to tower over the town on the riverbank, surrounded by a lush park of ravines, forests, and gardens modeled on the great royal landscaping of the eighteenth and early nineteenth centuries. The fortress, still standing in 1941, was the landmark that Nazi officials and postwar witnesses cited as indicating the place where Miropol's Jews were shot.

We parked the car and started to search for the location. A hand-drawn map, which I had copied from the records of a 1986 trial against the wartime Ukrainian militia in Miropol, revealed the relative location of the mass grave to the road, river, and forest, but there was no scale to measure distances and no legend identifying special markers or points of reference. As we walked along a tree-lined road that disappeared into the horizon, we were not sure at which point we should leave the road and enter the forest toward the river, which ran parallel to the road. I kept looking at the map — a squiggly line for a river, a grouping of triangles that we assumed symbolized the forest — expecting that at some moment it would all make sense, that we would find where we were and where we needed to go. But we were lost. Anatoly, Felix, and I tried several openings into the forest; some dirt paths seemed promising at first, but then they veered off in multiple directions. If we saw a clearing, or an oddly shaped, large depression in the earth, we imagined it might be the spot but then reminded ourselves that many seasons had washed over the surfaces, while runoff had carved the soil into new patterns. Pedestrians' shortcuts and hikes through the park had turned the entire forest floor into a web of paths; to an outsider it looked like a random constellation, not a route to a destination. We gave up. We abandoned the forest and started to walk along the road, back to our car. I reassured Felix and Anatoly that the trip had still been worthwhile, though in my mind I was calculating the wasted time and expense, embarrassed about my fixation with going to Miropol just to see what was there. And then a car came speeding toward us. I moved to the roadside to avoid it, while Felix, to my surprise, waved it down.

The driver, a middle-aged woman, pulled over and cranked down her window. She saw that she was being accosted by a westerner and local guides who looked lost, or in need of something. And she wanted to help. Her grown daughter was in the backseat. They were both wearing sundresses and high heels and, they told us, were on their way to a birthday party. They were in a festive mood, so it was a bit odd to explain that we were looking for the site where the Jews of Miropol had been murdered during World War II. I knew the woman might easily be offended or feel threatened, or at least in-convenienced. Instead, without much hesitation, the older woman motioned for us to climb into the backseat. Apparently she knew of the murder site and had decided to show it to us. Her daughter was visibly annoyed — she sighed while rearranging packages to make room for us in the small car.

We drove to a place that was closer to the river than any location shown on my map. By foot, we approached a single path overgrown with stinging nettles and bushes. We paused before going into the thorny muck. But our guide navigated it, in her dress, bare legs, and high-heeled shoes, pushing back the branches for me in my jeans and sneakers. I kept my head down. There were slippery roots, broken bottles, and sharp thorns. Our eager guide looked around while marching forward, and then she stopped: "Well, here we are, this is it." I saw nothing that resembled the terrain in my photo. We stood there in silence. And then the sunlight overhead caught my attention, causing me to look upward. As I did, I traced the steep wall of a ravine, with dangling roots exposed, right up to the top. The sandy precipice above looked like the spot where the Jewish woman had stood, bent over in her polka-dot dress and holding the children.

Based on decades of researching the Holocaust in Ukraine, I assumed that the pattern of killing across the country also applied to Miropol. Before a mass shooting, male Jews and local Ukrainians were deployed to dig a pit. When ravines were available, however, the genocidaires put the natural topography to work, forcing the victims to stand at the brink of the precipice to be shot and then burying their corpses where they fell at the bottom. But in fact, here in this small town there were multiple mass graves and more than one killing site. As I later learned, this particular ravine was not the site of the killing shown in the photograph. It was, rather, where the last Jews of Miropol, "the specialists" (also known as the craftsmen, or professionals with valuable skills, including the town's dentist), had been shot in early 1942. It being winter, the ground was too hard to dig pits, so the ravine served the purpose. And Nazi schemers saw no urgent need to dynamite the walls of this ravine to conceal the crime. But I did not yet know this information.

The woman who led us to this spot knew about it because her grandmother lived in Miropol and told stories about the war, including recollections of hearing rifle fire coming from the park.

Now our happenstance guide extended her hospitality even further by offering to drive us to meet her grandmother. It would be my first interview with a witness in Miropol. The grandmother spoke about the Ukrainian policemen who had killed Jews. They were locals. And, she added, the militia knew the victims. She spoke slowly, and not in a coherent narrative; she presented her memories in random snapshots. During the interview I noticed an ornate plastic clock on the wall, a classic piece of Soviet kitsch that no longer ticked. Given the woman's age and frail condition, we were conscious of taking up her time but also unsure about exactly what time it was, since the clock's tired hands trembled back and forth. After a while we turned off our video camera, thanked the elderly woman, and said our goodbyes to this helpful family.

Before leaving town, Felix, Anatoly, and I decided to visit the Jewish cemetery, hoping that perhaps we might find a Jewish survivor, or a descendant of one, living nearby. We found hand-engraved tombstones dating back to 1896, with some showing legible bits of Hebrew prayers and family names. Many were broken up into chunks and weathered smooth. One of the few stones that remained standing was in the form of a tree stump with hacked-off branches, symbolizing the death of a child whose life had been cut short. Mixed with the rubble of the tombstones were trash and pecking chickens.

We left the cemetery through an ornate iron gate that had stood the test of time despite recurring vandalism. The cemetery was tucked behind a cluster of prewar homes on the dirt road where we had parked our car. Unlike the gutted town center, remnants of Jewish life could be seen here, in the wooden houses, with porches and doorframes that once displayed mezuzahs and welcomed customers who needed shoes repaired or clothes mended. The weathered roofs curved downward, and porches sank into the muddy earth, hunched in silence like the exhausted elderly who have endured too much to speak.

3

THE *AKTION*: THE GERMAN KILLERS

THE MIROPOL "PORTRAIT" depicts the moment of a family's final destruction. The focal point is the woman and children, and our eyes move from them to the source of the action, to the armed killers. Tracking down these shooters lent urgency to my research. They might still be alive, possibly never held to account for the murder that the photograph clearly documents. I had worked on investigations with Nazi hunters. I had sat in the courtroom in Munich as survivor witnesses and historical experts came forward and accused the collaborator Ivan Demjanjuk, a Ukrainian guard at the gassing center of Sobibor who had immigrated to the United States after the war; I knew of his misdeeds, yet he lied and shamelessly concealed his face under the rim of his baseball cap. It was not outside the realm of possibility that one or more of the perpetrators in the Miropol photo might still be apprehended. The Ukrainian killers in the photograph were young men when they shot their Jewish neighbors. And what about the Germans? Had they retired comfortably in their hometowns and suppressed the wartime past, unaware that this photograph existed and made their faces visible, and possibly recognizable? My first task was to research these German perpetrators.

The two Germans in the photograph were not elite SS men and not regular army personnel. I could see that from their uniforms, which bore no markings of the SS or the Wehrmacht. I thought at first that they might instead be regular German police officers. During the Nazi invasion of the Soviet Union, Heinrich Himmler, the commander in chief of both the elite SS and the regular police forces in Germany, mobilized tens of thousands of police from German cities to serve as both mobile and stationary security forces in Nazi-occupied territories. Some neighborhood patrolmen from Hamburg or Bremen, too old for regular combat, were deployed for this purpose. These veteran policemen were teamed with a younger cohort, many of them highly trained, Nazified career officers, and together these men served as the foot soldiers of the Holocaust. Hitler framed World War II as a *Vernichtungskrieg*, or "war of annihilation," a titanic struggle against the rising tide of Judeo-Bolshevism, which in his view threatened to sweep westward into Europe and destroy civilization. It was, according to the fearful ideas that Nazi leaders propagated among ordinary Germans, a battle for survival. And, Hitler promised, the effort, unlike the Great War, was not going to end in defeat because this time the Germans recognized who the true enemy was. The German policemen sent to eastern Europe would do their part by murdering at least 600,000 Jews.

In the history of the Holocaust, the summer of 1941 was a critical period of escalation that reached a point of no return. In a matter of weeks, mobile Nazi killing units, which had begun by shooting all adult male Jews, expanded to a "root and branch" genocide, targeting women, children, and entire families. As the eminent scholar Raul Hilberg observed, "For every echelon of the Nazi regime, the summer months of 1941 mark a transition from uncertainty to certainty: therefore, every scrap of paper dating from that time and written [by those involved] acquires basic importance." One order, dated July 11 and bearing the name of a commander of a police regiment in Belarus, specified that the shootings should take place at the outskirts of towns and villages, that photography was not permitted, and that the killing should be followed by comradely evenings "to erase the impressions of the day." Three police regiments were sent into the Soviet territories, with one unit designated for Miropol. I spent many years digging through German judicial records related to Order Police Battalion 303 (Orpo 303), the unit that swept through the region; it was attached to Himmler's Higher SS and Police Regiment South. Its members shot Jews in Miropol in September 1941 before continuing on to the ravine at Babi Yar, near Kiev. One subunit then circled back to Miropol in late September for some "mopping up" operations. A witness recalled that this time the killers brought with them a gramophone from Babi

Yar; there they had learned that playing music during the *Aktion* made it more pleasant for all.

A postwar investigation into Orpo 303 started in earnest in 1965, when the official West German agency for investigating Nazi crimes received copies of SS documents, created by Himmler's command staff, which had been housed behind the Iron Curtain in Prague's Military History Institute Archive. From these documents, the agency identified former SS men who were alive in Germany and therefore could be prosecuted. How had these SS and police records ended up in Prague, along with the Miropol photograph? Near the end of the war, Adolf Eichmann, his secretaries, and other officials in Himmler's Reich Security Main Office in Berlin had sent truckloads of classified records to SS headquarters in Prague. There, most were burned, dumped in the Vltava (Moldau) River, or placed in caves with dynamited booby traps. But some, like these SS records in Prague, were found after the war and became critical evidence of Nazi atrocities.

These documents were now in the files of a chief prosecutor in Regensburg, which is where I searched through them. They held about eighty thousand pages of wartime documents, postwar testimonies of former policemen and witnesses, and legal correspondence pertaining to Nazi crimes in Ukraine. The investigators had pasted official wartime portraits of the police into albums. The headshots were like a police lineup — except the suspects were the police themselves. Carefully examining them, I sought to identify the killers in the Miropol photograph. I compared facial structures: cheekbones, eyes, hairline, the height and size of ears, scars, and other potentially identifying features. I read about countless massacres and crimes, including gruesome details: how the killers raped Jewish women before murdering them, how they took their lunch breaks and ate among the corpses, and how they kept tallies, as if mass murder were a competitive sport. These files had not been digitized, in part because of privacy laws in Germany. Each page, with its original stamps and the signatures of the killers, had to be read and searched for details possibly linked to the Miropol massacre — thousands of testimonies filled with names, dates, and the locations of crimes. They read like bloodstained pages. None, however, perfectly matched the details of the Miropol massacre of October 13, 1941.

I was apparently pursuing the wrong unit, stuck in an archival cul-de-sac. I returned to searching the main database of all postwar German investigations. Then a colleague pointed me to another possible lead in the German archives — one of the slimmest of the files. I had missed it because in it, the crimes that had occurred in the Ukrainian town of Miropol were erroneously attributed to a Russian town, Myropol. The German archivists didn't misplace Miropol in Russia. They misplaced Ukraine in Russia.

The case was opened one January night in 1969 when a retired German customs official, Kurt Hoffmann, appeared at the local police station of his hometown, Laatzen, a few miles south of Hanover, Germany. He announced that he wished to report a crime. The police officer on duty pulled out a form and typed up the details:

Crime Scene: Myropol Russia
Date of Crime: 1941
Punishable Offense: Mass Murder During the Nazi Period
Aggrieved Parties: Jewish and Russian People (unknown)

Polizistation (S) Laatzen
Pol.-abschnitt LK.Hannover
Reg.Bez.Hannover

(Genaue Bezeichnung der Dienststelle)

Geschäftszeichen: 194/69

Anruf: 86 40 63

Strafanzeige

DFB überprüft? Ja! - Nein!

Tatort: Myropol - Rußland

A.G.-Bezirk: —

Tatzeit: 1941

Strafbare Handlung:

Massenmord während der

NS.-Zeit

§§ _____ RStGB.

Geschädigt: jüdische und russische

Menschen (unbekannt)

Beschuldigt (Täter und Beteiligte):

a) Maurer

Paul HEISE

geboren am 18.8.1914

in Laatzen b. Hann.

Wohnung: Laatzen

Wiesenstr. 9

b)

geboren am _____

in _____

Wohnung: _____

Gegenstand: —

Wert (Höhe des Schadens): _____

Überführungsstücke: —

DIN A 4
Pol.-N 39

— Anlage

(Eingangsstempel)

Polizeistation (S) Laatzen,15.1.69
(Dienststelle)   (Datum)

Spurensuche
~~ist einzuleiten~~ — ist nicht erforderlich.

(Priebe) Polizeihauptmeister
(Name und Amtsbezeichnung)

Laatzen, am 15.1.1969 196

Der Rentner

Kurt Hoffmann

am 8 ten Sept. 1904

in Posen geboren.

in Laatzen, Lindenplatz 9 wohnhaft.

Fernruf: ---- , zeigt an:

1941 wurde ich zum Zollgrenzschutz
eingezogen und in Hildesheim aus-
gebildet. Nach meiner Ausbildung
kam ich nach Rußland. Ich war
in Myropol stationiert. Als eine
Umfrage gehalten wurde, wer sich
an Erschießungen beteiligen wolle,
meldeten sich meine damaligen
Kameraden

    Erich Kuska und
    Hans Vogt

freiwillig zu diesem Kommando.
Beide waren in Schlesien beheima-
tet. Ich habe später das Massen-
grab selbst gesehen; in zwei
dieser Massengräber lagen mindeste

This form made a strong impression on me: it was unremarkable, a typical bureaucratic instrument recording standard information related to the reporting of a crime. Yet the contents typed into the form reveal nothing standard. The crime had occurred more than twenty-five years earlier, the crime scene was in the Soviet Union, and the victims were identified as "Jewish and Russian people." Hoffmann divulged that he had been stationed in Miropol during the war and that in the autumn of 1941 his unit had participated in the massacre of Jews. This time, as I read the vivid testimonies from the investigation that Hoffmann's report set in motion, I realized that the detailed descriptions of the murder, such as the exact location in the park, the date in mid-October, and the attire of the Ukrainian collaborators corresponded precisely with the details I had gleaned from the photograph. And here I had found the German killers. They were customs guards.

Hoffmann explained to the policeman in Laatzen that in 1941 he had been drafted into the Reich Finance Ministry's customs border-protection services and trained in Hildesheim. Presumably he was part of the mass mobilization of Nazi forces needed to invade the Soviet Union in June 1941. After his training Hoffmann was sent to Ukraine and stationed in Miropol. One afternoon, he recalled, his commander informed the squad that mass executions were planned and asked whether anyone would like to participate. Two of Hoffmann's colleagues stepped forward: Erich Kuska and Hans Vogt. Following the executions, the witness Hoffmann explained, he went to the shooting site and saw two mass graves, which contained three to four hundred bodies, among them women and children. Hoffmann added that he knew at the time that they were Jews.

The police captain in Laatzen took down Hoffmann's statement and then spoke with him about its implications. He admonished Hoffmann that to make false accusations knowingly was a crime according to the West German code and punishable by imprisonment. Hoffmann acknowledged this warning, insisted that his statements were true, and implored the police officer to start an investigation. Hoffmann had no additional information about the whereabouts of the alleged perpetrators, Kuska and Vogt. Hoffmann left the station, expecting to hear more from the German authorities. The police officer noted his observations of Hoffmann at the end of his report:

> The person who filed the report did not give the impression of being a busybody. His statements were clear and forthright. Nevertheless I advised Mr. Hoffmann at least 5 or 6 times about the implications of knowingly giving a false testimony. He stuck with his story, and remained firm that the police station Laatzen accept the given report.
>
> There is no indication, no reason to believe that the reporting man is a mentally unstable person.
>
> When asked why he chose now to report this incident to the police, he put forth that the situation was not giving him any peace.
>
> In this regard, I have the impression that the reporting person [Hoffmann] knows more than he stated.

The police captain in Laatzen followed procedure. His station contacted the state criminal investigator in Hanover, who in turn inquired with the national office, located near Stuttgart in Lud-

wigsburg, for investigating Nazi crimes. The national office established that the October massacre in Miropol had not been investigated. One of the main suspects, Erich Kuska, lived near Bremen,
so the case was handed over to the main prosecutor's office there.
Hans Vogt was never found and played no further part in the proceedings. In the months that followed, dozens of testimonies were
taken from Hoffmann's wartime colleagues—German customs
guards who had witnessed and taken part in the killing of the Jews
of Miropol on October 13, 1941. Though the photograph itself was
not part of the West German investigation, the witnesses described
what we see in it. They also contradicted, and indeed lied about,
information that is evident in the image.

Erich Kuska, accused of shooting Jews and bragging about it
to his comrades, presented his version of events when summoned
to the Bremen courthouse on August 14, 1969. With a grammar
school education and background as a miner in Silesia, Kuska had
begun his wartime service as a border guard along the San River,
not far from the Nisko reservation, where Eichmann's men in Vienna "dumped" some two thousand Jews who were mostly chased
by gunfire over the river into Soviet territory. The German advance
into the Soviet Union as of June 22, 1941, brought him eastward
into the rear-area occupied zones of Ukraine. As for the crimes in
Miropol, Kuska claimed that whoever had accused him of volun-
teering to shoot Jews in Miropol was a liar, adding, "I have never
shot a person. I find it downright outrageous that someone accused
me to have shot persons when I could not even once harm a dog."
He asserted that his unit had been in Miropol for only a week; from
there, he claimed, he had been sent to Kiev on another mission

(other members of the unit stated that they had been stationed in Miropol for three months and had not been sent to Kiev). Kuska clearly had prepared his version of events to avoid prosecution, but he had not rehearsed it very well. Next he got to the real matter at hand, launching into a defense as to what he had witnessed and done in Miropol in October 1941.

According to Kuska, one morning the Ukrainian militia drove about forty men to a hill outside town. "One could see that they were Jews," he said. Then Kuska corrected his testimony, replacing the phrase "one could see" with the statement that "I heard" singing and bawling. He went on to testify that the Ukrainian militia, wearing civilian clothes and armbands and carrying rifles, were drunk. They shot wildly at the Jews who lay in the mass grave. Kuska said he was so shocked that he had turned away and left. But in his concluding statement he wished to stress that "he did not see a single German soldier, policeman, or member of the customs guards or SS at the shooting in Miropol." For someone who had only "heard" this massacre, he was able to present stark visual images of it. He correctly identified the Ukrainian militia's role, what they wore, and the weapons that they carried. He tried to minimize the number of murder victims, citing only forty men and excluding women and children. He argued that he saw no other Germans. But in order to observe their supposed absence, he would have to be present at the mass murder site during the killing.

The historian Christopher Browning pioneered a way of reconstructing micro-histories based almost entirely on the testimonies of victims and perpetrators. He developed tests of logic and veracity to set against mendacious statements like Kuska's. He asked, "How may a historian of the Holocaust use a variety of different, often conflicting and contradictory, in some cases clearly mistaken, memories and testimonies of individual survivors as evidence to construct a history that otherwise for lack of evidence, would not exist?"

The Absence of Evidence

The wartime documentation on Miropol is sparse. The town is mentioned in passing in police reports of the German military and the SS as either a stopover location or a temporary outpost. I had seen Miropol listed in the records of Himmler's command staff, which registered that Order Police Battalion 303 had passed through the town between July 30 and late September 1941, along with an SS infantry regiment, amounting to as many as two thousand men. In the US National Archives, I found the war diary of a Wehrmacht security division (454) active in and around Miropol, and an entry for October 3, 1941, regarding the deployment of Slovakian forces. Still, Miropol was not a major German outpost; it was just another town along the route to district headquarters in Zhytomyr, and therefore the paper trail relating to the massacres that occurred there is thin.

After January 1944, when the Germans had evacuated and Miropol was reoccupied by the Red Army, the Soviet Extraordinary Commission for the Investigation of Nazi Crimes began to collect testimony about the mass shootings. The commission's final report concluded that 960 civilians had been shot in Miropol over the course of two mass shootings of Jews, on October 13, 1941, and February 16, 1942. In fact, starting in August 1941 a subunit of a German killing squad reported the shooting of Jews who had allegedly refused to work and were supporting the resistance. But the dates in October and February are correct, and as we know, the Miropol photograph documents the massacre on October 13.

The victims in our photograph were the remnant of a community being destroyed after the first wave of killing in the summer of 1941 and before the final *Aktion* against the "specialists," or "craftsmen," and their families in February 1942. When the photograph was taken in October, Jews and non-Jews alike were aware of what the German word *Aktion* meant: not deportation to the promised land of Israel or even to a nearby labor camp, but a death march to the edge of town to be shot. Even today, the word *Aktion* rolls off the tongues of local Ukrainians. Like *Gestapo,* it is among the few German words integrated into the rural dialect.

No extant Nazi documents report the event pictured in our photograph. But cosmologists and astrophysicists have taught us that the "absence of evidence is not the evidence of absence." The fact that there are no Jews in Miropol today (at least none that openly identify as Jewish), and that documentation about their history there is sparse, does not mean that they did not exist there for centuries, until the Nazis and their collaborators brought them to near extinction. This is the logical fallacy that the Nazis counted on: the illusion of absence. The photograph dispels it. Working inductively from this one document, this photograph — we can uncover more sources and start to piece together what happened in Miropol on October 13, 1941, in spite of the erasure that perpetrators attempted during and after the war.

The 1969 Bremen investigation that Kurt Hoffmann initiated was not the only one to look into war crimes in Miropol. Between 1945 and 1986, separate attempts were made by prosecutors in Soviet Ukraine, Czechoslovakia, and West Germany to determine what happened there. There was no coordination among these investigations or any sharing of testimony. The photograph was never entered as evidence. As a historian, however, I have the advantage of collecting evidence of all kinds, across different countries, and I can draw conclusions based on historical knowledge and access to materials that have accrued over time, particularly since the end of the Cold War.

An important source of evidence regarding the few perpetrators, accomplices, and witnesses visible in the image — and those who remain blurry figures in the background, or may be present outside the frame of the photo — were eighteen Ukrainians who agreed to be interviewed in 2014 and 2016 about wartime atrocities they had witnessed or participated in. Some watched the mass shooting as adolescents, from hiding places behind the trees; others saw their Jewish neighbors being marched from the marketplace to the forest and heard the gunfire; some plundered Jewish homes and businesses and searched for gold and other valuables in the mass graves. One woman admitted that she had been forced to dig the pit at the massacre site. Their candid recountings make them vulnerable to attack by anti-Semites and extreme nationalists in Ukraine who wish to suppress this shameful chapter in their history; for that reason, when these witnesses are cited in this book, their surnames are abbreviated to protect them.

In 2016, some of these interviewees brought me to multiple crime scenes in town. Postwar generations, including the young mother and daughter I had met in 2014, assumed that there had been only one massacre, which had occurred at the large ravine. Conflicting local memories settled on this, and it made sense because of the prominence of the Babi Yar Ravine and the ravine in Russian literature as a place of darkness and despair. But the direct witnesses, the elderly, knew the exact location of particular killings of Jews, including the October 1941 shooting. These Ukrainians testified also that more officials of the German occupation had participated in the photographed massacre than can be seen in the image. The Germans had surveyed the forest for a suitable killing site, secured the bullets and guns, and identified those who would serve as grave-diggers, guards, and shooters.

Another source of evidence for me was the nearly four hours of videotaped testimony provided by Ludmilla Blekhman, the only known survivor of any massacre at the Miropol crime scene; she died in Israel in 2015 before I could meet her. She stated that her family had been shot in Miropol in September, but her account closely resembles what happened in October. All of these statements from Ukrainian witnesses were held up against the evidence presented in the photograph. They added details about many intersecting lives, places, and chronologies that fall outside the frame of the photograph itself.

The Chronology of Catastrophe

The photographer captured one second in time, but the planning, implementation, and cover-up of the murder occurred over several days. As I analyzed the testimony that had been quietly filed away in archives thousands of miles apart, this photo began to make sense as part of a larger sequence of events during "the fateful months" (in Browning's words) of Nazi decision making related to the "Final Solution to the Jewish Question."

The families massacred in Miropol were among the first to be gunned down in toto in the European Holocaust. In fact, Nazi leaders were emboldened by the ease and speed with which they could carry out killings in broad daylight as the Wehrmacht quickly occupied most of eastern Europe by the fall of 1941. Hitler predicted that Moscow would be conquered by October 15. In this euphoria of victory, Hitler and Himmler pushed forward with their plan to annihilate all Soviet Jews and then to expand the genocidal campaign to all European Jews. The plan was executed in stages, but rapidly. At first the mobile security task forces of the SS and police, the Einsatzgruppen, were instructed to destroy all Jews occupying state and party positions, targeting able-bodied men who might foment serious resistance on behalf of the Soviet state and attempt to protect their families. Then Himmler authorized the expansion of killing to women, children, and entire communities; this unleashed a torrent of anti-Semitic violence across the Baltic states, Belarus, eastern Poland, and Ukraine. Pogroms and mass shootings took place in and around urban capitals, in old fortresses and forests, along riverbanks, and in open fields and ravines. Centuries of Jewish life in the Pale of Settlement were turning into ash, rubble, and mass graves. Within a fifty-mile radius of Miropol, tens of thousands of Jews were gunned down in Berdychiv, Zhytomyr, Shepetivka, and Novohrad-Volynskyi. A bit farther away, at Kamianets-Podolsk, more than twenty-three thousand were shot at the end of August, and then in Kiev more than thirty-three thousand at the end of September. Where could the Jewish families in Miropol, completely surrounded and living in ghettoized conditions, go to escape this onslaught? The killing was not subsiding as the army and the Einsatzgruppen advanced. It kept increasing, averaging thousands of deaths per day in autumn 1941. An "exuberant" Hitler (who had returned from a tour of Ukraine in August 1941) sent out a rousing call to all soldiers in the east in early October. He commended them on the victories and the taking of more than two million Soviet prisoners. He described the Soviet "paradise," marked by unimaginable poverty, as a system created by "Jews and only Jews." He acknowledged Germany's allies, including the Slovakians:

> The world hitherto never has experienced similar events. The territory the German and allied troops have occupied is more than twice as large as the German Reich of 1933, more than four times as large as the English motherland. Since June 22 the strongest fortifications have been penetrated, tremendous streams have been crossed, innumerable localities have been stormed and fortresses and casemate systems have been crushed or smoked out. From the far north where our superbly brave Finnish allies gave evidence of their courage a second time, down to Crimea you stand today together with Slovak, Hungarian, Italian and

Rumanian divisions roughly 1,000 kilometers deep in the enemy's country.

The highest-ranking army official in Ukraine, General Field
Marshal Walther von Reichenau, "considered the extermination of
Jewish women and children to be pressingly urgent and should be
carried out in whatever form it took." Reinforcing Hitler's call to
the troops, on October 10, 1941, Reichenau issued his own "sever-
ity" order on "the conduct of the troops in the eastern territories,"
exhorting every soldier to accept fully and indeed mete out the necessary, severe retribution against "the subhuman species of Jewry,"
specifying the recently conquered territories in which revolts "as
experience proves have always been caused by Jews." One German
soldier, in a tank unit headed to Moscow at this time, pasted two
photographs side by side in his personal photograph album. One
shows a German reading Hitler's October 1941 call to all soldiers in
the east. To complement this, he placed next to it a second photograph — an atrocity image of a dead Jewish man who had been run
over by a tank.

By this time, Hitler had informed Himmler, the "architect of
genocide," that he desired the Reich to be "emptied and freed of
Jews" "as soon as possible." Plans were accelerated to deport Jews
from Berlin, Frankfurt, and Vienna to the east. Senior SS and
police officials explored the railway links to Ukraine, where Jews
could be shot in remote places like Miropol. Mass shootings were
one method of genocide, but not the only one. Himmler experienced firsthand how nerve-racking and messy these killings could
be when he attended the shooting of a hundred Jews in Minsk on

August 15, 1941; the event was allegedly filmed for Hitler. More-over, openly shooting all European Jews in the occupied eastern territories would have revealed genocide to the world and required resources that Germany could not spare during the war. Other pro-cedures, therefore, were being tested in different locations. About two years earlier, Nazi officials had started a program of murder-ing mentally and physically disabled Germans by means of poison gas released in chambers. Then, to kill institutionalized patients in conquered Poland, SS leaders and chemists had developed mobile gas vans; carbon monoxide from the running engines poisoned the victims. In September 1941, the SS at Auschwitz tested cyanide (Zyklon B) on Soviet POWs, and the experiment was deemed a success — in contrast to another approach, using explosives, which had failed the month before in Minsk. Himmler considered the pros and cons of gassing in mobile vans and stationary chambers as well as proposals from regional Nazi leaders in Poland, Serbia, and Germany involving the deportation of "their" Jews to the Soviet Union to be shot. As Christopher Browning determined, in the "brief twelve-day span between October 13 and October 25 plans to construct camps with gassing facilities emerged not only for Bel-zec but also for Chelmno, Riga, Mogilev, Birkenau, and possibly Sobibor."

Thus, Miropol fits into the chronology of catastrophe, the much-debated timing of the Nazi decision to murder all Jews and its first phase of implementation in the summer and fall of 1941. Yet timing and chronologies take on a different pace and length at the micro level of the Holocaust. In Miropol, as elsewhere across east-ern Europe, Nazi operations were rapid, and the sequential patterns are striking: prior to the killings, Jewish people are taken from their homes; peasants outside the town going about their daily business hear gunfire in the distance; occupation officials and local non-Jews, drawn to the sound, arrive at the scene; plunderers ransack the vacated Jewish homes, to the sound of that same gunfire; the Jews are forced to approach the killing site, to the sound of gunfire and screaming; they watch as their loved ones are murdered; and they face the killers, and their own death. Using hundreds of testimonies of Germans, Slovakians, and Ukrainians who passed through or resided in Miropol, and of the one Jewish survivor, I was able to reconstruct events just before, during, and after the photograph was taken on October 13.

Sunday, October 12, 1941

DAYTIME

Three German SS officers, whose names remain unknown, arrived in the town of Miropol, perhaps sent from the nearest headquarters, in Berdychiv. Shootings of Jews had occurred there in August and September 1941, so a suitable execution site already had been identified. The officers set about procuring local helpers to be gravediggers, corpse carriers, and guards and locating equipment, such as shovels and horse-drawn carts.

Most of Miropol's peasants were at home; many had returned from church services. Two of the German SS men entered the mud hut of Lydia S. The fifteen-year-old lived there with her mother. Unable to communicate in Ukrainian, the Germans approached

Lydia and gestured in a digging motion. Lydia's mother tried to intervene but was beaten down. One German brandished a pistol, and the other had a rifle slung on his back. They forced Lydia outside, where more teenage girls had been gathered on the road. The Ukrainian peasant girls — now a small squad of gravediggers — were brought under guard to the forest.

When they arrived at a clearing, the Germans began to shout: "Dig! You Russian pigs, *Kaputt* [you're finished]!" They sneered at the girls and sang to pass the time. After the girls finished digging out a layer a few feet deep in a circular area "about the size of a room," the Germans ordered elderly Jewish men to the site.

The Jewish men completed the pit and were killed on the spot.

The pit was eight by eight meters in size and ran one and a half meters deep. The Germans calculated that it would be big enough to accommodate the corpses of the remaining Jews in Miropol, mostly women, children, and the elderly. Satisfied with the preparations, the German SS officers returned to town to recruit the killers.

SUPPERTIME

The only German security personnel stationed in town were members of a platoon of customs guards, including Kurt Hoffmann, who were at the local canteen, eating and playing cards. Their commander, Commissar Nette, was in the middle of a game of Skat when three "uninvited SS men brusquely interrupted the game." According to Hoffmann, one of the SS officers loudly admonished Nette, "Why are there still Jews living here?"

Nette pulled back his chair, stood up, walked to the door, and motioned to the SS men that they should leave, stating, "I am not entirely in agreement with your interests."

The SS men walked out.

Leaving the Skat game unfinished, Nette rushed to his headquarters nearby.

Later he reappeared with the two of the SS officers at the platoon's barracks, which were located at the paper factory, not far from the forest where the pits had been dug. Upon their arrival, the men in the barracks jumped up, fell in line, and stood at attention. Evidently the SS visitors had informed Nette of the impending massacre and requested his assistance, because Nette asked the men, "Who will volunteer to participate in a shooting *Aktion*?"

Border policeman Erich Kuska stepped forward: "*Jawohl!*"

Border policeman Hans Vogt stepped forward: "*Jawohl!*"

The volunteers left with the SS officers.

Rumors circulated in town about plans to kill all the Jews. Even Jewish elders who had remembered Germans during the Great War as a cultured people realized now that they must prepare for the worst. The men gathered to decide on a plan for resistance. The father of twelve-year-old Ludmilla Blekhman visited a Ukrainian colleague and friend of the family and beseeched her to hide his three daughters. She agreed to help.

NIGHTTIME

The deputy chief of the local police in Miropol, a Ukrainian named Zavlyny, gathered his men and split them into two groups. About twenty local Ukrainian policemen (mostly from town and the surrounding villages) formed an outer cordon to seal off the town and prevent Jews from escaping to the forests and villages. Another twenty were told to force the Jews from their homes, gather them in the marketplace, and guard them until dawn.

The police instructed the Jews to pack their belongings quickly. They told them that they must leave their homes and go to a neighboring town for labor assignments. Ludmilla Blekhman and her sisters had not yet fled to the Ukrainian friend. Ludmilla packed her doll and put on her best blouse. It had been sewn by her grandmother, using fabric from the rabbi's widow's *kriah* (clothing torn as an act of grief). As Ludmilla and her family were leaving their home, their neighbor rushed in with her son, a schoolmate of Ludmilla's, yelling "Mil'ka, Mil'ka, get this fine coat! Mil'ka, Mil'ka, come here, here is a good Singer sewing machine." The schoolmate took the coat from the bedroom armoire while his mother grabbed the sewing machine. Furious about the betrayal of her schoolmate and worried about the fate of her home, Ludmilla glanced back as she was led to the marketplace. She saw more neighbors plundering her family's house, carting away bedding, towels, chairs, anything that was portable. Others assaulted them — throwing stones and bottles, grabbing the valuables the family carried — as she and her mother, father, grandmother, and two sisters walked on the road toward the marketplace.

The pogrom had begun. The town was engulfed in a great clamor. The yelling, screaming, and howling penetrated the walls of the German barracks, the clapboard cottages in town, and the mud huts at the town's perimeter. There were sounds of glass breaking and gunshots popping.

Ukrainian militia armed with clubs, tools, and Russian rifles chased Jews, bludgeoning some to death and shooting those who resisted or could not walk. They searched for Jews hiding in sheds and under floors. They stuffed valuables into their pockets. They chased young Jewish women, ripped off their clothes, and raped them. One policeman named Khutov searched for Ludmilla's older sister, who was among the prettiest of the Jewesses. Before the war, Khutov had wanted to court her, but she had spurned his advances, so now he took her.

In the town center, one Ukrainian family could not sleep because of all the commotion. A girl crawled out of bed to peek through holes in the walls. She saw an elderly, infirm Jewish woman being carried into the courtyard below. The old woman was wrapped in white bedclothes, and still in her bed. Ukrainian militiamen shot her and carried the dead woman away in her bed. A younger Jewish woman, the old woman's daughter, burst into the Ukrainian family's house, begging for shelter. They hid her in their cellar.

About two hundred Jews were encircled in the marketplace, about a third of the entire population still remaining in Miropol. A Ukrainian policeman named Les'ko yelled, "Who are the craftsmen? Two steps forward! Whoever has a family among the craftsmen, you may take them with you!" Pandemonium ensued as women and children rushed forward, and in the panic families were separated. Craftsmen lost sight of their wives and children. The dentist, who could not find his wife and small son, became hysterical.

The craftsmen and their families were separated into one group and allowed to stay in Miropol as essential laborers (until they were also killed a few months later in the local ravine). The rest were told that their labor was needed elsewhere, that they would be brought to a work assignment in the morning. They waited outside with their bundles of belongings, sobbing, shivering, praying, and fearing the worst. Some tried to bribe the guards, desperately promising gold, whatever they could offer to save their lives and their loved ones. During the night one Jewish woman, a seamstress in the town, escaped and made her way to a Ukrainian's house, begging for shelter and food. She was turned away because the family feared they would be killed too if they took her in.

Monday, October 13, 1941

DAYBREAK

Between 5 and 6 a.m. the Jews were lined up in a column and led several hundred meters toward the old fortress overlooking the river. As they walked, many cried, and some said goodbye to one another. Individuals who refused to go were shot on the spot.

Peasants, already tending to their cows, heard the cries and single shots of gunfire coming from the direction of town.

At 7:30 a.m. a German customs guard reported to his assignment in the horse stalls. None of his colleagues were there. He heard loud noises in the distance and walked toward what sounded like a deep chant. He saw a small one-story building, which housed the local police station and jail. Jewish women and children and some men of all ages were held there. He saw their faces through the barred basement windows. About a dozen mostly drunken Ukrainian police in brown overcoats danced and swayed around the building, waving their Russian rifles. The customs guard recognized the melody they chanted. It was the *Todeslied* (*Funeral March*).

The Jewish dentist was seen suffering in a public spectacle of Sisyphean torture. He was made to push a barrel of water up the hill, only to be beaten and then pushed back down the hill with the barrel.

At 9 a.m. another customs guard in Kurt Hoffmann's unit walked toward the forest, first passing through the ring of Ukrainian militia surrounding the town. He saw about a hundred Jews, crying horribly, through the windows of the police station. The Ukrainians then led them from the building into the forest.

Along the path the militia pushed groups of Jewish families. Fathers, husbands, brothers, and sons tried to shield their daughters, wives, sisters, and mothers from beatings. And when they fought back, the militia beat them with the butts of their rifles, shattered their skulls, or shot them on the path.

The executioners gathered at the pit. Four or five Germans, including Erich Kuska and Hans Vogt, appeared in the black uniforms of the customs police; Ukrainian militia wore overcoats and armbands.

The Germans had miscalculated. The pit was not large enough. The Ukrainian militiamen at the site ordered the Jewish men there to dig another mass grave.

At 10 a.m. the sounds of gunfire changed, from single shots to uniform firing. The sound reached the quarters of a detachment of Slovakian Security Service guards, who were also stationed in town.

The Slovakian commander, named Hrushka, told his company's scribe and photographer and two guards in the unit to investigate and report back. The photographer grabbed his Zeiss Ikon Contax. The three Slovakians passed through a cordon of Ukrainian guards surrounding the site, and then watched, standing about twenty feet from the killing. The photographer documented the Jews being killed.

The Ukrainian police escorted Jews in small groups from a nearby holding hut about sixty feet away to the edge of the pit. They taunted the victims by name. They unleashed their resentment against their richer neighbors, their more clever schoolmates, and their bosses in the paper factory. The victims were known to them from the dentist's office, the cobbler's shop, the soda fountain, and the collective farm.

They grabbed small children and babies by the legs and smashed their heads against the trees.

Lubova, a peasant girl living along the Sluch River, was gathering wood in the forest and heard the gunfire. She approached the site and hid behind the trees. She saw a column of Jewish women and children, and she saw Jewish mothers, who were holding children, being pushed into the pit.

The Vaselyuk family, or what was left of it after most of the men had been driven away or killed, was led to the execution site. One was a nurse who had been caring for her infirm grandmother Esya, shot the day before. They were surrounded by the militia, including Ukrainians they knew from town. Now it was their turn. The nurse, Khiva Vaselyuk, and the children were forced to the edge of the pit. Down below were the bloody bodies of her kin. Some still moved. Some women had jumped into the pit or were shoved in while holding their small children in their arms and hands, and were then shot "like fish in a barrel."

At noon a German customs guard, having observed the mass shooting for two hours, watched as Ukrainian police shot at anyone moving or trying to crawl out of the pit.

AFTERNOON

The Ukrainian militia returned to the Jewish quarter, searching for more Jews and their valuables. They demolished the houses, taking the materials to furnish and expand their own homes: floorboards, bricks, windows, dishes, cabinets, tables, beds, and pillows.

Peasants and other locals appeared with carts. One looter of Jewish houses and shops, discovering that there was little left to plunder — everything had been taken so quickly — spotted toothpaste on the ground, a real find.

The horse-drawn carts, normally used to transport hay, were loaded with bodies of Jews, piled up like wood. The coachmen gathered more corpses from the houses, marketplace, and paths. These were transported to the forest and dumped into the mass grave.

The popping of bullets continued throughout the day.

The German customs guards Erich Kuska and Hans Vogt returned to their barracks in the paper factory, about a mile down the river from the execution site. Known as a Jew hater, the forty-year-old Kuska bragged about what it was like to murder Jews, reenacting how he aimed at the nape of the neck and pulled the trigger.

NIGHTTIME

Ludmilla Blekhman regained consciousness and realized that she had not been shot; she tried to crawl out of the pit. Others, who were dying, pushed her up. She crawled across the moonlit glade strewn with corpses. As she fled into the woods, she noticed that her torn blouse, superstitiously cherished because the rabbi's widow's *kriah* was stitched onto it, was now stained with mud and blood. She knocked on the door of a small house belonging to the forester, and the woman who answered agreed to hide her for the time being.

The Subsequent Days

The hunt for Jews continued.

The Ukrainian police ordered locals, mostly young women and girls, to clean up the Jews' houses and to carry any corpses to the mass grave.

The Ukrainian girls who had assisted as gravediggers were ordered to cover up the mass grave with soil and lime. The ground was moving.

The German customs policeman Kurt Hoffmann visited the mass graves and saw that corpses were only partially buried and that limbs were visible.

CASE CLOSED

In a letter to Kurt Hoffmann of May 27, 1970, the senior prosecutor, Hoeffler, recorded that "I could not verify your claim" that Kuska had killed in Miropol. Commander Nette, who might have testified, "was killed defending Breslau during the war," and "our search for Hans Vogt yielded nothing." Hoeffler concluded, "For these reasons I am shelving the case, I am not pursuing Kuska and investigating Voigt [*sic*]."

While one of the killers, Vogt, could not be found, other Germans who were present at the massacre denied their crimes and placed the blame on the Ukrainians and the SS. The prosecutor believed the liars and questioned Hoffmann's credibility. In the summer of 2017, after identifying Kuska as one of the killers, I telephoned the Kuska family near Bremen and explained that I was researching their family's wartime history. They were not interested in dredging up the past and abruptly hung up.

There are reasons why West German prosecutors failed fully to investigate the massacres in Miropol. The political will was lacking to aggressively pursue "ordinary" policemen and customs guards; many had been allowed to continue these professions after the war. The crimes had been committed against non-German victims, mostly unidentifiable, and the crime scene was a remote village in eastern Europe, now located behind the Iron Curtain. At the time of the Miropol investigation, in the late 1960s, the German civil service was populated by former Nazis who wanted to keep their jobs and were allowed to do so; they posed no threat to West German democracy. In order to win this case, prosecutors would need a confession or testimony from multiple witnesses establishing that the suspect had not only committed the crime but also had acted with excessive cruelty or out of hatred for the victims. Additionally, in the case of Miropol, little hard evidence from the war could place the suspect at the crime scene on that day. Hoeffler, as senior prosecutor, did not press witnesses by challenging their contradictory versions of events and self-exculpatory assertions. He came to consider Hoffmann an unreliable witness (or perhaps a troublemaker) because he learned that Hoffmann, in a possible personal vendetta, had denounced a family member in another case of war crimes. The former German customs guards insisted that no Germans had shot Jews, or if Germans had participated in the killing, they must have been SS men. No documents or photographs were used as evidence in the West German case initiated by Hoffmann.

And yet the untruthful and self-serving statements of the customs guards do not erase the historical value of the testimonies concerning war crimes found in this case, as well as in others collected by West German investigators. The Ludwigsburg archive of West German testimonies amounts to about 500,000 statements, and these resulted in 6,487 convictions of German criminals (only 7 percent of the cases pertained to the murder of Jews). The testimonies can now be weighed, for veracity, probability, possibility, and logic, against one another, against wartime documentation, and against the accounts given by others present at the time — Jews, Ukrainians, and Slovakians.

The historian Saul Friedländer observed that scholars had failed for decades to write an integrated history of the Holocaust because they privileged Nazi documentation over other testimony. These academics were skeptical of the factual reliability of victims' accounts and those of other non-German witnesses speaking after the war. Unintentionally, many scholars thereby silenced victims and other subjugated civilians, such as the Ukrainian peasant girls forced to dig the mass grave, and inflicted upon them another form of historical repression — extending the power of the Nazis through overreliance on "official" German wartime documents (which, as we have seen, are spotty at best for small towns like Miropol). The privileging of Nazi records can perpetuate the perspective of the Nazi conqueror in Ukraine. Here Ukrainians were valued only as tools of genocide, their names and personal details left unrecorded. The documentation of the postwar case instigated by Kurt Hoffmann would not be the place to find the names or further information about the Ukrainian militiamen in the Miropol photograph. They appear as blurry figures in the photograph and would remain unidentified until 1985, when, as we will see, a determined Soviet prosecutor in Zhytomyr, Ukraine, tracked them down. They were eventually convicted.

Researching a wide range and depth of sources is essential to ethically and accurately re-creating history. Genocide involves a multitude of crimes, participants, and witnesses, and those involved have myriad motives and perspectives. Viewing the Holocaust from the German view alone, as many scholars did prior to the 1990s, led to erroneous assumptions: that the Jews rarely resisted going to their deaths; that the "Final Solution" was imposed by top Nazi officials in Berlin upon lower echelons and executed in strict obedience almost exclusively by the SS; that sexual violence was incidental and not an integral aspect of the Holocaust; and that killings were "industrial," implying that they lacked the brutality of other genocides. Other than the Bremen case of 1969, none of the testimonies used here to re-create the crime captured in the photograph, nor the photograph itself, were available to me or other historians before the end of the Cold War.

Writing history demands striving to capture it from every possible angle, not just the one best preserved in state archival records, which are rife with gaps and privileged classifications. In fact, the video testimony of the sole survivor of the massacres, Ludmilla Blekhman, is among the most reliable and detailed. Unlike the German suspects under investigation, this traumatized witness was motivated to speak truthfully and struggled to remember what happened when she recorded her testimony in 1997.

4

THE PHOTOGRAPHER

ASSUMED THAT THE photographer of the atrocity in Miropol was a collaborator, standing at close range in military uniform, helping to prevent the Jewish families from fleeing, and humiliating them by taking their photos at such a moment. In fact, I learned that later in the war, in May 1943 in Bratislava, he was denounced to the Nazi-allied authorities for "making photos that were not permitted" and that "worked against the New Order in Europe." It was on this occasion that the photographer's name first appears in the records and that the Miropol photograph, along with others, became the subject of an official inquiry. On that spring day in May 1943, Lubomir Škrovina, the owner of a radio shop in Banská Bystrica, was summoned to Slovakia's state security headquarters in Bratislava and interrogated by Filip Lisý, a secret service officer handling cases of Jews in hiding and illegal emigration.

Škrovina's profile as documented over the course of the investigation was curious. At the end of 1941, he had been discharged from the Slovakian army for health reasons after having served on the eastern front, in a security division in Ukraine, as both a guard and a company scribe. The Slovaks were allied with the Germans and — like the Romanians, Hungarians, Italians, Spaniards, and Finns — participated in Operation Barbarossa, the invasion of the Soviet Union in summer 1941. In Slovakia, all males of ages sixteen to sixty were required to serve either in the military or as a member of a radical fascist group, the Hlinka Guard. When Škrovina returned from his duties on the eastern front, he brought photographic film. In his home, he had a darkroom where he developed prints of his former comrades in arms and atrocities against Jewish civilians.

Officer Lisý confronted Škrovina with "engaging in monkey business" with Jews, or secretly protecting them, and also with stockpiling materials for the resistance movement within Hitler-sponsored Slovakia. Škrovina protested that these allegations were false, but he admitted that he had witnessed a massacre during his six months of service on the eastern front as a corporal in the field campaign. When Lisý's agents appeared at Škrovina's home on June 25, 1943, they asked him to give up all his photographs from the eastern front. He gave them this explanation: "In Miropol, Ukraine I had the opportunity to see the atrocity of the war, when Ukrainian militia and German finance guards used guns against partisans. Some of the partisans were shot because they resisted. I took pictures of it. After I arrived back home, I didn't show these pictures to anyone, and later on I burned them, as I didn't want them to end up in the wrong hands. These pictures were taken publicly with the approval of German commanders." Škrovina offered them dozens of other images showing "damaged Russian tanks, Ukrainian cannons, and Ukrainian people at a funeral." Since none were considered suspicious, "no pictures were confiscated" from Škrovina's home in 1943.

Ukrainian witnesses whom I eventually interviewed in Miropol referred to all Germans in uniform as either "soldiers" or "Gestapo." But Škrovina offered a different and significant detail: he referred to the Germans at the massacre site as "finance guards." And in fact as we know — as the photograph attests — he testified correctly. If we look closely at the German uniforms, we see that they are neither those of the SS nor the Order Police: the sleeve cuffs and buttons on the jacket and the emblem on the cap are the wrong shades of color, size, and symbols. If the killers were regular Order Police, their uniforms would have the white embroidered eagle and wreath on the upper left sleeve; there would be twice as many shiny buttons on the coat, about ten visible above the belt. The cap emblem would be smaller, and the cuffs and collars would have black trim. The German killers were attached to the Reich Finance Ministry. They were Kurt Hoffmann's comrades in town, there to check cargo and packages in the local train station.

At his interrogation Škrovina, who was characterized by the person who had denounced him to the authorities as a "gangster," "a leech on the body of the Slovak nation," "a big show-off," and a "fox who can outsmart anyone," retorted that he knew who had denounced him. It was a man named Krakovsky, a member of his unit in Ukraine and a former employee. Škrovina had previously fired Krakovsky because he was embezzling money from Škrovina's radio shop. By providing this information, which Lisý was able to verify, Škrovina convinced the Slovak secret police that Krakovsky had the motive to commit mischief. Škrovina was let go, even though Lisý continued to compile a list of serious offenses worthy of further investigation. Škrovina was hoarding and hiding supplies such as copper wire and tires. He kept Communist literature in his home — rare books about Lenin and the Communist Party — as war booty from his time on the Russian front. He illegally possessed a gun. He was seen consorting with Jews in the black market. At this time the Slovak Communist Party had ties to Soviet partisans in Ukraine and sought to reunite Czechoslovakia and do away with the independent state of Slovakia, which Hitler sponsored. The fact that Škrovina had been in Ukraine, kept literature about the Soviet Union in his home, had technical skills as a radio maker valuable for the resistance movement, was married to a Czech, and was interacting with Jews made him a likely source of opposition to the German-friendly regime in Slovakia. Perhaps Lisý was sympathetic to the resistance movement, or Krakovsky had been right about Škrovina's ability to "outsmart anyone." Škrovina — who was in fact a Slovakian member of the resistance — had outsmarted the police investigator.

Although the 1943 file does not contain the photograph in question, it does hold important clues about what happened in Miropol. Škrovina admitted to openly taking pictures of the massacre. He referred to a series of photographs that, if discovered, might offer a visual narrative of the sequence of events — and also might incriminate him or other Slovakians. The other wartime sources regarding the Miropol massacre, such as the German documents and Soviet investigations, establish only that Slovak units participated in security operations. Local witnesses remembered non-German units in town but referred to them as Hungarians or Romanians.

When Škrovina told Lisý he had burned his photographs of the massacre, he was not telling the complete truth; he had kept the negatives. In 1941, when Škrovina arrived at the crime scene to document the massacre, his Zeiss Ikon Contax was loaded with film that could capture eight impressions. He took at least five photographs that October day in Miropol, memorializing the murder of the family that was first brought to my attention at the DC Holocaust Museum in 2009 as well as that of the other victims documented in four more Škrovina photos held in the Prague archives. In the second photograph in Škrovina's series, one woman dressed in white is crouching at the same spot as the family and her armband with the Jewish star is visible.

I studied the entire series that Škrovina took on the eastern front. It is clear from this work that he was encouraged to use his skills as a photographer to document the unit's routines, the group's camaraderie, and the local events he witnessed in Ukraine, including the violence of the Holocaust. This was a war journal in visual form. His five prints of the Miropol massacre cohere as a narrative. Škrovina wanted to create a visual record, and the intentional ordering suggests that he knew in advance how things would unfold, that he must have seen other rural massacres as his unit marched east with the German Army. It is unmistakable that at the center of his narrative, he meant to place the scene of the killing of the mother and children.

Škrovina used different angles at the shooting site in his attempt to document both the sequence of events and to capture "the entire scene," as he put it.

The killers shown in the first three photographs remain as the core group: two Ukrainian militiamen led by the two Germans. But in the second photograph, which depicts the murder of one woman — this must have occurred moments before or after the death of the family — we see a third German official, also wearing the uniform of the customs police, who is facing in the direction of the camera. Hoffmann identified Vogt and Kuska but not this German. In the third photograph depicting the shooting, Škrovina chooses to eliminate all but the victim and the German killer from the frame. The variety of angles and number of photographs suggest that Škrovina took the images, as he stated openly, in full view, and that he was allowed to move around the scene. The killers were focused on their task, not attending to or distracted by the camera at the center of the action as they exerted their extreme power over victims — perhaps they vainly liked being photographed.

Škrovina captured an image of the pit into which the victims fell. We can see that the victims there were predominantly clothed women and children.

Škrovina was eventually to explain that the bodies seen along the path in the final photograph were "persons murdered on their way to the mass grave"; they were killed "because they refused to go to that mass grave." This is an important statement and observation. Often wartime German reports claimed that Jews were shot "while trying to escape," branding them as dangerous criminals. Perhaps more famously, some observers described Jews being forced to their deaths as going passively, like "sheep to the slaughter," that is, resigned to their fate as G-d's punishment. But these people in the photograph, lying on the path to the forest, were killed because they *resisted* their own murder. They were fighting for their lives, and those of their families too. Ludmilla Blekhman, the only known survivor of this mass killing, remembered that her father pushed through the ring of guards as part of a plan to create an opening through which the community could run away. Her father stayed behind, sacrificing himself to the Ukrainian guards and yelling to his daughters, "Save yourselves!"

Missing from the images are the Slovakian guards and the Ukrainian girls. In the division of labor in this instance of the Holocaust by bullets, the Ukrainian girls were the lowest in the hierarchy of collaborators, but a rung higher than the Jewish men.

Together they dug the pits. The Jewish men were killed immediately after digging, and then the girls were shooed away. At least one curious girl crouched behind the trees and watched the mass killings that followed. Other peasant girls were brought back to cover the bodies and clean up the mess: they had to collect body parts scattered around the site and place them in the mass grave.

Škrovina survived the war, but barely, as a member of the resistance movement centered in Banská Bystrica, Slovakia. In the decade following the war, he settled down with his wife and son, after losing a second child in an accident in the early 1950s. Škrovina continued to operate his radio shop, and he taught at the technical high school. He cherished his wartime Zeiss Ikon Contax and began to show his now adolescent son how to operate the camera.

Then one day in 1958, the Czechoslovak State Security Apparatus and Soviet KGB summoned Škrovina to be questioned about his wartime service. Fifteen years had passed since Lisý had interrogated him, and now the context was radically different. His examiners were not Nazi agents, but Soviet ones. A new generation seeking to cleanse Slovakia of its wartime fascist collaborators renewed the pursuit of justice. Anyone who had been a member of the Slovak People's Party or a member of its radical paramilitary wing, the Hlinka Guard, was suspect. The Czechoslovak Communist Party had seized power in 1948 and within ten years had transformed the country into a Soviet satellite through Stalin-style collectivization, political purges, and show trials of high-ranking leaders, who were executed for treason. In 1954, the leader of the Slovak

Communist Party was sentenced to prison for being a "bourgeois nationalist." In addition to overturning the polity, the new generation of Czechoslovak Communists sought to eliminate Slovak autonomy. KGB-like investigators scrutinized military records and determined which Slovakian units had supported Hitler's forces in Operation Barbarossa.

The photographs made by former Slovakian soldiers active in the east, including Škrovina's, set off this 1958 investigation. The secret police confiscated snapshots and albums from suspects' homes and during interrogations presented these photographs to the suspects and to others, who were then pressed to identify more persons, units, and locations, and to describe the associated crimes. These statements would lead to the next arrest. Photographs captured the crimes during the war and turned the wheels of justice after it.

When, on September 2, 1958, Škrovina was called to the Ministry of Interior in his hometown of Banská Bystrica, interrogators pressed him about the series of atrocity photographs taken in Miropol. Under pressure, his former comrades from his military service in Ukraine had identified Škrovina as a photographer. During this preliminary questioning, Škrovina admitted that he had photographs and agreed to hand them over the next day at his workplace. He was allowed to go home that night. The secret police, however, followed him back to his apartment and then stormed in, knowing that the first thing Škrovina would do upon returning home would be to stash or destroy the most incriminating photographs. The police arrested Škrovina in the presence of his son, searched the home, and confiscated several 4.5-by-6-inch photographs and sixty-six negatives from his time in the east. Škrovina was detained for forty-eight hours. In 2016 his son recalled this harrowing time: The police had taken away his father because of some mysterious wartime photographs. Why were his photographs dangerous? Would his father return home?

Responding to interrogators, specifically about the photograph that is the subject of this book, Škrovina stated, "As far as I know, the murders were carried out by the soldiers of the German SS-Army and local militia. I took the photos on my own initiative." He used his "own camera, a Zeiss Ikon [...] a device which I still have at home." Then he described what he had experienced and seen in Miropol. Škrovina dropped his earlier specific reference to the German killers as customs officials. Attuned to his Soviet audience, he also refers to the victims not as partisans, as he did in 1943, but rather as "progressive" (*pokrokových*) citizens in the Ukraine, more concretely in Miropol, and then, when he recounted what happened that day, he stated specifically that the murdered were "civilians of Jewish faith."

PROSECUTOR: Tell us what happened on the day of this photo?

ŠKROVINA: One Sunday morning, probably in October 1941, I was woken up by soldiers from the company, saying that German soldiers were detaining citizens of Jewish faith. And that they could hear shootings close to the town of Miropol. Then later we learned that the Germans were shooting civilians. Based on this information, I was sent with 2 other Slovak soldiers by our company commander First Lt. Hrushka to find out what was happening. I took my camera with me. We went to the hill in the forest at the edge of town, near the citadel where the civilians were being held. And then what I saw — the Germans [*sic*] were bringing those people in groups toward a clearing in the woods where there was a dug out pit in which corpses of the murdered citizens already lay. When they brought around 10 people to the pit, they ordered them to undress [*sic*; they are mostly clothed in the photos], and then they shot them in the back of the head. And I took pictures. All the persons in the photos, which I submitted to you, were murdered. And I personally saw it. I would also like to point out that the prints were made to capture the entire crime scene.

PROSECUTOR: In photos 3, 4, 5 [referring to the three images of shootings] you can see that the murders are committed both by the German SS soldiers and the Ukrainian military members. Testify whether these militia members were citizens of Miropol?

ŠKROVINA: As far as I know the members of the militia were citizens of Miropol. These militiamen knew very well the local conditions of the area, as well as the citizens [Jews] who were arrested and murdered [...]

Škrovina estimated that as many as three hundred Jews were killed that day.

He explained that he took the photographs to remember his wartime experience, as a souvenir of the war.

In 2017, Škrovina's son recalled that his father had trimmed one negative to remove a Slovak guard pictured in the image. And yet Škrovina had stressed in 1958 that his "prints were made to capture the entire crime scene." Was this the assertion of a photographer-artist? It seems more likely that by claiming that his prints showed the entirety of the scene, Škrovina was hoping to obscure the fact that he had removed the Slovakian guards, apparent collaborators, from the evidence. In this way, he could more easily present himself as having no alliance with any such collaborators among his countrymen, and instead cast himself as an onlooker and photographer: a witness to the crime, not an accomplice.

The questioning concluded that night, and then Škrovina was released. But since he had named his commander and others in his unit, the investigation continued. The detectives turned up more photographs taken by other Slovak guards. Škrovina himself was forced, to his deep regret, to give up his original negatives. When he was interrogated again, in June 1959, he specified that the victims were "people of Jewish religion" who were murdered by the German SS and the local Ukrainian fascist militia. And he insisted that he took the photos "in secret." After this session, the examiner noted on the protocol that "I must say that he [Škrovina] does not look like a person whom we can trust. Based on the fact that the pictures were taken from such a close distance, one cannot state that the pictures were taken without the acknowledgment of the persons doing the killing." The investigators were also suspicious of the fact that Škrovina had kept the photographs in the years since the war and had not revealed them to the authorities.

The Czechoslovak investigators knew that Škrovina had been part of the anti-Nazi resistance and that he was married to a Czech woman, but this did not clear him as a suspect in wartime crimes

against peaceful Soviet citizens in the east. Škrovina was not a
card-carrying Communist Party member, so his political loyal-
ties were in question. The investigators concluded that Škrovina
might have been "one of the active participants in the mass murder of Soviet citizens, but it is very hard to prove this claim." The
regional office of the Ministry of Interior recommended forward-
ing to "our Soviet comrades" the statements, photographs, and
information about the German and Ukrainian killers gleaned
from Škrovina's testimony and photographs. And yet no additional information about communications with German, Russian,
or Ukrainian offices exists in the file. It appears that the photographs were not shared with East German authorities or with the
Ukrainian KGB.

The written testimony contained no additional information
about what happened that day in Miropol. A handwritten note
at the end of the file suggests that the investigation was dropped
fourteen months after it started, on November 10, 1959, as "it was
not possible to identify persons in the photographs." Although
the case was propelled by the visual evidence, the inability to
deeply research the photographs and identify Slovak accomplices
halted it.

And so this investigative file containing Škrovina's original
4.5-by-6-inch prints of Miropol was eventually transferred to the
Security Services Archive in Prague. In 2016, I requested all files
pertaining to this case. I specifically asked for the dozens of missing
negatives, which Škrovina had sought to recover before he died, in
2005. Since the files were digitized, archivists insisted that I did not

need to see the originals. These, they explained, were more onerous to extract from cold storage; doing so would accelerate the deterioration of the paper and prints. I should be content to look at the materials on the computer screen. While I appreciated their concern for conserving their collection, it seemed to run counter to the purpose of the archives: to support research. I needed to see the originals because any mark on the front or back of a document could reveal a clue. Besides, I had learned that the tedious exercise of digitizing thousands of pages could not be completed without some human error. What if one page, front or back, had been missed? Eventually I was permitted to study the original prints, but the files contained no negatives, so I could not verify whether Škrovina's Miropol prints had been altered or cut.

What do the photographic choices reveal? What do the images tell us about their creator? Why did he take the photographs? Why did he keep them?

I met Škrovina's children in Slovakia in September 2017, and they generously shared their family history and collections. Škrovina's son allowed me to poke around in the attic. I found an old cabinet with folders containing the father's childhood drawings. His daughter kept a suitcase filled with his photographs, wartime letters, and certificates; it also contained one of Škrovina's favorite smoking pipes. That pipe is one of his distinguishing features in group photographs with his wartime comrades, such as this 1941 shot, showing Škrovina seated in the middle.

The personal papers in this family's archives make it clear that Škrovina had a vivid imagination and a steady hand. As a child he drew sweeping curves of ships made to look like colorful sea dragons and also penned precise architectural cross sections of buildings. And so it was with his photography: we see both the artist and the mechanical draftsman at work, paying attention to overall composition but also rendering details with exactitude. While stationed in Miropol he sought to escape the horror and tedium of the war by sketching portraits and landscapes. Now I found myself, decades later, starting to draw my own portrait of Škrovina.

Škrovina's son recalled that his father had attended a technical high school, leaving his hometown at the age of fifteen, after his father died. He ventured to the nearest city, Banská Bystrica, and ended up working in a munitions factory there. From records of Škrovina's 1943 interrogation, we learn more. The photographer came from a family of Czech farmers in Brezno, and after four years in a technical factory in Nove Mesto nad Vahom and then working at the munitions factory, he took over a radio shop in Banská Bystrica, in 1939.

Škrovina refused to join trade unions and political movements. His interrogator in Bratislava in 1943 later noted that Škrovina had not been "in the past nor in the present, a member of a political party of association." In letters to his wife written in 1941, Škrovina scorned the Slovakian fascists by referring to their party newspaper as a rag, joked that he might end up in jail for his insubordination, and constantly sought ways to dodge his military duty.

When I interviewed Škrovina's children, I did not show them the photograph of the shootings. I asked them questions about their father's life and character, his hobbies, favorite stories, and sayings. His children knew that their father was traumatized by his wartime experiences, but they did not pry. I learned from them that he was an outlier, at times free-spirited. He was a risk taker, a romantic.

Škrovina's daughter remembered that her father liked to pull back the carpets in their large living room in order to roller-skate and have dance parties. He was a lady's man, though deeply devoted to his wife. During the war his wife, whom he affectionately wrote to as "My Bohu" (among other affectionate variations on her name), was targeted for deportation as part of the Czech minority in Slovakia. He risked marrying her, and he protected her and her mother from harm and persecution. Škrovina liked to be outdoors, skiing and windsurfing. In his photography, his son made clear, he liked to capture everyday scenes and nature and to take close-up portraits.

What about Škrovina's message to us as a documentary photographer? Was he trying to testify in some way? In the words of the historian James Curtis, a specialist in early American photography,

> If we are to determine the meaning of a documentary photograph we must begin by establishing the historical context for both the image and its creator. A documentary photographer is an historical actor bent upon communicating a message to an audience. Documentary photographs are more than expressions of artistic skill; they are conscious acts of persuasion [. . .] Far from being passive observers of the contemporary scene, documentary photographers were active agents searching for the most effective way to communicate their views.

In the letters that he sent to his wife from Ukraine, Škrovina pined for his dear Bohu, imagining that they were listening to the same music and expressing how terribly he longed for her. And yet the correspondence served a purpose other than such intimate exchange. Škrovina and his wife were partners in a secret and dangerous attempt to document the crimes of the war and to distribute his images to resistance organizations. They numbered their letters to detect if any had been intercepted. One month into the Ukrainian campaign, Škrovina was sending rolls of film to his wife and asking her to process them and send him copies of the prints — which indicates that he didn't believe that these early images, prior to the Miropol shooting, would engage the military censors. By this time, Škrovina had passed through parts of western Ukraine where the

German military had openly carried out pogroms. One "trophy" image taken by Škrovina or a member of his unit shows severely beaten Jewish men and a woman on a street, in pools of blood. Slovak colleagues and a German soldier pose behind the corpses like hunters with a fresh kill. On July 25, 1941, Škrovina wrote to his wife that he was sending her two rolls of film, with sensitive images, to be developed, telling her, "Please develop the film and send me copies of the prints. Do not use a Jewish film developer who might destroy the film or anyone who might be unreliable, even if you have to pay more, tell the developer that these are rare photos."

Škrovina understood that while these photographs might not put him in definite peril with the censors, they would be offensive to Jews.

As Škrovina continued eastward, German violence against Jewish civilians escalated from pogroms to systematic genocide, from selective killing of men to mass shootings of entire families and communities. His letters reflect the horrors:

14 August 1941

Dear Bohulenka,
[...] please don't send me the *Gardinista* [the Hlinka Guard newspaper] anymore, I am fed up, bored. We listen to the radio, the music and the noble sounds do not fit the environment of smashed windows, rough wooden benches [...] If I described to you some of the other grotesque images in my mind, you would be horrified [...] my thoughts are quite black [...] I don't know if this is really happening or not but it seems that the black color of my hair has seeped into my imagination, and my sideburns begin to turn gray [...] there are so many things to write to you but it is not possible.

A few days after Škrovina attended and photographed the murder in the Miropol Park, on October 13, he sunk into a deeper despair, telling his wife only that "I am not going to write much today because I feel miserable."

Back home, the Slovak government, under the president Father Jozef Tiso, had issued a series of anti-Jewish laws along the German model of the Nuremberg Laws. Tiso met for tea on October 20, 1941, with the German *Reichsführer* of the SS police, Heinrich Himmler, and Foreign Minister Joachim von Ribbentrop. They discussed the "Solution of the Slovakian Jewish Question" and agreed that Germany could help Slovakia become free of Jews by deporting them to the Nazi-occupied eastern territories.

Perhaps Škrovina's despair turned, at this time, to outrage, enough to embolden him to write a longer letter on October 19:

> Dear Bobanku,
> I got your letters today, number five and an un-numbered one, perhaps number six.
> Bohulka, send Hudoba [unidentified] the package. Do not be afraid. Put in it one pair of long summer underwear and some foot wraps. Then send him two round batteries, but with a small adjustment. Let Krakovsky do it. [Škrovina's employee was likely acting unwittingly as courier.] They must not look any different from the others. Then put the films in them. Be sure not to include any valuables in the package.
> [...]
> Regarding the release of that material, it wouldn't be bad, but think hard about what to release, then adopt the radical solution and <u>stick to it</u>. Regarding Krakovksy, do what you think is best [...]

My dear one, I am terribly, terribly sad. Four months is a very long time after all. A truly difficult test.

Disgusted by the war, missing his wife, and perhaps content with the photographic documentation he had secured, Škrovina began to seek ways to get out of his military service and return home. He was losing his mind and his moral bearings.

Nov 7 [or 11; illegible] 1941

Dear Bo,
I am not me in this new world, I am not myself [...]
Time is running fast, I am trying to get off the front, we are making our own alcohol, killer stuff, my soul mate please write to me, Hello to mom.

Škrovina was allowed to return home for the Christmas holiday in December 1941. He feigned an illness to avoid being sent back to Ukraine and joined the resistance. Father Tiso was following through with Himmler's offer to help deport thousands of Slovakian Jews to Nazi-occupied Poland. The first Jewish deportees to arrive at Auschwitz were young Slovakian women, in March 1942. Jews considered more valuable to Slovak society, such as male doctors, received a "yellow slip," a dispensation that only Tiso could grant, sparing them temporarily from deportation. Škrovina knew that deportation to the east meant death. He sheltered Jews in his home and helped some escape to the forests, including two doctors who had yellow slips. One of them was Škrovina's neighbor, Dr. Ladislav Gotthilf, an obstetrician/gynecologist with a wife and a five-year-old son. When Bohu became pregnant, Dr. Gotthilf cared for her and in October 1942 delivered Lubomir Škrovina Jr. into the crossfires of Nazism and Stalinism. Some time in 1943 or the first half of 1944, Gotthilf joined the medical corps of the Slovak resistance movement encamped in the mountains and forests around Škrovina's home, and brought his wife and son with him.

Slovakia stood in the maelstrom of the struggle over eastern Europe: Hitler sought to retain the client state, Stalin aimed to extend Soviet Communism across eastern Europe, and the western Allies supported the restoration of the nascent democratic Czechoslovakia under the statesman Edvard Beneš, who was in exile in London. Our photographer was among the thousands of Slovaks on the ground who participated in the Slovak National Uprising (August 29–October 28, 1944). The Slovak coalition of thousands of anti-fascist fighters (including members of the Democratic Party, the Social Democrats, and the Communist Party) was logistically supported by the Soviet air force, British intelligence, and the US Army Air Force. In response, the Germans occupied Slovakia, setting off a revolt that culminated in the national uprising. The Free Slovak Radio exhorted patriots to overthrow the Hlinka dictatorship and to liberate Slovakia from German rule. In Škrovina's hometown, Banská Bystrica, the center of the resistance, the Slovak National Council declared its will to restore the free state of Czechoslovakia. Yet lack of coordination among these diverse forces, as well as the Soviet diversion of its promised support to Poland and Hungary, resulted in a tragic defeat. Himmler's brutal Waffen-SS and mobile killing unit (Einsatzgruppe H) quickly descended on the region, adding to a combined police and military force that amounted to forty-eight thousand soldiers. The campaign of terror and reprisals targeted the partisans in the mountains and forests around Banská Bystrica; about one hundred villages were razed and some five thousand civilians and partisans were killed. On November 10, 1944, German SS and Slovak fascists seized Ladislav Gotthilf, his wife, Eveline, and their seven-year-old son, Michael. They were taken to an anti-tank ditch at the edge of the road, shot, and dumped in a mass grave.

After months of fierce fighting and public executions, the Red Army gained control over Banská Bystrica on March 25, 1945. Tiso was taken prisoner by the Americans when the war ended, on May 8. He was sentenced to death and executed in 1947, along with thousands of other Nazi collaborators who were, according to one historian of the era, detained in "every police station, every school, church or public building." In spite of his commitment to the Slovakian resistance, Škrovina's military service complicated his profile. During this early postwar period of "wild retribution," he went into hiding until things settled down.

Before Škrovina died sixty years later, in October 2005, he did two things related to the photographs. In 1994, in post-Soviet independent Slovakia, he wrote a letter to the minister of the interior to request the return of his photographs and negatives of "Jewish civilians executed in the Ukraine." He said he had wanted to document the Ukrainians' killing. He understood that his images uniquely showed their direct role. Indeed, this was the feature of Škrovina's visual documentation that immediately caught my attention. Jewish survivors described Ukrainian collaborators as "the worst," often referring to their brutal excesses as guards at gassing centers. Yet there was nothing in the German wartime documents about the mass shootings in 1941 to indicate that Ukrainians were formed into execution squads, since officially, the non-German oc-cupied population and indigenous police auxiliaries were not sup-posed to be armed with guns. But two of the Miropol photographs document Ukrainians as shooters, using Soviet rifles.

Škrovina took a second action concerning his photographs to-ward the end of his life. In July 1997, he donated the camera he had used to take the Miropol photographs to the newly established Museum of the History of Jews in Bratislava. In the donation ac-knowledgment letter, the museum director stated that the camera would be displayed in a future exhibition on the Holocaust. At the time of his donation, Škrovina urged the museum director to find his photographs and negatives in the Czech archives. His sixty-six negatives were not found. As an independent scholar, and then with the help of the United States Holocaust Memorial Museum, I again sought to recover the negatives, also unsuccessfully.

In September 2017, I went to the museum in Bratislava. I wanted to inspect the camera, thinking that perhaps the apparatus itself would somehow reveal more about the photographer. It was oddly thrilling to hold it. I photographed the camera from every angle and documented the model and serial number. His Zeiss Ikon Contax has a Novar lens 1:4.5 and a 75 mm focal length; it uses 120 mm film, which produces larger negatives with crisper images and more tonality than many other cameras of the time, but fewer shots per roll of film.

The photographs Škrovina made with his camera capture what he could not put into words. In *On Photography* (1973), Susan Sontag writes about photographers as conflicted moral agents, operating with mixed motives concerning conscience, taste, and the need to document reality. Škrovina's picture taking may have helped him make sense of the disorienting reality before his eyes, or perhaps the lens shielded him somewhat from the atrocity unfolding before him. "Photographing is essentially an act of non-intervention," in Sontag's view. But this characterization of the atrocity photographer as a passive witness is not entirely in line with what we have uncovered about Škrovina. For him, photographing the event, trying to capture "the entire scene," was both an expression of defiance and a turning point.

Sontag argues that the photograph is a "material vestige" of its subject, a stimulus for remembering or reexperiencing the event and people in the image. Škrovina was haunted by what he saw, heard, smelled, and felt. He wrote to his wife that it felt as if the blackness of his hair was seeping into this brain, turning his hair gray. There was nothing he could do, or so it seemed, to save those victims at that scene in October 1941. But being there certainly shaped his subsequent choices and the risks he undertook, which affected him and his family. He refused to stay on the front, feigned illness, spent months in a nerve clinic, then resumed contact with Jews in his town, including sheltering some in the attic of his family home. He helped Dr. Gotthilf secure a place in the forest with his comrades in the Slovak National Resistance, although Škrovina ultimately could not save him or his wife and child. Škrovina was antifascist and anti-Soviet. He had felt no pride wearing any government-issued uniform. He hated the war.

The political philosopher and German Jewish émigré Hannah Arendt described images of the Holocaust as an "instant of truth." The Miropol image became Škrovina's testimony against the fascists, the war, and the mass murder of innocent women and children. It was, as he wrote in a letter to his wife, "material" for the resistance. It was to be handled carefully but with resolve.

The pioneering Civil War photographer Mathew Brady reportedly stated that "the camera is the eye of history." When Škrovina looked through his viewer and pressed the button on his Zeiss Ikon Contax, he captured meaning that he could not grasp at the time. Or, as the French theorist Georges Didi-Huberman elaborated 150 years later, the image exists *"in the eye of history* [...] in a moment of visual suspense, as the 'eye' of a hurricane," in a "flat calm" with clouds that "make its interpretation difficult."

Škrovina experienced and saw things that October day in Miropol that existed outside the edges of the images. I have been trying to recapture these things as well. When his photographs and oral and written testimonies are combined with other sources in German and Ukrainian archives, and with the testimonies of local witnesses, we can get closer to capturing the entirety of the scene. Among the sequential images, the most blurry one gives a view from the edge of the pit, looking down onto the clothed corpses below. At the Security Services Archive in Prague, I could zoom in and out of the digital scan on a large, illuminated screen and compare it with Škrovina's original print, which was even brighter. Looking at the tangled heap of bodies, I suddenly saw the polka-dot dress. I made out the left arm of the woman and traced it to the little boy's hand, which she still held.

5

THE SEARCH FOR THE FAMILY

W HEN THE ETHNOGRAPHER S. Ansky traveled in and around Miropol in the early years of the twentieth century, preparing to write what would become the most famous Yiddish play in modern times, *The Dybbuk* (1914), and in the process collecting an archive of eighteen hundred regional folktales and images, one story stood out. Local Jews relayed this tragic tale passed down since the mid-seventeenth century, when pogroms engulfed the region. According to the legend, a bride and groom were on their way to the canopy to be wed but along the way were brutally murdered by the Cossack Bogdan Khmelnitsky. To remember the slain couple, synagogues erected small monuments, which came to symbolize the fragility of Jewish existence. The betrothed embodied the future, procreation, and the continuity of Jewish life. Ansky, reflecting on the tale, remarked that the "couple was like a tree chopped down just as it began to blossom."

This legend resonates too in the essential sense of the Miropol photograph. Murdering mothers with their children is the ultimate evil. In all my years of researching the Holocaust, the theme of the family ran through everything I read. It was there in plain sight, and yet I had not reflected on it as such. Perhaps it was too difficult to face. I joined my colleagues in referring to victims in terms of large numbers: six million Jews, the populations in Warsaw, Minsk, Berlin, Vienna, and so forth. Ironically, we have inherited these versions of death from the Nazis, who relegated human beings to numbers killed, cargo processed in gassing factories, or entire regions made *Judenrein* (free of Jews).

Or I calculated genocide as the individual loss, as one testimony, one biography, and one name read aloud on the memorial day of Yom HaShoah. I attempted to change the focus from the numbers to the individuals by researching and publishing the work of one semi-anonymous diarist named Samek, who was shot while resisting his murder in western Ukraine. In Samek's first diary entries he explains why he put pen to paper. After lashing out at the world for its abandonment of the Jews, Samek dove into a tunnel of grief concerning the loss of his sister, deported to Belzec. He wrote to document the existence of his family members who had disappeared into oblivion. He could not bear the thought that he was the only one left in his family, that those whom he loved most had *all* been murdered brutally. It hurled him into an existential crisis.

Many, or probably most, Jews struggling to survive reasoned to themselves, "If I myself perish, maybe my son will survive me. Or else one of my daughters, or my old father." As one eminent survivor, the novelist Piotr Rawicz, recalled, "They wouldn't admit the possibility of the whole family's being wiped out, for that would take away even the hope of revenge. How could they possibly believe that there would be nobody, after they had gone, to recite the funeral prayers [. . .]?"

The Miropol photograph documents the final moments of a Jewish family. I was determined to identify this family, but how? I had already scoured the Nazi documents and postwar German investigations concerning Miropol. As is typical for these types of sources, rarely does a Jewish name appear. Occasionally in postwar investigations Jewish survivors provided witness statements. The investigation in response to Kurt Hoffmann's 1969 testimony eventually identified the German killers in the customs guard unit. But the prosecutor made no effort to track down witnesses from Miropol itself or to contact Jewish organizations with links to survivors. Perhaps he assumed that there were none. The German records were not a likely place to find a Jewish family name in Ukraine. I turned my attention to former Soviet regional archives and to Jewish genealogical databases.

When, in the wake of the Nazi retreat, the Red Army returned to Miropol in early 1944, the Soviet Extraordinary Commission for the Investigation of Nazi Crimes began to collect testimony about the mass shootings there. The commission's final report, in the Russian state archives, calculated that 960 civilians were shot in Miropol and that two mass shootings of Jews occurred, on October 13, 1941, and February 16, 1942. Only four testimonies were attached to the report, from local Ukrainians or Jewish evacuees or soldiers who briefly returned to the town, but there was a list of 214 Jewish names. These are ordered alphabetically, with birth dates, so one can discern family units.

I went back to the photograph to place the woman and children in it against the birth dates and family configurations on the list. The woman appears to be anywhere from young to middle-aged. But the boy was old enough to walk, so perhaps between the ages of two and five, and therefore born between 1935 and 1940. The Soviets listed the Jewish victims by surname and in family units.

In this digital age of research, names and locations are key to tracing the victims in sources such as the International Tracing Service Archives, the tens of thousands of videotaped oral histories at the Visual History Archive at the University of Southern California, the Fortunoff Video Archive for Holocaust Testimonies at Yale University, and the Pages of Testimony held at Yad Vashem. These and other paper and digital collections, such as the European Holocaust Research Infrastructure, which virtually unites the collections of 2,165 archives in fifty-nine countries, have opened up a transnational vehicle for mining the records strewn across regional and state archives. Over the years I periodically checked the online finding aids and databases by entering "Miropol," but with paltry results; I found two Ukrainian laborers originally from Miropol who had registered as displaced persons after the war in Germany.

Mostly the return was "no items found." The archives are massive, but they are made up of rather fragmentary records and personal effects — identification cards, birth certificates, last notes scribbled and thrown from deportation trains or over camp fences, creased family photographs, pocket watches, Magen Davids — the bric-a-brac of human existence, inert yet waiting to be claimed and pieced together into an empirical account.

A collection amassed by Jewish survivors and their families, Yad Vashem's Pages of Testimony contain nine thousand boxes of 2.7 million pages of postwar inquiries and statements. In 2013, UNESCO designated it a "Memory of the World Register." However, 95 percent of the victims registered in the database are from western and central Europe, not from eastern Europe, where the majority of Holocaust victims resided. Of this majority one million are still not registered. We do not know their names. In fact, half of the missing, unidentified Holocaust victims were murdered on the territory of Ukraine, and most of them were children.

I kept studying the lists and looking for more. At Yad Vashem, I found a list from a 1980s postwar KGB investigation of the Miropol massacre that contained 238 names. With the 214 names first collected by the Soviet Extraordinary Commission in early 1944, I had uncovered close to 450 victims (there were duplicates). Though the lists were incomplete — they named fewer than half of the total 960 victims murdered in Miropol in the Holocaust — they were all I had to work with. As I analyzed the lists, I noticed that there were very few names of single people; those appearing alone were usually elderly women, such as Chaya Kupnik, born in 1860, listed on one line. There were few young and middle-aged men, since most had been evacuated with the Red Army. I focused on the boys born between 1935 and 1940, and any family remnants with small children. I began to draw genealogical trees to map the generations of loss. Since the Nazis wanted to cut down those trees and eradicate them, root and branch, somehow restoring them on paper in this way combined research and memorialization.

In the end I identified eleven separate family units by cross-referencing names from the war crimes investigations and the Pages of Testimony. One surname stood out as a possibility: Rapaport. Dina Rapaport had been killed in the Miropol Park in 1941 with her baby, according to the Page of Testimony filled out by a relative. In the file there was a reference to an attached photograph of a Jewish child killed in Miropol. I requested the originals from the archivist, hoping for a miracle, or at least another clue. The archivist returned with the folder and opened it — it was empty. Decades before, the archivist explained, the reading room at Yad Vashem had no proper security system, so many things had gone missing from the files. Why would someone steal a personal photograph of a murdered child? Was a relative here on a desperate mission to recover and grieve that lost child? Or maybe the photograph had been merely misplaced or loaned out somewhere.

I turned my attention to another name. Esya Brontzovskaya was a single elderly woman who was listed in both the wartime Soviet investigation records and in the Pages of Testimony at Yad Vashem. In the Pages of Testimony, I read that Esya was related to a family killed in the Miropol Park and that she had a grandson about the age of the small boy in the photograph. The family tree I could re-create showed that she was related to a family named Vaselyuk.

I noted this and continued searching through the Pages of Testimony, from A to Z, for anyone from Miropol or the surrounding towns. On my last day in the archives, I reached V. And there, copied on the Page of Testimony for Khiva Brontzovskaya Vaselyuk, was this family photograph.

I gasped. Someone had drawn an arrow pointing to the woman standing to the far right, in the sleeveless dress. This must be Khiva. The little boy in the sailor suit reminded me of the child in our photo. Maybe the older child with the headband could have been the one on Khiva's lap as they were being murdered? I asked the archivist to check the original file for the photograph (I was researching the digital copies on a computer screen). The archivist learned that the photograph was kept by the survivor who completed this Page of Testimony. However, there were special notes in the archival file about the back of the photograph (information not available in the digital database). The portrait had been taken in the summer of 1941 (shortly before the massacre in October). The persons in the photograph were identified as women and children from the Sandler and Vaselyuk families. The smallest child, in the sailor suit, was named Boris Sandler (b. 1938) and to his left was another boy, named Roman, who was the child of Khiva Vaselyuk. The archivist told me that fewer than 1 percent of the millions of Pages of Testimony contain photographs, and photographs from 1941 are especially rare. Captured on film when the war and the massacres of Jews in Ukraine were underway, the women stare at us with serious expressions, perhaps feeling angry, and fearful. The name of the elderly widow Esya had led me to this file. She is not pictured here, although she was the grandmother of Khiva. I found Esya's surname, Brontzovskaya, on another list with two male names without birth dates: Grigory and Leonid. This family portrait shows a family past the time when it contained men; the aunts, sisters, mothers, children, and grandchildren were trapped in Nazi-occupied Ukraine and facing a deadly future.

I felt a rising excitement: Khiva Vaselyuk and the two children could be the victims depicted in the Miropol photograph. But I had to be sure. At the bottom of the form was the name of the submitter, a descendant named Svetlana Budnitskaya, a surname that was not on the list of victim names from Miropol. Her address was Southfield, Michigan, and there was a telephone number.

I rushed back to my hotel room in Jerusalem. It was 10 a.m. in Michigan. I called the number, and an elderly woman with a Russian accent answered:

Hello, yes, I am Svetlana Budnitskaya.

My name is Wendy Lower, I am a professor of history and a scholar of the Holocaust in Ukraine. I am calling you from Jerusalem; I am doing research at Yad Vashem. And I found the Page of Testimony that you submitted and the photo that shows the boy, Roman Vaselyuk.

Yes. [*quiet*]

Please tell me about that little boy?

They shot him, the fascists did, with his mother.

And the other child, Boris, do you know him?

[*silence, then sobbing*] Send me a letter, I will tell you all I know. I will give you more photos, I have more photos. Those fascists how they schiess [shot]! [*starts to wail, catches her breath, and then becomes loud, outraged*] And what they did to my grandmother, Esya. She was paralyzed in bed, they carried her, in her bed, threw her in the pit alive!

A pit?

It was near the ravine along the river, in the park, in a ditch. Roman was my cousin. Please come to me. I will help you!

In the historian Petrovsky-Shtern's words, "The family was the nucleus of Jewish life, for the shtetl to survive and Judaism to prevail; there was nothing more important than a strong family. The family was about life and life only." He also notes that "the Jewish family was patriarchal in men's imaginations only. The golden age shtetl was entirely matriarchal."

In addition to working outside the home, as many Jewish women did in Miropol — at the paper factory, the local school, the hospital, and in shops in town — most Jewish mothers were expected to manage the household and feed, clothe, and bathe their children, as well as uphold Jewish traditions by preparing weekly Shabbat meals and annual celebrations. In the Hebrew series of verses that teaches the alphabet, Jewish youth learned about the ideal maternal figure, the "*Eshet chayil*," or woman of valor, the wife who "rises while it is still nighttime and gives food to her household and a ration to her maids, from the fruit of her handiwork she plants a vineyard [...] She spreads out her palm to the poor and extends her hands to the destitute. She fears not snow for her household, for her entire household is clothed with scarlet wool. She opens her mouth with Wisdom, and the teaching of kindness is on her tongue. She anticipates the needs of her household, and the bread of idleness, she does not eat. Her children rise and celebrate her; and her husband, he praises her: 'Many daughters have attained valor, but you have surpassed them all.'"

In Miropol, the Jewish family had endured the intense assaults of nineteenth-century Russification, the loss of male providers during the Great War, and Soviet assaults on Judaism (including the seizure of communal property), pushing public religious observances and traditions into the domestic realm. Ludmilla Blekhman, the lone survivor of the massacre in Miropol, remembered that her mother had trained her in family traditions and the female roles of running the household, cooking special cakes at Passover, preparing Shabbat dinner. Fathers taught sons formal religious laws, texts, and prayers. As diarists and memoirists have stressed, the Jewish family was a source of material and emotional sustenance. Parents provided shelter, food, the security of tradition, and the comfort of affection.

During the Holocaust, Ludmilla's parents were faced with unprecedented decisions. One can hardly imagine the conversations that parents kept from the children. In the first days of the German occupation, Ludmilla's older sister was brought to the cellar, and her parents instructed her to "never go out." If her existence was documented in the official record, she might become a target of extinction by the Germans. If she could avoid the mandatory registration of all Jews, she might survive. On the eve of the mass shootings, Ludmilla Blekhman recalled, police forces descended and rumors of doom circulated. One was that a pit had been dug and was so deep that one would need a ladder to climb out of it. The Jewish elders gathered to devise a plan of escape. They determined that "the children must survive!" Each family was asked to identify a sympathetic and bribable Ukrainian who might hide the children. The adults would attack the police and go down fighting. They attempted this during the *Aktion,* but nearly all of their Ukrainian neighbors betrayed them.

Ruth Kluger, who survived Auschwitz-Birkenau because of her mother's bravery and acuity, experienced firsthand the awful challenges faced by Jewish women under these extreme circumstances: "We were raised to make gefilte fish, not to resist, to defy the men." Women were taught to obey, to sacrifice, and certainly not to abandon family and children. The weight of this tradition, and how deeply it was internalized in gendered roles and expectations in the family unit and dynamics and in the minds of individual Jewish women, is one explanation for why so many Jewish women went to their deaths with their children. They had already taken on the role of head of household when their husbands were sent to camps, were murdered, or fled. They cared for the remaining children and the elderly while they themselves feared for the future, and as they met unthinkable deaths together. Mothers helped children pack bundles and dressed them as they were ejected from their homes, and held their hands as they were marched closer to the sound of gunfire in the forest. Mothers comforted children, often not their own, even as they were filled with an unfathomable fear of suffering and death.

Some might explain these acts as a reflection of a female trait, the ability and desire to nurture. Of course women wanted to survive as individuals, and some abandoned or even killed their own children to survive. But most of the evidence shows that Jewish women tried to protect their children and sacrificed themselves. Perhaps beyond their maternal instincts, they also acted on another understanding of familial survival and duty to a community that was faced with extinction.

According to the sociologist William J. Goode, across time and different cultures the family unit has served the same basic functions: ensuring survival, performing labor, providing sustenance, socializing and acculturating its members, and educating them. It has been a conveyor and enforcer of a given society's norms, especially gendered ones, which uphold social conventions. In some but not all societies, the family is expected to provide love and comfort to its members. Indeed, kin altruism has been decisive for the survival and evolution of humankind. Family stories, traditions, and ritual practices, passed down and accrued over generations into collective wisdom and a way of life, improved the chances that each newborn infant would reach adulthood. These things are precisely what genocidaires seek to destroy socially, culturally, and biologically.

As I reflected on the experience of the collective suffering of the Jewish family, I realized how definitive a feature the annihilation of the family was in the ideology and perpetration of the Holocaust. In Germany, the political discourse at the time spoke of the nation in genealogical terms, as a family, which according to Nazi thinking was a racial community, the *Volksgemeinschaft*. Non-Aryans had to be extirpated, root and branch, from the national family tree. In 1920, the founders of the Nazi Party unveiled their manifesto, the so-called Twenty-Five Points, which called for the restoration of a Greater Germany, the removal of Jews as citizens of the German nation, and the promotion of a racial state. Point Twenty-One declared that the state must care for the nation's health "through the protection of mother and child." A quasi-Christian sanctification of the mother and child ran alongside the Nazi idealization of the Aryan family. Images of Holocaust victims, like the Miropol photo of the Madonna-like mother and her child, reveal how a western aesthetic valuing maternal love and sacrifice can be simultaneously consecrated and desecrated. Nazi policy was two-pronged: family welfare and family destruction.

In German eugenic thinking, the key racial unit was the family, the source of reproduction and Germanization. Ethnic Germans deemed to be of good Aryan stock were resettled in family units. Human value was measured in genealogical charts and blood types. Pseudo-scientific and culturally prejudiced racial theories were considered dead serious matters at the time. All applicants to the SS, Himmler's elite organization, had to prove their racial purity based on a family tree stemming back to the eighteenth century. The same was required of their potential female mates; Himmler himself passed judgment on these matches. He expected SS men to father at least four sons: "We stand or die with this leading blood of Germany, and if the good blood is not reproduced we will not be able to rule the world." Himmler calculated that two sons could die in the war to conquer the world, and the other two could continue the family lineage.

As for those deemed "inferior" — potential pollutants in the "Aryan" bloodstream, particularly Jews, as well as Roma, Slavs, and the mentally and physically disabled — they faced a barrage of discriminatory acts and were forced to undergo certain biological procedures. Among the more extreme examples were restrictions on marriage, forced sterilization and abortions, the confinement of Roma families to "Gypsy camps," and the breakup of Slavic families, with some members serving as conscripted labor for the Reich and some few children, deemed "racially valuable," kidnapped and assimilated into adoptive German households. The first victims of Nazi mass murder were German children thought to be genetically defective, or "useless eaters," because of physical or mental disabilities. Under pressure, their parents entrusted them to the state for treatment, and the state then euthanized them. By progressively overcoming taboos against such actions, the Nazi government was able to escalate its program of killing: from murdering disabled children to murdering all the disabled, from mass shootings of Polish civilians to the genocide of the Jews.

Eliminating enemy races and resistance cells, according to Nazi thinking, necessitated the destruction of the family. If the Gestapo uncovered one member of a family carrying out acts of sabotage, the entire family was punished. The concept was known as *Sippenhaft*, or kin liability, a medieval legal practice that the Nazis transformed into an instrument of terror and genocide. When the July 1944 plotters failed in their assassination attempt against Hitler, their wives, children, and other relatives were arrested, sent to concentration camps and orphanages. According to Heinrich Himmler, "the men of a guilty family, in many cases of the whole clan are to be executed on principle, the women are to be arrested and taken to a concentration camp, the children are to be removed from their homes and concentrated" in Reich territories, where they were tested for their racial value. On December 1, 1941, the Einsatzkommando commander Karl Jäger submitted a lengthy tally of 137,346 Jews who had been shot, bragging that his unit had "achieved the goal of solving the Jewish problem in Lithuania." He added that, however, some Jewish laborers were desperately needed and that these remaining male Jews "should be sterilized immediately to prevent reproduction. Should any Jewess nevertheless become pregnant, she is to be liquidated." Several Nazi decrees forbade pregnancies and births in the ghettos of Lithuania. Police escorted women in the late stages of pregnancy, who had visibly violated the ban, to doctors who were forced to carry out abortions. Strict rationing, heavy labor, and squalid living conditions led to the undernourishment and therefore decreased fertility of young adults, which lowered birth rates among Jews. In the perpetrators' minds, they were "engaged in a battle with the generative force of the victim group," targeting "the life force as such, attempting to destroy (via families) the civilian world in its totality" (according to the genocide studies scholar Elisa von Joeden-Forgey).

The exchange between Hitler and his Croatian ally Marshal

Slavko Kvaternik, on July 22, 1941, is especially revealing. Hitler spoke frankly about his intention to wipe out all the Jews on the continent of Europe and warned that "if any State for whatever reasons allows even one Jewish family to remain, then this bacillus herd would become a new source of degeneration."

As the mass killing of Jews commenced in the summer of 1941, Heinrich Himmler, apparently attempting to overcome his men's inhibitions, explained that Jewish children had to be exterminated because they would grow up to avenge the murder of their parents. Married and the father of a young daughter, Gudrun (whom he affectionately called "Puppi" [little doll] in the captions of his own family album), Himmler understood that many of the Einsatzgruppen leaders, who served as mass shooters, were husbands and fathers, "and they winced as they pulled their triggers on these helpless creatures who reminded them of their own wives and offspring at home." General von Reichenau of the Sixth Army, whose soldiers conquered Ukraine and were stationed in Miropol at this time, agreed, fuming that any disorder caused by orphaned Jews jeopardized troop discipline. He and his colleagues, referring to Jewish babies and toddlers locked in a schoolhouse in Biela Tserkva, insisted that "this brood must be stamped out!" In early July 1941 a member of Reserve Police Battalion 105 wrote home to Bremen that "Jews are free game [. . .] One can only give the Jews some well-intentioned advice: Bring no more children into the world. They no longer have a future." A regional commander in Einsatzgruppe C (Sk4a), Heinrich Huhn, who ordered Ukrainian militiamen to kill children in Radomyshyl' (ninety miles from Miropol), recounted after the war that at the ghetto liquidation in Zhytomyr, women were allowed to hold their infants in their arms, which he viewed as a more humane and orderly approach to the killing.

For the German killers, these young ones were irrelevant "useless eaters," an irritant, or sources of sadistic amusement. The children at the killing actions were unruly; they did not understand orders, did not obey, cried, and tried to run away.

The Nazis and their allies exploited love of family to deceive and torture Jews. Hungarian ghettoization of Jewish families like those from Munkacs, imprisoned in a brickyard, included the establishment of a "mint" — "the place where sadistic gendarmes and detectives tortured Jews into confessions where they hid their valuables." Wives and children were forced to watch their husbands and fathers suffer beatings conducted with canes, truncheons, and electrical rods, which were often deliberately applied to the genitals. Hungarian police stormed fifteen-year-old Max Eisen's home deliberately on Passover in 1944, when the family was gathered for the Jewish holiday. All were ordered to gather their belongings for deportation to the east (to Auschwitz). The police tried to maintain order, telling them to "stay together in column, you will stay with family." And at the Birkenau ramp, German SS officers carrying out the selection told Max Eisen, "Go to the right, you will see your family tomorrow."

The euphemisms and terse reports of Nazi killers obfuscate the suffering of the families, perhaps a tacit acknowledgment that depicting these familial relations would humanize the victims too much. At the police station where one of the Ukrainian killers in our photograph was located in 1943, about a hundred miles from Miropol, a German gendarme patrolling the area submitted this brief report:

> Pohrebysche, Gendarme Station
> On May 7, 1943, 21:00 hours, following a confidential report, 8 Jews, that is 3 men, 2 women, and 3 children were flushed out of a well-camouflaged hole in the ground in an open field not far from the post here, and all of them were shot while trying to escape. This case concerned Jews from Pohrebysche who had lived in the hole in the ground for almost a year. The Jews did not have anything else in their possession except their tattered clothing. The burial was carried out immediately on the spot.

The description of eight Jews, adults and children, indicates that this was a family unit, or perhaps one or two partial ones. No names are provided. This group had likely managed to survive on the run and in hiding until 1943 because of the aid of local Ukrainians, who provided shelter, food, and perhaps the rags they wore. But it seems that the goodwill of the locals had been exhausted. It took only one denouncer to bring the group's survival to an end. The Germans and their collaborators hunted Jewish families like this one, down to the very last mother, father, son, and daughter.

Hitler's allies appreciated the importance of including entire families in the measures they took to solve their nations' "Jewish problem." When the Slovakian president Father Tiso organized the first deportations of European Jews to Auschwitz, in March 1942, the call for six thousand Jews was changed to a demand for "family transports." According to the historian James Mace Ward, besides "ostensibly honoring natural law by not tearing apart families, the shift solved the problem of providing for the aged and very young in the absence of 'work capable' Jews." But many young Jews volunteered for deportation in the hopes of sparing their families the hardship. Among the deportees was a talented young Jewish woman named Helen Spitzer, a graphic artist and mandolin player from Bratislava who appeared at the deportation spot expecting to go to a summer camp with other girls, like "serving in the Peace Corps," she later told me. She never saw her parents again.

A lack of focus on the family as a meaningful category reflects more than an intellectual blind spot. Some of the worst stories of the suffering of victims of genocide and mass violence, the ones we can barely stomach, the ones that cause us to turn away in revulsion, center on the family. The fact that the photographer Škrovina focused on the mother and child was not by chance. The maternal image contains its own gendered aesthetic in the history of visual culture, but our photographer also understood he was capturing the ultimate act of barbarism, what would later be given the name genocide.

In Miropol, Ukrainian policemen and German customs guards took the "opportunity" to pull the trigger and blow away a family. In the photograph, the little boy is barefoot and dressed in his suit coat. He holds the hand of the woman, who, I now thought, might be his aunt. Perhaps the little boy abided or hesitated when instructed to walk with her to the edge of the pit. He had already seen others in his community, perhaps even his cousins, aunts, grandmothers, and grandfathers, being shot.

Most of the children were pushed into the pit, and some were then shot from above, as one German witness put it, "like fish in a barrel." Testimonies from the Sonderkommandos who worked in the gas chambers reveal that the weaker children and the elderly were found at the bottom of the pile of corpses; they had been pushed to the bottom by the stronger victims gasping for air. Nella Rost, who collected testimony in Krakow, observed that we need a new language to describe a mother "hearing the screams of her children being buried alive."

At war's end no Jewish family in Nazi-occupied eastern Europe was fully intact, and the small number of Jewish children who survived were orphans or left with one parent or a surrogate. And what haunted these child survivors for the rest of their lives, what they were unable to overcome, were memories not only of their own physical suffering but that of a parent or sibling.

Thus the family runs through the Holocaust as a major factor in Nazi racial ideology and its implementation, and in the testimonies of victims and survivors. It continues today in the active second- and third-generation movements and annual gatherings. The theme of family, as we've seen, can be key to conducting research on the Holocaust in genealogical records, in oral history, and in the material found in private family collections. And among the most common of these private sources is the family photograph. For the millions deported or forced into hiding or ghettos, the object most often packed and brought along, besides jewelry and currency, was the family photograph.

The father of genocide studies, Raphael Lemkin, lost forty-nine relatives. Yet in Lemkin's definition of the crime of all crimes, the family as the fundamental unit targeted in acts of genocide rarely appears. It is implicit in the term he coined, *genocide,* which combines the Greek word *genos,* denoting lineage, ancestry, or kin, and the Latin suffix *-cide,* meaning "slay, kill, or chop down." Two elements of the crime refer to the family: the taking away of children and the prevention of births. Since destroying the reproductive family unit is the sine qua non of biological erasure of any group that genocidaires deem the enemy, should we pay more attention to the plight of families in the history of genocide, and in prevention efforts today?

Family does not appear in the United Nations Convention on the Prevention and Punishment of the Crime of Genocide of 1948, which defines the victim as a "national, ethnic, racial or religious" group. It is implied, though, as a part of the target group. In the deliberations leading up to the UN convention, Soviet representatives had objected to considering political and class groups as victims, probably owing to Stalin's attacks on nationalists, non-Communists, peasants, and capitalists. Legal scholars at the time and since have debated what constitutes a target group, referring to clans and tribes as familial units claiming common descent. In Lemkin's explanation of genocidal acts that prevent life, he stressed the deliberate separation of families as a policy of depopulation, as well as the forced removal of children and measures, such as sterilization, to end procreation. Family appeared in indictments that defined war crimes and crimes against humanity as "any injury done with the intention of extermination, mutilation, or enslavement, against the life, freedom of opinion, the moral or physical integrity of the family, or the dignity of the human being, by reason of his opinion, his race, caste, family or profession."

At the 1948 Nuremberg military trial against members of the SS

Einsatzgruppen that led mass shootings in Ukraine and elsewhere in eastern Europe, the leading American prosecutor, Ben Ferencz, who interacted with Lemkin at that time and would later lead the cause of the International Criminal Court, made a powerful opening speech, confronting the killers in what he called the biggest mass-murder trial in history. Ferencz's words seem to speak to our Miropol photograph:

> The number of deaths resulting from the activities with which these defendants have been connected and which the prosecution has set at one million is but an abstract number. One cannot grasp the full cumulative terror of murder one million times repeated. It is only when this grotesque total is broken down into units capable of mental assimilation that one can understand the monstrousness of the things we are in this trial contemplating. One must visualize not one million people but only ten persons — men, women, and children, perhaps all of one family falling before the executioner's guns. If one million is divided by ten, this scene must happen one hundred thousand times, and as one visualizes the repetitious horror, one begins to understand the meaning of the prosecution's words, "It is with sorrow and with hope that we here disclose the deliberate slaughter of more than a million innocent and defenseless men, women, and children."

But Ferencz's calculation was an exception. There were no major discussions among the legal framers of the genocide convention or prosecutors at Nuremberg about the family as a category of analysis for understanding extreme acts of barbarism. Lemkin and other legal scholars focused on the anti-natal measures debated in the international eugenics movement and brutally implemented, in genocidal proportions, by the Nazis (through sterilization and forced assimilation). This is surprising because at this time of post-war restoration in Europe, the theme of family ran through other foundational legislation and campaigns to restore civilization by reuniting families and creating new ones.

Indeed, the international community made the rights of the family a priority. Within a day of the adoption of the UN convention on genocide, on December 9, 1948, the General Assembly issued the Declaration of Human Rights. In Section 3, it states, "The family is the national and fundamental group unit of society and is entitled to protection by society and the state."

The sun was setting over Jerusalem as I sat on my bed at the Prima Park Hotel near Yad Vashem. Files of victim lists, hand-drawn genealogical charts, and copies of the Miropol photographs were within reach. I had just finished the telephone call with Svetlana in Southfield, Michigan, and could still hear her agitated voice, how she inhaled, searched for English words, then spoke them in her Russian accent. I studied the faces in the family portrait memorialized in her Page of Testimony. They stared at me with no joy in their eyes. The women pressed their lips firmly together. The children looked frightened and confused. I compared my action shot of the murder with this family portrait. I wanted to match the little boy in the sailor suit, Boris Fila Sandler, with the boy in the suit who was being murdered. I thought Khiva could be the woman in the polka-dot dress. The delicate legs of the child slipping from the mother's lap in the gunfire could be traced to the torso, shoulders, round face, and sad eyes of the child Roman, Khiva's son, in the portrait. The faces in the family portrait stared at me, while the ones at the murder scene were not visible, obscured in the puff of smoke.

There was more work to be done to illuminate the family's story after this compelling telephone call with Svetlana, but my research itinerary was next taking me from Israel back to Ukraine to conduct forensic work at the mass-murder site with an investigative team. Still much progress had been made. I had the photograph of the murder, and I now had in my possession this rare family portrait, taken after the Nazis had arrived, one that indelibly showed each face as each wished to be pictured. The women are posing one last time for the camera: "We are what is left." "We were here." "Remember us!"

6

EXCAVATING HISTORY

Every village and town, every forest brims with graves looming
from a distance, as a historical lesson and a warning. Once the
living witnesses are gone, then those graves will speak volumes.
They will accuse the whole world, with an eloquence a hun-
dredfold mightier, of having committed, or having failed to act
against the cruelest of crimes.

— *Samuel Golfard, diary entry, April 11, 1943, Peremishliany, Ukraine*

Two YEARS AFTER my first road trip through Ukraine, in
1992, before I had seen the photograph and knew Miropol

only by name, Jewish religious organizations started to survey mass graves of the Holocaust. The Jewish Preservation Committee of Ukraine had identified 495 such sites. A more recent estimate of the number of mass graves in Ukraine, compiled by the Catholic-Jewish organization Yahad–In Unum, is 916. The US Commission for the Preservation of America's Heritage Abroad published a list of 1,500 cemeteries, mass graves, and synagogues, drawn up over a five-year period (1995–2000). This mapping of Jewish life and death requires the work of teams of local authorities: mayors, historians, genealogists, wartime witnesses, and Holocaust survivors.

Researching the Holocaust is a form of excavation, digging for traces of a people driven to near extinction. It often involves topographical clues as much as artifactual ones. At the mass graves in Ukraine, Yahad–In Unum researchers have found bones as well as Stars of David, wedding rings, dolls, and family photographs — buried objects that tell us what was most precious to the victims.

I had studied the Miropol photograph as evidence of the Jewish history of the town. It had led me to a routine Nazi *Aktion* on a small town's Jewish community in Ukraine and to an act of resistance by a photographer. It had given rise to an understanding of the centrality of the family in the phenomenon of genocide. Now the photograph sent me to the place where Škrovina once stood and where the victims remain. The Holocaust at Miropol left its mark on riverbanks, ravines, fields, and forests. This scarred landscape could be read as an extra-textual source.

As the forensic archaeologist Caroline Sturdy Colls observed, "The Holocaust sits between history and memory; it is neither a closed chapter nor still occurring." Exhuming the history of the

Holocaust disturbs sites and souls and raises important ethical questions. Anyone who participates in an onsite investigation, interviewing local witnesses and searching for remains, becomes a recorder, a disrupter, and a subject of this history. One violates Jewish religious law and the basic human right, as articulated by the United Nations Commission on Human Rights, "to rest in peace [as] a general principle of humanity."

In Miropol the landscape is another piece of evidence to triangulate with the other sources: first and foremost the photograph but also German and Slovakian wartime documents, postwar testimonies and oral histories, and artifacts such as the camera. Topography reveals how the perpetrators planned and carried out the crimes. Mass-shooting sites were often located at the outskirts of town, not far from a road, so that the victims could be brought by truck or made to walk to their deaths. A nearby fortress, barn, or shed may reveal other aspects of the event. Such sites were often used to hold the victims while the pits were prepared and during the mass shootings. In these holding pens the victims were forced to give up their valuables and often subjected to additional tortures. Wives and daughters were raped in front of husbands and fathers. Sadists among the German officials and local collaborators outdid one another in choreographing spectacles of barbarism, forcing orthodox Jewish men to shave their beards, dance on shards of glass, ride each other like animals, and eat their own feces. How visible and audible might these degrading displays have been to the local population, to the forest ranger, to the young cow herder, to the railway workers, to the children in the village school?

The event left its mark on local memory and on the ground itself. The digging of the mass graves in 1941, and after that, the decomposition of corpses created unusual depressions and mounds, a proliferation of new vegetation, and topographical mayhem of various kinds. I was not sure what I would find after seventy years. When I returned to Miropol in the summer of 2016, I discovered another disturbing fact of forensic archaeology: human bones rise to the surface.

The physical crime scene allowed me to draw upon more than forensic archaeology. Here I could test the veracity or reliability of different statements about the experiences of the victims and the actions of the perpetrators. How close was the center of town to the shooting and to the barracks where the photographer was billeted? What sounds could have been heard, and what could have been seen from the perimeter, from the grazing fields, the train station, the marketplace, the paper factory, and the local school?

In most cases of homicide, perpetrators are individual adult men, and so are their victims. We know that genocide is different. The killers murder in groups and their victims are entire families. Genocidaires develop systematic methods. They kill in broad daylight, mostly in secluded settings and pastoral landscapes.

The most famous mass shooting of the Holocaust occurred at Babi Yar. One of the few known photographs of the site at this time shows German officials picking through heaps of clothing; the image does not depict the mass murder. We need to pair this photograph with one of the most significant documents of the time, a brief report stating matter-of-factly that "Sonderkommando 4a in collaboration with Einsatzgruppe HQ and two Kommandos of Police Regiment South [including Orpo 303] executed 33,771 Jews in

Kiev on September 29 and 30, 1941." This, the largest mass shooting up to this point in time, happened over two days, on the outskirts of a capital city. It could hardly be kept secret. At least forty copies of this terse, post-action report were distributed across Berlin, to the SS, the police, the army, and the Nazi Party. Such reports were routinely read, discussed, analyzed, and copied, so that the 1941 mass shootings in Ukraine and across eastern Europe were widely known in the government and the party. Word spread across Europe as witnesses traveled home on leave or to other posts, eventually reaching a Jewish man in Dresden, Victor Klemperer. He noted in his diary in April 1942 the "ghastly mass murders of Jews in Kiev. The heads of small children smashed against walls, thousands of men, women, adolescents shot down in a great heap, a hillock blown up and the mass of bodies buried under the exploding earth."

The scale of the Babi Yar ravine killing has overshadowed the scope of the murders that occurred across Ukraine in smaller towns such as Miropol. Only now are we discovering the local shooting sites and human remains, raising the death toll of the Holocaust in Ukraine from an estimated 1.1 million to 1.5 million Jews. The Miropol massacre was replicated hundreds of times in the countryside, forests, riverbanks, and ravines of Ukraine. Each site contains its own history.

For the investigation of the mass grave in Miropol, I asked the Yahad–In Unum team to join me. The team had years of experience in Ukraine, using archival records to plot murder sites of the Holocaust, matching bullet casings to identify the murder weapons, identifying human remains, and collecting witness testimonies from local Ukrainians. The major force behind Yahad–In Unum's success has been Father Patrick Desbois, a French priest who has been awarded human rights honors from the United Nations, the German government, and the United States Congress; he has been featured on *60 Minutes* and other media outlets.

I know Father Desbois, and in preparation for the work I shared whatever material I had on Miropol, a location the team had not yet investigated. The archival material included maps of mass graves, as well as lists of names of Ukrainian police, local witnesses, and victims. Yahad–In Unum's team, a critical partner to me in Miropol, was especially skilled at collecting oral histories from Ukrainian villagers and eyewitnesses, which I needed, since my Ukrainian language skills were rudimentary.

Historians usually conduct research alone and do not go to sites outside of archives to carry out fieldwork as part of a team — and certainly not one that includes international investigators, interpreters, and videographers reporting to an eminent Catholic priest. But research on the Holocaust has grown into a multidisciplinary endeavor, bringing together myriad professionals and laypersons in a rare case of international solidarity, something that sadly was not available to the millions of victims during the war.

In Miropol, we planned to collect testimonies and establish basic facts that had been filtered and distorted by more than seventy years of Sovietization. Lead investigators on the Yahad–In Unum team briefed me about what to expect in Ukraine. They told me not to divulge, during interviews with Ukrainian witnesses, that most of my source material came from KGB investigations. Mere mention of the KGB would arouse old fears of spies, and the witnesses would clam up. At the site of the mass grave, which I had identified based on maps used in a 1986 Soviet Ukrainian trial against the wartime Miropol militia, we would search for bullet casings to establish that the ammunition was German. It might be possible to measure the dimensions of the mass grave or graves and estimate the number of persons killed. These colleagues were doubtful that we would find one of the former policemen, or even the families of policemen. The locals tended to withhold such information, out of fear and respect for the privacy of the children and grandchildren of the killers. In small communities like Miropol, family histories are familiar to everyone, and tacit pacts of secrecy exist as to who was a wartime traitor, a Soviet patriot, or a Ukrainian nationalist, making it hard for outsiders to gather information. Yet some of today's elderly, who were children during the war, do want to talk; some wish to clear their conscience before they die.

Our investigative team — historians, interviewers, interpreters, a videographer, a cameraman, and a driver — started by casting a wide net to identify anyone who had been living in wartime Miropol. During the day, Yahad–In Unum's investigators worked in two pairs, a younger Ukrainian couple and a middle-aged one; they walked and drove around town, attempting to engage the elderly. At night they reported back to the team and me about possible interview subjects, including those who had witnessed the mass shootings and any persons who had some memory of or interaction with Jews in Miropol.

On our first day in Miropol, while we waited to hear back from the investigators, we pulled out the trial sketches of the mass graves. We traveled by van on the road leading from the central marketplace to the fortress and continued into the forest on a dirt road paralleling the river. I remembered the road from my first visit to Miropol, with Anatoly and Felix in the summer of 2014. But this time we drove past the ravine. One Soviet sketch showed that there were at least two shooting sites, and the larger one, with multiple mass graves, was in a forest clearing farther down the road.

We reached the end of the fortress grounds, where the dilapidated Soviet military compound stands. We could see a dirt path veering into the forest and decided that this route, on the east side of the Sluch River, might lead to the location of the mass shooting. We got out of the van and walked into the forest, looking for the clearing indicated in the sketches. Only a few hundred meters in, we saw a nursery of pine trees, rows of glistening saplings drenched in light accentuated by the dark frame of the thick forest. We recognized the rectangular lot from the satellite images on Google Maps and knew the massacre site should be along the eastern edge of this pine-tree nursery. We turned east and picked up our pace, in anticipation of discovering it. A narrow, bumpy footpath led us into a strange landscape, a forest bed of muddy mounds with circular trenches — what forensic archaeologists call the halo effect.

The anthropologist and forensic expert Katherine J. Powell, who has written extensively on police methods for detecting the burial of human skeletal remains, explains that the initial digging and any later exhumation of graves makes a significant impact on the environment. Usually plants, multiple seasons of fallen leaves, and other debris are found on a forest floor. When the Miropol pits were created in 1941, the diggers cut through multiple layers of soil, of different colors and textures. The top layers mixed with the earth below, disrupting the baseline and the natural layering of sediment above it.

Decomposition changes the nutrients in soil and its acidity. Some plants and fungi, including nettles and certain mushrooms (ammonia fungi and post-putrefaction fungi), thrive under the new conditions. Children's bones decay faster than those of adults because of their higher collagen content. Thus the Jewish children in Miropol, who are more difficult to identify in wartime documents than are adults, are also less likely to be uncovered and identified as human skeletons.

When the soil was returned to the grave to cover the victims, it underwent a process of resettling or consolidation, which created the unusual topography of trenches and mounds. The plant life recolonized in a way that is inconsistent with the vegetation of the surrounding area. In moist environments like this Ukrainian forest, the displaced soil was less compact than that of surrounding areas and produced more vegetation.

The presence of the victims also interferes with the environment. We can see in the photograph that the Miropol victims were clothed and inhumed — placed into an ecosystem. Decomposition begins with bloating and the release of bodily fluids; the earth has to expand to absorb this. Maggots, mites, and flies, as well as jackals, boars, and other scavengers, burrow in and feed off the remains. One German butcher stationed with Nazi occupation officials in wartime Chudniv, a town neighboring Miropol, was questioned after the war about the crimes against the Jews. While he denied participating in or directly witnessing mass shootings, he knew about them, and recalled that one day when he was slaughtering a boar, he found human limbs inside the animal.

The geological impact of the Holocaust by bullets is irreversible, and yet it is easy to overlook because the forms of evidence are subtle. I was standing on top of one of the mounds, absorbing the entire scene around me — pillars of tree trunks, canopies of branches, and taps of light rainfall. The chugging sound made by a train in the distance echoed off the trees eerily, like a salvo. I noticed that our French videographer had put down his camera and was reaching down into the muck of leaves to pick up something. It was white. He brushed aside the dirt and began to identify its rounded contours — it was a fragment of an adult human skull. He pointed to the imprints on the bone, intricate markings, which I later learned were cortical sulcal patterns. These traces represent the convolutions of the pulsating cerebral cortex. Each individual has a unique configuration. I reached down too and lifted up a wet clump of leaves and soil. I separated my fingers to sift through it, and white shards appeared in my open palm. I had grown up playing outside in the yard and in forests, gathering sticks and building forts. This white matter was nothing like anything that I had held before. It was hard, partially round, with blunt-toothed edges, like part of a cog. It was the remains of a human vertebra. I asked how it could be that these bones were so easy to find after more than seventy years. Had animals or other scavengers dug them up?

Perpetrators sought to dispose of bodies quickly and easily, and they put nature to work to facilitate the process. The soil was used to suffocate; the rivers used to drown; the precipice of a ravine used to pull victims struck by bullets down into the natural pit below;

the walls of the ravine dynamited to cover up the bodies. The Nazis went further to destroy the evidence of their crimes. They produced quicklime chemicals to accelerate decomposition of bodies at the killing sites. They repurposed wheat grinders to crush the bones.

The SS killer who had organized the mass shootings of Jews in the region of Zhytomyr, including those in and around Miropol, was Colonel Paul Blobel. He was assigned to a new task in 1942 — the exhumation and burning of human remains. In August 1943 his Sonderkommando 1005 (Jewish prisoners sworn to secrecy) was based about ninety miles from Miropol in Rivne (Rowno). Blobel ordered the offices of local police to provide a list of all mass graves, with brief descriptions of their locations. The cryptic list indicates two hundred sites: "Szepetowka, in forest, 3 graves; Slavuta, in forest, 1 grave, in the gravel pit, 1 grave; Laktschi, 1 km south of town, in the quarry; Melnija, 2 km west of the town in the sand pits, 1 grave; Gorochow, 1 km south of town, 100 meters from the path, 1 grave; near the quarry; next to the river, next to the Jewish cemetery."

Blobel assigned Sonderkommandos to the grisly work of exhuming and burning the remains, and then these laborers were routinely killed to complete the cover-up, just as other Jews had been killed after digging the mass graves now being revisited.

In the 1949 Geneva Conventions, the rights of civilians killed in time of war were extended to include an honorable burial and a marked grave. There was nothing honorable about this open site in Miropol, with its scattered fragments of bones. The secular and religious violations suffered by the Jews murdered in Miropol's forest seemed unending. Ukrainian witnesses described the wartime Jewish community as observant — over two decades of Communist rule, despite its brutalities, could not undo centuries of religious belief and cultural practices. A former Ukrainian schoolmate of a Jewish family in town recalled that, although the Jewish prayer house had been destroyed, along with the Orthodox Christian church, in the 1930s, the Jews remained very religious. They prayed at home. She could see at night, through the windows, how they sat together, holding hands by candlelight.

The site had produced human remains, bones not meant to be found, as well as extraordinary memories tied to this place in the forest. Petro G. and Leonid U. had been grazing cows in fields near the mass-murder site. Leonid recalled three shootings, which he saw while crouched in the forest. As he struggled to describe the layout of the scene, we handed him a pen and paper. He drew a sketch that matched the archival records. We noticed how he became transformed as he spoke; his tone and mannerisms became childlike, as if he had returned to that time in his life. He started to sob as he explained that his mother would have beaten him for revealing these secrets. She had told him, "Do not go into the woods!"

The Universal Jewish Encyclopedia (1941) contains a lengthy entry on burial customs, the kind that this community would have understood and observed, as one can see today in the historic Jewish cemetery in Miropol. The Burial Society in Miropol laid down rules of conduct, including punishment for anyone who "opened his mouth or used bad language in the home of the dying or at the cemetery." The ancient Hebrews regarded burial as being "gathered unto one's people" (Genesis 49:33). Bodies were not to be buried at the same time, in the same grave; this would violate the peace of the dead. A deceased person had to be prepared, washed, and clothed for the afterlife. Women's hair was shorn and, in some traditions, bequeathed as an act of remembrance. Human remains were not to be disturbed except to be transferred to the Holy Land of Palestine or reunited with family in a family plot. Desecration of a grave was considered an act of wickedness. According to Halakhic law and Jewish burial customs, the soul remains attached to the body, to the bones. To disturb a grave is to disturb a soul.

For decades the unprotected state of the mass graves in Miropol remained an unsettled issue, though not one constantly in the public eye. Things changed in the 1980s. Jewish survivors and relatives of the murdered who had immigrated to Israel and Canada returned to the town. One of them, named Kremer, had lost eighteen members of his family. Another was a successful businessman named Rapaport, whose family members appear on the first victim lists handwritten by Soviet investigators. These surviving relatives, including men who had seen the hell of the battlefront, were now determined to avenge the murders of their loved ones on the home front and to make sure their families were honored with a proper burial. They pressed the regional authorities to do something about the unprotected mass graves in the forest. Everyone knew of their location and vulnerability to theft and natural disturbance. The local non-Jewish population was interested in them insofar as they might contain Jewish gold and other valuables or the remains of former Red Army soldiers, prisoners of war, or members of the Soviet resistance.

When I interviewed the retired mayor in 2016, he recalled having met Rapaport in Miropol in the 1980s. True to the tradition of Ukrainian hospitality, the mayor had hosted him with a hearty meal and goodwill toasts of fiery vodka, raising shot glass after shot glass to the friendship of the peoples and world peace. Rapaport announced that he would like to invest in the local paper factory, still a vital industry for the town; the facility had historically been managed by the Jews, including his own father, who had been shot in the forest. The mayor brought this proposal to the municipal leadership, including representatives of the Communist Party. They rejected it as suspicious, an example of capitalist manipulation and foreign interference.

Before my first research trip to Miropol with Anatoly and Felix, before the 1980s exhumations, the mass graves in Miropol had already been disturbed many times: first by the so-called black diggers, local plunderers looking for gold; then officially in 1945, when the Soviet Extraordinary Commission (Excomm) carried out a superficial exhumation; and then again in 1986, when the investigation was reopened. In the two official instances, locals were requisitioned to dig the site. The Miropol commission in 1945 consisted of eight investigators, medical and legal experts supported by local leaders in the church, schools, and police, who summoned witnesses. Its final report was not complete. It accounted for two killing actions in which Jewish victims were shot and buried four hundred meters from town, in the park. But there were at least three killing sites in the forest park: two at the location in the photograph near the pine nursery and one at a ravine near the park's entrance near the Sluch River. Also, the final report did not discuss the pogroms that accompanied the shootings. The fact that there is a report on Miropol at all (though the file is slim) attests to the scope of the work of Soviet investigators during and immediately following the war.

At the time of the second Soviet exhumation, in October 1986, more than forty years had passed since that day in the park pictured in the photograph. But still the hard evidence of the crime was buried: the bones and the bullets. And so the senior KGB investigator, Major Mikola Makareyvych, contacted a forensic doctor and a ballistics specialist. The team worked in Miropol for about ten days, collecting statements and forcing three identified suspects to retrace the steps of the column of Jewish victims to the forest.

The witnesses and collaborators knew the exact locations of the shooting sites and pits. For the purposes of the investigation, Makareyvych decided, it would be sufficient to begin exhuming in three areas (including the site in the photograph). The bulldozer pushed through the soil's top layers of leaves and mud, tearing apart the tangle of roots and overturning trees. Then laborers from the paper factory who wanted to help started to dig with shovels and by hand. About one and a half meters into the earth, they discovered a layer of lime, and below that, soil mixed with human remains. Dr. Bitman, a bespectacled forensic scientist in a white lab coat, was especially meticulous because (according to the recollections of Miropol's mayor) he was Jewish. Bitman lifted the bone fragments with his gloved hands, carefully placing them on sheets of paper. He brushed away the soil and lime and lined them up like puzzle pieces that might fit together: jawbone, frontal skull, shoulder blade, hipbones, a vertebra, the bones of a man, a woman, children. Bitman signed this official photograph, which documents an assistant organizing the human remains at the same crime scene where Škrovina had been present with his camera.

Фото №2 Систематизация костных останков
Эксперт   С. Битман

In our 2016 interview with a guard who had been assigned in 1986 to protecting the site, he recalled expressing shock when the doctor showed him the smashed skulls of two children and hand bones tied with barbed wire. "I remember that vividly," he told us, as we searched the site with him nearly twenty years later. As he recounted the history of the exhumation, he stopped and pointed to a weed-covered mound, stating, "Oh, here is a grave that we did not open."

The bones that were recovered were placed in five coffins. One contained the children's bones, another the former head of the Jewish community; he could be identified because he had a leg deformity, which Dr. Bitman discovered among the remains. Why did more bones surface when I visited the site in 2016, thirty years later? It could be a case of soil erosion. Perhaps the roots of trees, the digging of plunderers, or the scavenging of animals pushed them to the surface. More likely it was a combination of these forces and other disturbances. When we interviewed the guard, he stated that he had to chase away curious people who were poking around; also, in 1986 the bulldozer had plowed through the mass graves and overturned the soil with the bones.

After we notified the Jewish community and a rabbi in Strasbourg about the unmarked and unprotected site, I informed colleagues at the German national memorial in Berlin, which had funding to care for such burial places. In 2009, Father Desbois had stood in the German parliament, the Bundestag, and argued that the German government had cared for decades for the upkeep of hundreds of thousands of Wehrmacht and SS graves in eastern Europe. Who should care for the gravesites of Holocaust victims? Chancellor Merkel's government allocated funds in response to Desbois's plea.

Within a week of my report to the German authorities, a team arrived to mark the site. They surveyed it, about two hectares of land adjacent to the former Soviet military base and the tree nursery. They brought a geo-radar scanner to see if the earth showed signs of a mass grave. But the effort failed. The terrain, they explained, was too overgrown with tangled roots. They could not manage to get the signal into the ground to detect gaps and holes in soil layers; proper scanning to determine the scope and depth of the graves would be time-consuming and costly. To protect and memorialize this site, given its location near the restricted land of the former military base, would entail government negotiations. Besides, I was told, there are hundreds of other towns with mass graves. They cannot possibly cover them all.

7

THE MISSING MISSING

PHOTOGRAPHS DOCUMENT AND recall the past; they depict what is now gone, and they conjure up emotions. Survivors retelling their life stories on film hold up personal photographs at the end of an interview. They cling to the photographs because they often are all they have of loved ones who were disappeared or killed without a proper burial and without a formal death certificate documenting their existence. When I researched photographs as an element of the Shoah Foundation testimonies (searching more than fifty thousand videotaped survivors), I dis-

covered a pattern. Survivors presented snapshots of wartime atrocities as well as family photographs, exhorting viewers to look at the
atrocity shots, declaring, "This is what happened to my family, and
to Jews across Europe." Survivors, in this way, beseech us to remember. Their identification as victims starts with their family history
of persecution and the experiences of loved ones who were unable
to emigrate from Europe and whose exact fates remain unknown.
We know what happened to the family in the Miropol photograph,
yet they are among half a million unidentified Holocaust victims in
Ukraine.

World War II introduced a new understanding of the depths
of human cruelty in the massive crime of genocide; this era also
opened up a new chapter in international humanitarian relief and
rehabilitation programs, aimed mostly at assisting refugees, searching for the missing, and reuniting families. Millions of civilians
and prisoners of war in Europe had been forcibly relocated and
detained in tens of thousands of sites run by the Nazis and their
allies: concentration camps, labor camps, ghettos, and killing centers. The uprooted in Europe included hundreds of thousands of
orphaned children. At war's end, the Allies implemented the Yalta
Agreement to repatriate displaced persons (DPs) to their countries
of origin. The Allies took on the enormous challenge of caring
for "stateless" Jews and orphans who had no home to return to; to
house them they used available sites such as the former concentration camp Ebensee, a twelfth-century monastery near Dachau, or
Feldafing, a former Hitler Youth Camp in Bavaria. The Jews among
the displaced persons, numbering about 250,000, called themselves

by the Yiddish or Hebrew term for "remnant," *oysgevortzlte,* "a person ripped from his roots," or *di nisht dershtokhene, di nisht gehargete, di nisht gekoylete:* "the not killed, the not slain, the not gunned down." The term *survivor* came later. In the immediate aftermath of the war, Jews said, "I am what is left," not, triumphantly, "I am a survivor." The novelist Meyer Levin recalled in his autobiography, *In Search,* that traumatized Jews who appeared in the European offices of Jewish relief agencies presented a fragmented account of what had happened, using words and locations, such as Treblinka, that he had never heard of. As Levin described it, these Jews all had their own mental snapshots, which in 1945 could not be "properly developed."

A ragged sixteen-year-old Ludmilla Blekhman returned to liberated Miropol on June 30, 1944. She wore the shirt that she swore had saved her. It was all that she had left of her former life. Her home was demolished; all her family's personal possessions were gone. Ukrainian neighbors had ripped the wooden planks from the floors and walls and carted them away for firewood or other uses. Realizing fully that all she hoped for — her family and her home — was gone, Ludmilla began to cry as never before. She had suffered many nights living like an animal in the woods, hiding in fields and forests, wading through swamps, fending off rats. She had been arrested by the Gestapo and under torture had maintained that she was a Ukrainian peasant girl. For two years and nine months, she had been on the run, in constant fear and hunger, pretending to be someone she was not while grieving the violent murder of her parents and siblings. And when the war was over, she realized that she was indeed utterly alone. In a 1944 letter, Ludmilla wrote to a distant aunt and uncle in Moscow: "Dear Uncle Ilya and Aunt Fanya, I received your letter drenched in tears. Yes, I have neither father nor mother, nor sisters [...] I have no one. Somehow I miraculously survived."

Ludmilla thought about all the people who had betrayed her family. One of them was Nadia, the close friend of her older sister. They were schoolmates; each was the kind of girlfriend you share secrets with, the kind you pose with in a photograph to seal your friendship for life. When Ludmilla returned to Miropol, she went looking for Nadia. But she did not embrace her as an old friend. She confronted her. Nadia had served as a translator for the Germans. Ludmilla cried out to her: "You betrayed us! Please give me that photo you have, posing with my sister." The photograph was Ludmilla's only trace of her sister.

As survivors gradually returned to life, rehabilitated with rations and medicine administered by Allied military personnel, Red Cross nurses, Jewish welfare agencies, and United Nations relief workers, their immediate concern was to find loved ones and reunite with family members. In the offices of the Central Tracing Bureau in Hamburg and Munich, aid workers set about helping ten million people find one another, processing sacks of letters from people writing to register their lost loved ones or greeting children who appeared, seeking their parents. The German radio broadcasted names and birth dates, whatever information the children could provide. Surviving Jews made inquiries and searched for traces of their missing relatives, hoping for miracles but assuming the worst.

In the first year after the war, the Allies, under the terms of the Yalta Agreement, repatriated most of the refugees. An estimated 4.2 million Soviet citizens, soldiers, and civilians were shipped back to eastern Europe — and to Russian gulags if they were suspected of collaboration with the Nazis. Others registered in the displaced persons camps, aiming to start new lives beyond war-torn Europe. But about 3.585 million were reported missing. The vast majority were from the territories of interwar Poland, including western Ukraine. They were "Jews and various categories of racial deportees [who] were exterminated in such large numbers, and often without record"; aid workers and tracing services found it impossible to determine their fates. These were the *registered* missing. What about the *missing* missing? Half of the victims murdered in the Babi Yar ravine on September 29–30, 1941, have not been named. The same is true for the Miropol massacre. For roughly half of the victims, there were no surviving family members, as there were for the Vaselyuk women and children photographed in Miropol.

Already in early 1944, the Supreme Headquarters of the Allied Expeditionary Forces had established the Central Tracing Bureau (renamed the International Tracing Service in 1948) to deal with "the tracing problem," defined as "the process of determining the location of persons whose present whereabouts, alive or dead, are being sought by their relatives, friends or governments." The Central Tracing Bureau sought "to establish the fate of those missing who cannot be found alive." This was arguably the biggest bureaucratic and humanitarian challenge ever undertaken, and the process continues to this day. According to the bureau, society could not be reconstructed until "basic human relationships had been restored." The living wanted confirmation of the deaths in their family, definite evidence, for psychological, legal, and other reasons. Those tasked with responding to inquiries quickly came to realize "the thoroughness and brutality with which the Fascist agencies extirpated their enemies."

What traces could be used to find loved ones? In the foreground of the Miropol photograph is a pair of men's shoes. When I first studied them, I wondered if they belonged to a father, brother, or uncle of the women and children being murdered. I surmised that he, as head of a household and its protector, was killed first, in front of his family. The silence of those empty shoes also reminded me of the numerous Holocaust museum displays featuring victims' shoes. At the United States Holocaust Memorial Museum, visitors stand before a glass wall behind which piles of shoes have been curated in pairs. Small red-leather Mary Janes belonging to a girl, sturdy black heels with decorative stitching belonging to a woman, flat brown oxfords with laces belonging to a man — each marked with impressions unique to an individual's feet. At the Szeged synagogue in Hungary, more than three thousand Jews were detained on the eve of their deportation; they were beaten, subjected to body searches, and forced to give up their valuables, including their shoes. Here in this postwar 1945 photograph from Szeged we see women searching through the shoes of the dead and missing Jews.

Few records, as we've seen, documented the individual mass-shooting victims by name. Neither Stalin nor Hitler accepted the international norms for the treatment and return of captured civilians and soldiers stipulated by the Geneva Convention of 1929 or The Hague Convention of 1907; these standards included providing lists of the names of prisoners to inform families and pave the way for eventual repatriation. When Nazi leaders evacuated their offices, fleeing before the advance of the Red Army into Germany, they destroyed camp and prisoner records. As the Jews and Poles were destroyed in the Warsaw uprisings of 1943 and 1944, for example, the offices in the ghettos and the city that housed their records were also incinerated. Jews deported to gassing centers and killed upon arrival were not registered by name or given a unique prisoner identification number in the camp records. They might appear on a deportation list, but their eventual fates were not documented. For Jews in rural areas of Ukraine and the Soviet Union, like Miropol, who were shot on site, the Nazis and their accomplices did not bother to list the names of those killed. They did not even bother to write up a descriptive report of the massacre; the genocidaires were obligated only to register, in writing or by oral statement, that the *Aktion* was complete. They rushed to make Europe *Judenrein*, to erase Jews from history and memory, not to document each one for posterity.

At the International Military Tribunal at Nuremberg, during the afternoon session of February 27, 1946, a member of the Soviet prosecution team questioned Samuel Rajzman, who had been deported in August 1942 with his family and eight thousand other Jews from the Warsaw ghetto to Treblinka. Rajzman provided one of the first detailed accounts of the gassing facility, including the bogus train station, replete with signs for the ticket and telegraph office and a restaurant. This was all a ruse meant to calm the Jews, who were gassed upon arrival. But when Rajzman arrived at Treblinka he was assigned to a labor commando in charge of loading the clothing of the "murdered persons on the trains." After two days there, his mother, sister, and two brothers arrived. He watched them being led to the gas chambers. "Several days later when [I] was loading clothes on the freight cars, my comrades found my wife's documents and a photograph of my wife and children. That is all I have left of my family, only a photograph."

Determining the fate of the missing when the paper trail was thin or nonexistent took time and required efforts that spanned continents and involved myriad agencies. Welfare workers and newly established tracing agencies worked feverishly, realizing that the likelihood of establishing the whereabouts and the fates of the missing depended on living witnesses, such as Samuel Rajzman. Survivors and relatives abroad posted notices in newspapers, wrote letters to international and local authorities, and made inquiries with former neighbors. But the success rate was not high: for Jewish organizations in New York, less than 20 percent; in London, around 9 percent; and in Warsaw, the Jewish Joint Distribution Committee's rate of documenting the fates of the missing was between 10 and 20 percent. The German Jewish paper *Aufbau,* popular among émigrés in New York, served as an outlet for this effort, publishing lists of missing relatives and obituaries honoring the murdered and documenting their existence and their fate. On *Aufbau*'s page of death notices in February 1946, one can read that Joseph Schaeler and his wife Elisabeth "died the martyr's death in the gas chambers of Auschwitz in the night from March 16th to the 17th, 1943." Over time relatives gave up their searches as they realized that a sister, mother, brother, father, or child was among the millions murdered. Their loved one was no longer findable. In the historian Jan Lambertz's words, "When did the 'missing' become the perished? When did the tunnel of grief begin?"

The survivors needed some form of documentation that officially vouched for who they were, where and when they had been born, and what had happened to them during the war. Among the largest group of survivors were Soviet and Polish Jews who had been evacuated quickly or had otherwise escaped the Nazi occupation. As refugees and deported laborers, they trudged bad roads and unfinished railway routes, and they languished in overcrowded camps and desolate junctions within inner Russia, Kazakhstan, Uzbekistan, and the Middle East.

Svetlana Budnitskaya and her family were among those evacuees. She was about five years old when she, her mother, and her brother were sent to a labor camp in inner Russia. Their father had been drafted into the Red Army, and they reunited in 1945. Their search for family began when they journeyed back to Miropol. Svetlana's father inquired about his sister, Khiva Vaselyuk; his mother, Esya; and his nieces and nephews. He learned that there were no Jews left in Miropol. They had been shot in the park. He was told that in October 1941 his own mother had been carried to the mass-shooting site in her bed and thrown into the pit. This was the story that local Ukrainians told him then and that Svetlana repeated to me in 2016.

One of our witnesses in Miropol, Zinaida L., knew the Vaselyuk family and had seen the grandmother Esya murdered in her bed. When the Yahad–In Unum team and I visited her to film her testimony, we found her seated calmly on her front porch. Her daughter, presumably taking leave from her regular workday, sat beside her. When we opened the front gate, the chickens and dogs became excited, clucking and barking in a frenzy. The cottage was quaint, with a fresh coat of blue trim and colorful flowers in well-tended beds. Garden flip-flops and weathered shoes of different sizes were lined up by the front door.

We went inside the home, where Zinaida sat upright at the center of the couch. She was uneasy about being filmed. She combed her hair but looked away from the camera. She knew what we wanted to hear about, so she immediately launched into her wartime experiences. During the occupation her father was privileged. He had special skills as a railway engineer and could help repair the lines, so the Germans compensated him with a Jewish home in the center of town, where there were paved sidewalks. It had been the hat maker's house. Zinaida knew for sure because she saw the textiles and tools in the cellar. She recalled that horrible night:

> At that time, during the German occupation, we were not allowed to use power. There was no electricity at night to light our homes. We used kerosene lamps. And one night I was just a child but distinctly remember it was by candlelight and it was late, just before midnight, and we heard screaming, crying, clamoring outside under our window. Though my father told me to stay in bed, I disobeyed him because I was afraid and curious. At daybreak I went to the window and looked out. My father tried to chase me from the window. But I went back to see. I saw on the pavement, that sidewalk, that a column of Jews were walking along there, crying and screaming. There were thirty or forty people, including children. They were forced to gather and then march toward the park. It was horrible. And then later I heard the gunfire. I heard it myself. Days later the Polizei continued to search for the Jews. I saw something else. From our house we could see below to a courtyard another Jewish house. And there were stables between and we children were curious, we wanted to see what was happening at that Jewish house behind ours. We placed planks under the window of the barn, so that we could see out, we were curious children. And I saw this old woman being carried out in a bed, and the policemen shot her dead in the yard in her bed. She was too old to walk.

Zinaida continued to explain that the elderly woman was the grandmother of a young Jewish woman who had managed to escape. And she had fled from the house before the Polizei came. She was running, looking for a hiding place. And she came to Zinaida's house and was hiding in the garage. She had seen what happened to her grandmother. And that young woman had no parents. They had been taken earlier that day to the shooting. Zinaida's family hid this Jewish woman for one week in their cellar. They fed her. Zinaida's father had connections to the partisans and he took her to them, in the woods. He tried to save her, but Zinaida did not know what happened to that woman.

Was "that woman" pictured in the Vaselyuk family portrait? Could she have been the mother of the little boy Fila, as Svetlana had called him? We showed Svetlana's family photo to Zinaida, but she did not recognize anyone in it.

There are problems with this testimony. Zinaida was a child at the time, and whatever she saw, she probably could not make sense of then. She likely drew on the memories and stories of others to do so, and then to narrate the events to me. However, core elements of her story match Svetlana's. To my knowledge she had no contact in Michigan with Svetlana, who was evacuated during the war. And it is extremely unlikely that they ever crossed paths after the war. But the intersecting stories of these two individuals are remarkable. The Vaselyuks' family tragedy had clearly passed from local memory to history.

Esya's granddaughter Svetlana settled, after returning as an evacuee from inner Russia, in Ukraine, in Zhytomyr, the largest town near Miropol and the district capital. She completed her schooling, married, and had two children. After her mother died in Ukraine in 1992, she and her husband immigrated to the United States with her elderly father, to join her son near Detroit, Michigan. This was my next destination. I booked a ticket to Detroit and drove with a videographer to Svetlana's home in Southfield. After years of archival research and interviews with Ukrainian witnesses who could not identify the family in the Miropol photograph, I believed that this visit with Svetlana might conclude my search for the missing family.

When I arrived, I was warmly greeted by her son, daughter, and granddaughter. All of us became acquainted over lunch and then proceeded to the living room, where the cameraman was setting up. We completed the paperwork necessary to deposit the interview in the archives of the United States Holocaust Memorial Museum. Svetlana's story was not among the more than 100,000 audiovisual testimonies archived thus far. As a child evacuee, she did not self-identify as a "survivor" of the Holocaust, but rather as part of a displaced family of the Great Patriotic War.

She and I sat together on her couch. Svetlana had prepared for my visit by gathering her photo albums, all stacked up, with glossy, soft vinyl covers. I grew up with albums like these; they were very popular in the 1980s and '90s but now archivists and conservators detest them because their adhesive chemicals hasten the deterioration of photographs. Often when we peel back the clear covers, these original images tear.

Svetlana was anxious to open her albums. It did not seem like the right moment to point out that a shoebox might be a better place to preserve her family photos. She eagerly pulled back the plastic covers and lifted the images so that we could get a closer look and also check for any markings on the backs of them. There were black-and-white images of the world that was prewar Ukraine and of Svetlana's hometown, Miropol. Svetlana had no physical location where she might honor the remains of her grandparents, no gravesite to visit to say Kaddish. But she had these photographs. She ordered them by generation. The prewar photos showed her extended family looking proudly at the camera: in one image, her mother smiles while reclining on a rock while vacationing in Crimea, and in another, she plays in the forest of the Miropol Park. It is the same park where the ravine descends into the Sluch River, the park where the Jews were shot and I had discovered the bones. The photograph popped out on the page for me because of the polka-dot dress Svetlana's mother wore. It matched the fabric of the dress worn by the woman at the moment of death at the center of our 1941 photo. In the Soviet economy, consumer products offered little variety. In the 1930s that polka-dot material was probably mass-produced and distributed to local seamstresses or tailors to customize for their clients. Svetlana's mother's father was one of the tailors in Miropol.

Svetlana's stories were memory shards from her disrupted childhood. At times she became confused and presented stories that she had read about in the samizdat collection of survivor testimonies, *The Black Book of Soviet Jewry*. I asked Svetlana about other Jews from Miropol, if she knew any more information about families who lived there. She replied that she had no ties there and knew no one currently living in Miropol. She was living out the rest of her life in Michigan, between two worlds, as a Ukrainian émigré of Jewish heritage in a Detroit suburb, in a middle-class community of ranch-style homes, yawning yards, and cracked sidewalks. At the end of our interview I pulled out the Miropol atrocity photograph. She briefly looked at it and then turned away. She could not, or perhaps did not want to, identify anyone in it. She was growing weary, and wept. I realized that the interview was over. I should not have upset her with this violent image depicting what had happened, possibly to her relatives — the woman might have been one of her aunts and the children, her cousins. Svetlana would be unable to make a positive identification anyway. She had been five years old in 1941. Moreover, the victims' faces are barely visible.

The missing as subjects of history will elude us. Try as I did, with all the advantages of modern technology and access, I could not identify the family with certainty. Svetlana was not an eyewitness to events in Miropol. Ludmilla Blekhman, the only known survivor of the massacre, died in Israel in 2015 before I could interview her and show her the photograph.

In another attempt to find someone who might recognize the family in the photograph, I conducted interviews with Ukrainians in Miropol who had ties to the Jewish community during the war. They had faint and fading childhood memories of the Jews. Antoniya C. and Fanya T., both born in 1926, remembered the names of their Jewish classmates and friends who had invited them for Jewish Passover meals and treats. These were sensory snapshots: classic childhood recountings of sweets, first tastes of melon and ice cream, warm hospitality, the care given to them by the dentist (who went mad when the Nazis killed his wife and child in 1941), the prewar sightings of Jews' beautiful dresses and embroidered hats in the marketplace, and the cleverness of a skilled female bookkeeper who worked at the paper factory. Ukrainians remembered playing hopscotch and hide-and-seek with their Jewish friends, who spoke "their Jewish language" (Yiddish). One recalled that the last time she heard that language was when the Jews said goodbye to one another in the marketplace and recited Hebrew prayers while being marched to the forest. I wrote down any Jewish names that were mentioned by the Ukrainians, and some were not on the lists in the archives. But each time I presented the photograph at the end of an interview, the subject looked and, with a shake of the head, turned away.

8

JUSTICE

THE PERPETRATORS IN the photograph did not go missing after the war. Their fates are known. We've seen that Kurt
Hoffmann denounced the German killers to the authorities and
that one was questioned in 1969 but then released. They got away
with murder, as most of the lower-level German perpetrators did.

But not the Ukrainians pictured in the photo.

When the Germans evacuated Miropol in late 1943, they left
most of their Ukrainian police collaborators behind to contend

with the Red Army liberators, who arrived on January 6, 1944. These men had to conceal themselves and establish alibis and records of patriotic service. They joined the Soviet partisans and slipped into the rank and file of the Red Army. Some relocated to hide from neighbors who knew them and what they had done. They took on new identities and married, lying to spouses about their wartime activities.

In Miropol, the worst offenders were finger-pointed by the local population and resistance fighters, and they became targets for reprisals. In 1944, the Red Army arrived with intelligence operatives (SMERSH units), interrogators, and military field tribunals. The police who could be caught were treated in a vindictive, expedient manner. They were marched to the town center, where the population was gathered. The officers were seated, their hands tied behind their backs. The charges of war crimes were read aloud, the guilty verdict declared, and the death sentence carried out immediately. A makeshift gallows was erected, and the police were noosed and made to stand on top of a truck, which then moved slowly away as a Soviet official pronounced the men "traitors to the homeland."

The peasant girl Lydia S., who had been forced to dig a pit for the mass shooting in 1941, was there to see the proceedings. She was nineteen at the time. Decades later she described a vivid memory of one Ukrainian policeman, who had bashed the heads of Jewish children against the trees in the forest; this man was left hanging in the town center, his tongue protruding. Three police officers were executed at the spot where the Jews had been gathered to march to

their murders — in front of the *aptheka* and across from the Vaselyuks' house. These officers were left on display for several days.
Then their bodies, with bound feet, were tied to horses, dragged
through town, and discarded at the edge of the Jewish cemetery.
There was no place for them among Christians, alive or dead, as
they were traitors; even their corpses were exiled from the community. The families of the Ukrainian policemen were also interrogated and judged. Some were punished with deportation and hard
labor in inner Russia.

In the Soviet Union, according to Article 56 of the criminal
code, there was no statute of limitations on Nazi war crimes. After
the first wave of vigilante justice and summary executions had been
carried out during the Red Army's reoccupation of Ukraine, Soviet prosecutors cast a wider net and routinely processed and sentenced entire groups of former policemen, and often their families,
to twenty years of hard labor.

During the amnesty of the mid-1950s, these sentences were reduced to ten years, so that most of these "traitors to the homeland"
were released and could return home. Then in 1965, the Kremlin
declared that the fascists who had committed crimes during World
War II would be punished wherever they were and no matter how
long they had been hiding from justice; these people could not
count on forgiveness and the erasure of their crimes. Once people
were listed in the Soviet name index and on the KGB's lists, they
could be summoned to provide more names of "Nazi collaborators." This was an elastic term, encompassing anyone suspected of
consorting with Nazis or abetting them, or anyone who might be

a Ukrainian nationalist. A person's wartime past hung in the air overhead like the sword of Damocles. At any time the KGB could come knocking, drag you into the interrogation room, and perhaps sentence you to twenty years of hard labor, or another twenty years if you had already served time, based simply on the denunciation of a neighbor. This was a dark undercurrent of the Great Patriotic War and the annual Victory Day ceremonies: the laying of wreaths, the speeches, the veterans' parades. The shadow of the war was extended through the oppressive power of the Soviet system.

Identifying and documenting a defendant's wartime activities proved complicated because millions of Soviet citizens had been uprooted, deported, relocated, and gone missing. The tradition of naming via the patronymic reference and the frequent use of common first names meant that one could easily end up tracking down the wrong Ivan.

The senior KGB investigator Major Mikola Makareyvych was determined nevertheless to find the Ukrainian policemen who had committed war crimes in the Zhytomyr district. He checked the records and lists of Ukrainian policemen in the nearby town of Miropol. The Soviet Extraordinary Commission's report from 1945 had named the notorious Roman Kovalyuk, who had allegedly fled to the west.

I had learned about Kovalyuk in 2016, when Yahad–In Unum and I interviewed Ukrainian witnesses about the photograph. His name came up in several statements; then I checked the 1945 Extraordinary Commission report, and he appeared there too. A collective farm worker before the Nazis arrived, he was described as a wife beater, a drunk, and a greedy sadist who had volunteered for the police and enjoyed the war years, which gave him new power and access to plunder. He filled his shack with valuables belonging to Jews, including furniture, dishes, and carpets. We interviewed his former neighbor, who explained that Kovalyuk had returned to Miropol after the war, where he continued to terrorize the population and his own family. During the interview, this former neighbor stood up, walked to the window, and pointed across the field to another cottage: "Over there, that is where he lived."

We walked to Kovalyuk's home, which was boarded up and abandoned. The low, heavy door was unusually small, made of thick wood and secured with an iron padlock. We peeked through the slats of a shuttered window and saw broken teacups, soiled rags, empty canning jars, legless chairs, and used hypodermic needles. An overturned china cabinet rested on a floor of split wooden planks and dirt holes. Among the debris one item stood out: a photo album, with a bright Soviet-red velvet cover; its loose pages had fallen out. We later learned that the album and the house belonged to the policeman's son, Kolya. The neighbor told us that Kolya could not tolerate his father, especially as the two aged. When his father was confined to bed, Kolya stabbed him to death.

Makareyvych was not able to prosecute Kovalyuk, but there were other policemen to be found. Witness statements in the 1945 report identified them by surname: Zavlyny, Gnyatuk, Rybak, and Les'ko. Zavlyny had been immediately arrested by the Soviet Secret Police

(NKVD) after the war and executed. Decades later, Makareyvych tracked down Nikolai Rybak, Ivan Les'ko, and Dmitri Gnyatuk and indicted them in the summer of 1986. These are the mug shots from the arrest records of Rybak and Gnyatuk.

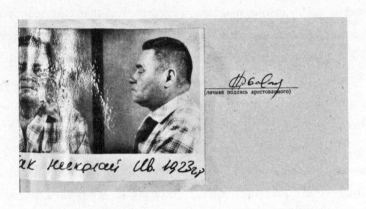

Rybak, a retired carpenter with a grammar school education, was living with his wife and two daughters in the neighboring region of Vinnytsia, in the town of Kirovohrad. On paper his wartime record looked clean: a Soviet military ID stated that he was in a partisan unit in Moldova, and an official document certified that he was a decorated veteran who participated in the victorious siege of Budapest. He had just been honored at the fortieth-anniversary ceremonies celebrating the end of the Great Patriotic War. Les'ko, whose street name during the war was "Nightingale," had been a potter and sold his goods at the Miropol marketplace before the war. He played the trumpet in the village band and worked as a guard at the paper factory. During the war Les'ko was known, at roundups of Ukrainian forced laborers, for his rousing speeches, which praised the invincibility of Hitler's Germany. He was also the Ukrainian policeman who was seen standing at the marketplace when the Jews were gathered there on October 12, yelling, "Who are the craftsmen? Two steps forward! Whoever has a family among the craftsmen, you may take them with you!" The German authorities compensated Les'ko with an empty house that had belonged to a Jewish family. When he was arrested, in Donetsk in 1986, he had no prior record of being investigated. Gnyatuk, the son of a blacksmith, had sold his grandfather's house on Pochtovaya Street in Miropol in the mid-1960s and moved to nearby Polonnoye. Makareyvych found out from local witness statements that the Ukrainian killers in the Miropol Park had worn repurposed Red Army coats marked with armbands, and they shot Russian guns or carbines. And indeed, we see in the Miropol photograph the Ukrainian police in their overcoats with armbands, firing Russian rifles.

All three had served in the Miropol police in the fall of 1941.

After Makareyvych confronted them with numerous witness testimonies, all three confessed to shooting Jews in the park and in other locations. Gnyatuk already had been convicted for being in the police, tried (on July 11, 1944) by a military tribunal in Zhytomyr, and sentenced to twenty years' hard labor. In the wake of the 1955 Soviet decree "On the Amnesty of Soviet Citizens Who Collaborated with the Occupiers in the Period of the Great Fatherland War, 1941–1945," his sentence had been commuted to ten years; this occurred on April 20, 1956. In 1944 his membership in the police had been enough to sentence him. Now in 1986, Makareyvych had more: clear testimony and evidence that he had committed murder in Miropol.

At first Rybak objected to the charges, stating that he had been forced by the Germans to kill, that he was following orders. But Makareyvych found a witness who painted a different picture. A girl who had fancied him in those days (she liked his dark "hedgehog" hairstyle) testified that she saw him with a rifle at the rounding up of Jews. She secretly followed him and the Jewish column to the park. She heard the bullets and the shouts, the weeping and the pleading. She was afraid to get too close to the clearing but out of curiosity climbed one of the bigger trees and hid in the branches. She could see everything happening below, including Rybak, who was aiming and firing his rifle with alacrity. Makareyvych found, in captured German records about the police training school in Berdychiv, that Rybak's name was listed as having graduated in 1943 with the assignment of squad commander and the rank of *Unteroffizier*, or NCO. Rybak had not ended his career with the police force after the 1941 shootings, a lie he had repeated to interrogators. He had signed up for the German police academy and had been promoted.

In 1986, the same year that Makareyvych arrested the Ukrainian policemen who shot Jews in Miropol, Soviet Ukrainian filmmakers released a documentary, *From Memory to Retribution*. It was in English, for western consumption. In the film, the narrator claimed that seven thousand Ukrainian "bourgeois nationalists" guilty of war crimes had found safe haven in the United States. The film depicted Ukrainian police as auxiliaries in Nazi mass-shooting operations. In his interrogation on October 9, 1986, Gnyatuk spoke openly and matter-of-factly about how he shot Jews; he remained more guarded about admitting his role in the deportation and abuse of Ukrainian laborers. Allegedly he had warned Ukrainian neighbors about the impending roundups of laborers and sheltered these neighbors in his house. Perhaps that is why he was able to remain in town and avoid denunciation after the war. Or he had gained the sympathy of local people who believed that justice had been served in another way. Gnyatuk's neighbor testified that his family was cursed. She explained to Makareyvych that during the war, when Gnyatuk was in the police, his two children were playing in the garden on Easter 1943 when they found a grenade, and it detonated.

These three defendants were among the more than 10,500 local men mobilized in stationary and mobile wartime police units in Ukraine. In the countryside German policemen were vastly outnumbered by the local militia — the average ratio was 1:18 — and in most villages and small towns, as in Miropol, there was no German police station. Nazi leaders knew from the start that they would need to rely on local inhabitants to secure and govern the occupied territories, even though Nazi racial ideology deemed the Slavs "inferiors," among those destined to "disappear" as the German population increased. Hitler authorized Himmler to establish non-German auxiliary units in late July 1941, a few weeks into the invasion of the Soviet Union and the occupation of Ukraine. At about this time German soldiers had already advanced through Miropol, and SS officers and German police in the mobile killing units (EK5) had begun their "security" operations. The new mayor, who had been approved by the German Army and the SS police as politically reliable, called a town hall–style meeting and made general announcements about the Nazi liberators and the end of Judeo-Bolshevism. He then imposed curfews and wartime rations, and demanded the surrender of weapons belonging to individuals. When the mayor called for volunteers for a new police force, several men stepped forward, noticeably some of the worst elements of the community. Witnesses described them as riffraff, criminals, and anti-Semites. Not long after the militia was formed, in early September 1941, a pogrom occurred. The Ukrainian nationalist underground reported that it had been instigated by drunken militiamen; some of them wore the armband of the "people's militia" nationalist movement.

Makareyvych opened the investigation in early 1986 and completed it on December 5, 1986. During that time, he made several trips to the crime scenes in Miropol. (This is when, as we've seen, he ordered the bulldozing of the massacre site depicted in our photograph.) On at least one occasion the defendants and other local witnesses were present, and Makareyvych asked the defendants to reenact what had happened — what they had done to their fellow "peaceful Soviet citizens." Gnyatuk stood at the crime scene and pointed out where he was positioned with his rifle and did the shooting, alongside two Germans whom he did not know. He said he stood to the far left of the pit and that his colleague Les'ko was at his right side, in the middle. They shot the "citizens of Jewish nationality" in small groups. Rybak and Les'ko were each also asked to describe what happened; their three verbal accounts were compared, and their reenactments recorded in photographs, including the one shown here.

On January 5, 1987, the district court in Dzerzhinsk heard arguments in an "open session" concerning the criminal case against the three. Two Jews, Ludmilla Blekhman and Maria Feferberg, testified on behalf of their murdered relatives. Ludmilla identified Rybak and Gnyatuk as the murderers of her family and described the hunting and the gunning down of these loved ones. Ukrainian women told how, when they were girls, the Germans had forced them to throw soil over the victims, though many of them were still alive. Gnyatuk confessed to killing the family Gitsko in their home. He shot the parents in the garden next to the kitchen in the middle of the day and then pursued the children, as in a "kind of hunting."

The mayor of Miropol was present at the open session as a representative of the town. He remembered that during the proceedings the policemen — who are in Škrovina's photographs — sat in silence. They did not prepare a defense. They had no alibis. Gnyatuk and Les'ko received the death sentence and were shot on January 28, 1987 (but not in public). Rybak was young, seventeen years old, when he did the killing and therefore was sentenced to fifteen years in a Soviet prison.

I asked the mayor whether, after serving his sentence or upon the collapse of the Soviet Union, Rybak had returned to town. The mayor tightened his lips and physically pulled back. "I will not state," he said. He then asserted, "We were all victims of the war. We all lost family members in the war, we all suffered. My own father is still missing in action."

I then pursued a different line of inquiry. "Have you been threatened by former policemen and their family members?" The mayor replied, "Well, the policemen's family members spoke with people whom I knew, and they tried to get to me, to arrange a meeting to tell me that I spoke too much, I had betrayed them and should keep to myself. But I replied that my words did not seal their fate. Their fate was already determined when they committed the crimes and betrayed their homeland."

In the mid-1990s, Security Service officials in newly independent Ukraine reviewed the case files and determined that there were no grounds for rehabilitating Gnyatuk, Les'ko, and Rybak. They had been "reasonably brought to criminal responsibility." Rybak had been sent to a high-security forced labor camp. He was not heard from again.

The investigations and punishments of the Ukrainian police-men in Miropol did not concern the Holocaust. They were not an attempt to reckon with centuries of anti-Semitism culminating in the brutal murder of Jews by Ukrainian neighbors. Officially there was no anti-Semitism in the Soviet Union, and no one spoke openly of the Nazi genocide of the Jews. According to the elderly mayor of Miropol today, everyone knew what happened to the Jews in town during the war. All peaceful Soviet citizens suffered and millions died in the Great Patriotic War, regardless of nation-ality.

The trial against the Ukrainian killers was in many ways typical of the late Soviet period: a quietly handled case involving the KGB office at the provincial (*oblast*) level, local experts, and witnesses, followed by public memorial ceremonies led by the mayor. Atten-tion was paid to following procedure, authenticating evidence, and documenting the investigation with photographs of the witnesses at the crime scenes. Dozens of witnesses were summoned and protocols transcribed, producing an extensive flow of paper like that of a modern criminal investigation and trial. The prosecution established that the defendants were the same persons listed by name as members of the militia during the occupation, that they were in Miropol at the time of the murders, that local witnesses had identified them as the killers in accounts that could be corroborated, and that there were indeed victims' bones at the crime scene. The Ukrainian KGB obtained wartime evidence from other archives beyond the local one in Zhytomyr to confirm this information. The accused confessed to murdering peaceful Soviet citizens, specifically Jews.

The prosecutor's files do not contain extensive briefs from historical experts tasked with providing context (including historical documentation) for crimes occurring more than forty years earlier. No wartime photographs were presented by witnesses; the fascist conquerors had cameras, but the Ukrainian peasants and militia did not. The local participants proved most valuable. They could bear witness to the Holocaust by means of their vivid memories. They did not need a Nazi photograph to prove what they had experienced and could explain directly. This small-town trial conducted in the waning years of the Soviet Union against these local police traitors received little publicity, unlike the media coverage of the atrocities at the camps and trials featuring camp commandants in the immediate aftermath of the Holocaust.

Starting in the spring of 1945, journalists were encouraged to visit

the Nazi death camps to document the horrors as General Dwight
D. Eisenhower had witnessed them at Ohrdruf, inspiring a public
statement and new policy: "The things I saw beggar description
[...] The visual evidence and the verbal testimony of starvation,
cruelty and bestiality were so overpowering as to leave me a bit sick
[...] I made the visit deliberately, in order to be in a position to give
first-hand evidence of these things if ever, in the future, there devel-
ops a tendency to charge these allegations merely to 'propaganda.'"
On April 19, 1945, General Eisenhower cabled General George C.
Marshall, urging him to bring in journalists and members of the
US Congress to tour the camps so that the horrible truth of Nazi
atrocities would become known to the public. Margaret Bourke-
White was among the journalists. She interviewed ordinary Germans and took a now-famous photograph of Elie Wiesel in the
barracks of Buchenwald. In her memoir, she explained how viewing the horror through the lens of a camera served as a welcome
filter: "There was an air of unreality about that April day in Weimar, a feeling to which I found myself stubbornly clinging. I kept
telling myself that I would believe the indescribably horrible sight
in the courtyard before me only when I had a chance to look at my
own photographs. Using the camera was almost a relief; it inter-
posed a slight barrier between myself and the white horror in front
of me."

Eisenhower ordered that visual evidence be collected to guard
against forgetting and disbelief. The photograph was invoked as a
force of truth and justice. "Pictorial reporters," as they were called
in the 1940s, compiled splashy montages with bold headlines; no

historical information or detailed captioning seemed necessary. This was a visual salvo of atrocity evidence from the battlefield and liberated concentration camps, rather than an explanation or a story. The titles were blunt: "This Is Nazi Evil," or "This is the collapse of civilization," or "The Pictures Don't Lie," or "Holding the Mirror up to the Huns."

After the Holocaust, the photographs fueled the Allied and victims' drive for retribution and justice against Nazi perpetrators. One such perpetrator was Oskar Waltke. In 1942 SS sergeant Waltke orchestrated a public spectacle of terror that was captured in a chilling photograph, showing the leaders of the Jewish community in Lemberg (today Lviv), Ukraine, hanged from the terraces of the ghetto and left on display. Twenty years later, in the 1960s, criminal investigators caught up with Waltke and questioned him. Waltke flatly denied his leading role in the mass murder of tens of thousands of Jews in western Ukraine. Confronted with the photograph as incontrovertible evidence, Waltke was forced to admit his participation. The West German court sentenced him to eight years in prison. In December 1941 another SS officer, Carl Strott, forced more than two thousand Latvian Jews, mostly families of women, children, and the elderly, to the dunes of the Baltic coast at Liepāja. They were made to undress in the frigid temperatures. In yet another act of torture and humiliation, Strott forced the Epstein family to pose for a final portrait moments before they were shot together. The matriarch standing upright at the center looks directly at her killer while her granddaughter turns away in anguish. Unbeknownst to Strott, a Jewish laborer working in Strott's headquarters discovered the film, developed it, and safeguarded this photograph until the end of the war. The image survived; the Epstein family did not. Thirty years later, in another rare instance of a conviction by a West German court, Strott was sentenced to seven years in prison. These and countless other photographs documented the killing machinery and its operators, provided the ground for initiating investigations, and led to convictions. These images have become part of the public record and part of our collective memory of the horrors of the Holocaust.

Unofficial, personal, and clandestine snapshots of murder have unmasked the guilty in the private domain too. They can surface in completely unrelated contexts, many years removed from the place where the images originated. In 1961, a middle-aged German woman was at her neighborhood beauty parlor in Hanover, sitting under a dryer and turning the pages of an illustrated magazine. One article caught her attention. It was an essay on the mass shootings of the Jews in Ukraine. It featured a black-and-white wartime photograph with this caption: "The last Jew in Vinnytsia." There on the page, a gaunt Jewish man in a crumpled suit coat kneels before a corpse-filled pit; he faces the camera. A crowd of smiling German men, wearing uniforms indicating that they are members of various Nazi forces, surrounds the man. One officer stands directly behind him, posing casually. His SS jacket is unbuttoned, one hand is on his hip, and the other grips a gun pointed at the back of the Jewish man's neck.

The *Hausfrau* holding the magazine could not believe her

eyes. The killer pointing the gun was her husband. Could she live with the knowledge that she had married a murderer? She kept examining her husband's wartime face close up. It showed no emotion. "Maybe he had shot hundreds in cold blood. Maybe he did so voluntarily." She went home to confront him, but he had already fled.

Atrocity photos can reveal fundamental truths about the human capacity for evil and, as evidence of wrongdoing, help turn the wheels of justice. The Miropol photograph was hidden away during Makareyvych's investigation. The impetus for the trial in 1986 was not a photograph but rather the fortieth anniversary of the war's end, which prompted the Soviet state to intensify its hunt for Nazi war criminals before it was too late. A crime-scene photograph was not necessary to convict since enough living witnesses were present at the scene to accuse and bring evidence against Rybak, Gnyatuk, and Les'ko; they then confessed to shooting Jews in the park on October 13, 1941. But when all the living witnesses are gone and cannot testify to what happened in the remote villages of Ukraine, what then will drive the quest for truth and justice? New evidence, especially photographs, can put things in motion, both within the courts and without, leading to other forms of redress. We all know about the power of the image, both stills and film footage, in this visual age. The naked girl, crying and running from a napalm attack in South Vietnam, or more recently, the photograph of Alan Kurdi, the three-year-old Syrian Kurdish boy in a red shirt who washed up on the beach of Bodrum, Turkey, to name just two images, produced a collective shock as they circulated in the mass media. Images like these can mobilize protest. They can even help bring about changes in government policy, to provide succor and refuge to the afflicted. Atrocity photographs in particular can become unifying, ethical calls to action and justice, if we choose to look.

EPILOGUE: THE SHOES

WHEN THE FIRST liberation photos of the Holocaust appeared in *Life* magazine and went into wide circulation, shocking images, such as Lee Miller's close-ups of the corpses in the death trains at Dachau, outstripped the human capacity for rendering experience into words. These lapses between seeing, comprehension, and words are evident when viewing our photo. The empty shoes and the crumpled coat exist there as questions, as gaps in knowledge. They remind us of the victims whom we cannot see, the many who were murdered and remain missing.

Prior to and during the Holocaust, empty shoes figured in abstract art, literature, and photography as symbols of humanity, and the use of shoes to depict loss is not only a postwar curatorial technique of Holocaust museums. As historical sources of material culture, shoes have come to aestheticize absence and mourning on a large scale. These stanzas from the Yiddish poet Abraham Sutzkever's "A Load of Shoes," written upon the discovery of his deported mother's shoes in the Vilna ghetto in Lithuania, capture this sense:

> [. . .] *The feet from these boots*
> *With buttons outside*
> *or these, with no body?*
> *or these, with no bride?*

Where is the child
who fit in these?
Is the maiden barefoot
who bought these?

Slippers and pumps,
Look, there are my mother's:
her Sabbath pair
in with the others [. . .]

January 1, 1943

In Sutzkever's poem, empty boots, slippers, and pumps exist somewhere between the living and the dead, among the children, maidens, and brides at a wedding or observing Sabbath. His shoes dance and patter; they stimulate our ability to imagine the past and provide poetic testimony to the lives of the wearers — unlike those haunting but inert objects we see today enshrined behind glass in Birkenau or bronzed as a memorial alongside the Danube River in Budapest.

One photograph too can pass across time and space, from its creator to family members, prosecutors, curators, historians, and the viewing public. It can put things in motion and elicit from those who study the image or are questioned about it an avalanche of information and emotion. It tugs at our ethical sensibilities. At first sight, it shocks, repels, seems impossible. The afterlife of the photograph, though, can become an ongoing story, with twists and turns. Like testimony given in words, it can be subject to manipulation, such as cropping or airbrushing.

Single sources—including an unexamined photograph—can potentially create a false sense of "knowing" the Holocaust, or at least some aspect of it. It is too easy to call up an image, such as the entrance gate at Auschwitz, as representative of a collective memory and a history; it is more challenging to learn the myriad, divergent stories of those who made this history and to grapple with the horrible truths of this and other Nazi slaughterhouses. The abstraction of empty shoes, enshrined, has become this kind of passive image.

Holocaust photographs are core historical sources that should be researched as thoroughly as written documents. Our photograph depicts "a world of fact," as one scholar put it. More than a stable imprint of the past or a "transfer of the real," it is a testimony. Our photographer communicated his message through the subjects, focal point, depth of field, and composition of his images. The series at Miropol imparts a chronology of events. Over time images may yield more than witness statements, which are circumscribed by the limits of memory, language, or knowledge acquired in subsequent events, and marred by other influences. Yet the photograph is not frozen, perfect, and impervious. Like all historical sources, it is inherently biased and open to different interpretations over time. The Miropol photograph captured stories that the photographer did not see when he took the picture.

Like flawed testimonies and memories, photographs can mislead because they can never completely capture the reality of the event pictured, or those involved. The Jewish man who was murdered, perhaps with his family, is not there, although his empty shoes and crumpled coat remain. We cannot see beyond the frame of the image—we can't turn 360 degrees to take in the entire setting of victims waiting to be killed, other possible onlookers, including our Slovakian photographer and his comrades, and more German officials. The papers strewn amid the bullet casings at the edge of the mass grave could be German lists or Jewish identity documents.

As readers and viewers, we project our own subjectivity and historical knowledge onto photographs of the Holocaust. From our standpoint, we know what will happen next. At the time, though, the Miropol victims understood that their family, the Jews in their village and perhaps across their country, were under attack and being killed. They may have believed that they would face a dark, uncertain future of slavery and pogroms because the Germans had conquered their town and were advancing on Moscow. They could not have grasped the extent of the Holocaust from their vantage point in the autumn of 1941; the tragedy that would occur across all of Europe would not be evident until the summer of 1942, when the mass deportations to the Aktion Reinhard gassing centers (that is, Belzec, Sobibor, Treblinka) and to Auschwitz-Birkenau were in full swing. Still, by mid-October 1941, Škrovina was not the only witness to express outrage over the barbarism of the Nazi war in the east. Prime Minister Winston Churchill had already digested intercepted German police reports of the mass shootings of Jews and POWs, and he was searching for the words to describe the scale of the brutalities. In a radio address on August 24, 1941, he declared, "We are witnessing a crime without a name." The international jurist and Holocaust survivor Raphael Lemkin gave it a "name": *genocide*. Our photograph captures that nameless stage of the Nazi realization of the "Final Solution."

Atrocity images, especially the rare ones that attest to acts of genocide, the crime of all crimes, offend and shame us. When we turn away from them, we promote ignorance. When we display them in museums without captions and download them from the internet with no historical context, we denigrate the victims. And when we stop researching them, we cease to care about historical justice, the threat of genocide, and the murdered missing.

ACKNOWLEDGMENTS

This book, like many projects devoted to Holocaust education and memorialization, started at the United States Holocaust Memorial Museum. I am grateful to many colleagues across the museum's departments, in the library, archives, collections, and the Jack, Joseph, and Morton Mandel Center for Advanced Holocaust Studies; they supported me in myriad ways. Thanks especially to Vadim Altskan, Judith Cohen, Caroline Waddell, Elliott Wrenn, Megan Lewis, Vincent Slatt, Michlean Amir, Sarah Ogilvie, Robert Ehrenreich, Radu Iaonid, Suzanne Brown-Fleming, Neal Guthrie, Natalya Lazar, Elana Jakel, Daniel Newman, Anatol Steck, Elizabeth Anthony, Jo-Ellyn Decker, Jan Lambertz, and Geoffrey Megargee. The staff historians Jürgen Matthäus and Elizabeth White read the manuscript and provided critical comments and corrections. The museum's Mandel Center sponsored two summer workshops in 2014 and 2017 that I participated in, one on collaboration and the other on photography. Both experiences expanded my research and connected me to resident fellows and experts, including Waitman Beorn, Gabriel Finder, Carol Zemke, Daniel Magilow, Daniel Hoffman, Dorota Glowacka, and Valerie Hébert. Furthermore, Ján Hlavinka, Michael Kraus, J. Luke Ryder, Noemi Szekely-Popescu, Marianna Kramarikova, Gabriela Hlavova, Ray Brandon, Anna Mallard, and Lauren Fedewa brought more sources to my attention and helped with translations. The Holocaust survivor and museum volunteer Liya Kaplinskaya devoted many hours to deciphering and translating handwritten Soviet witness testimonies. My analysis benefited from exchanges with John Roth, Peter Hayes, Benjamin Frommer, Paul Jaskot, David Shneer, Björn Krondorfer, Dieter Pohl, and Timothy Snyder.

During my research stay in Israel I received tremendous support from Yael Granot-Bein, Arieh Kochavi, and Annika Friedman at the Strochlitz Institute for Holocaust Research at Haifa University, and from Rita Margolin, Daniel Uziel, and Arkadi Zeltser at Yad Vashem. I also benefited from conversations with Arkady Brazin, the descendant of victims killed in Miropol, and was grateful that he responded to my queries on JewishGen.

In Europe, I teamed up with colleagues at Yahad–In Unum in Paris and benefited greatly from the contributions of Father Patrick

Desbois, Patrice Bensimon, Andrej Umansky, Kateryna Duzenko, Alexis Kosarevskyi, and the rest of the Ukraine team who joined me in Miropol. The Starovoitov family hosted me during my trip to Miropol in 2014, as they have done so generously and lovingly since my first trip to Ukraine in summer 1992. The Ukrainian historian Alexander Kruglov responded to my requests for KGB documents, which he generously shared and helped me decipher. At the German state archives in Amberg I received extra assistance from Jochen Roesel; at the German federal archives in Ludwigsburg from Peter Gohle; and at the Prague Security Services Archive from Svetlana Ptacnikova, Veronika Chroma, and Jitka Bilkova. Peter Rendek at the Institute for the Study of Totalitarian Regimes was one of the researchers who first showed me the Miropol photographs. The children of the photographer Lubomir Škrovina, Lubomir Škrovina Jr. and Jana Škrovina, generously shared their parents' personal collections and opened their family home to me.

Closer to home in California, I was named the 2015 Yom HaShoah Scholar in Residence at the University of Southern California. This USC Shoah Foundation fellowship advanced my research in the Visual History Archive, thanks to the staff and scholars there, namely, Stephen Smith, Wolf Gruner, Crispin Brooks, Ita Gordon, and Katerina Kan, who provided excellent suggestions and leads. I shared the photograph with law enforcement officials and appreciate Kevin O'Hara's assistance in analyzing the smoke at the crime scene. At Claremont McKenna College, I used my 2018 sabbatical to draft several chapters and received significant research funds from the dean of faculty's office to cover travel and translation costs. Also critical to the completion of this book was the support of the college's Mgrublian Center for Human Rights. With the necessary backing of Margaret and David Mgrublian and the center's advisory board, I was able to hire student research assistants Lucie Kapner, Henry Schulz, and Julie Kim to track down sources, and the assistant director, Kirsti Zitar, helped me edit the book proposal; with Professor Hilary Appel, Kirsti stepped in to run center programs when I was on leave with support of colleagues in the history department, especially Gary Hamburg, Lisa Cody, Heather Ferguson, Sarah Sarzynski, and Jonathan Petropoulos, who offered to read chapters and recommended texts and different approaches.

My brilliant agent at Writers House, Geri Thoma, helped craft the book proposal, and she successfully placed it at Houghton Mifflin Harcourt. I had the good fortune of working with executive editor Deanne Urmy, who is every author's dream. Deanne committed fully to the project and became a trusted confidante and critic. I thoroughly enjoyed discussing the research material with her and admire her mastery of structuring a narrative and refining prose. Editorial assistant Jessica Vestuto recovered my endnotes and eased us through all the frenetic tasks necessary to produce a book. I also acknowledge the fine work of Lisa Glover, lead production editor, and manuscript editor Susanna Brougham.

Family and close friends shared this research journey with me in many unselfish ways: as hosts during my travels, as sounding boards, and as sources of inspiration, consolation, constancy, and joy. Thank you, Christof Mauch, and many thanks to our beautiful sons, Max and Alexander Mauch, the Moylans, the Connors, the Lowers, the "Chickens," the Ades-Lawlors, Valerie Henry and family, Tracy Brown, Arbol Verde colleagues, and Melly. When I found myself struggling to complete this study amid life's other challenges, they, along with my partner and fellow historian of the Holocaust, Jonathan, helped me stay on track intellectually and emotionally. One of Jonathan's favorite quotes is from the eminent Holocaust scholar Raul Hilberg, who stated toward the end of his career that "there is no finality. Findings are always subject to correction and reformulation. That is the nature of the empirical enterprise. Since historiography is also an art form, there is inevitably a striving for perfection. Yet the reality of events is elusive, as it must be, and the unremitting effort continues for the small incremental gains, no matter their cost, lest all be relinquished and forgotten." I am grateful to all who have helped, including those I do not name here. I can only hope that our collective efforts constitute an incremental gain.

NOTES

.

Abbreviations

ABS	Archiv Bezpecnostnich Slozek, Security Services Archive, Prague
ASA	Amberg Staatsarchiv, Amberg State Archives, Amberg
BAL	Bundesarchiv Ludwigsburg, German Federal Archives, Ludwigsburg
GARF	Gosudarstvennyi Arkhiv, State Archive of the Russian Federation, Moscow
ITSA	International Tracing Service Archives, Bad Arolsen, Ger-

many (now the Arolsen Archives, International Center on Nazi Persecution)

NARA	US National Archives and Records Administration, Washington, DC
SBU	Arkhiv Sluzhby Bezpeky Ukrainy, Security Services Archive, Kiev
USHMM	United States Holocaust Memorial Museum, Washington, DC
USHMMA	United States Holocaust Memorial Museum Archives, Washington, DC
VHA	Visual History Archive, USC Shoah Foundation, University of Southern California, Los Angeles
YVA	Yad Vashem Archives, Jerusalem
ZSA	Zhytomyr State Archives, Ukraine

1. The Photograph

page

2   *Miropol, Ukraine:* The places featured in this book have a multilingual imperial history, reflecting the rich mix of local cultures as well as the dominant languages spoken by Polish, Russian, and German rulers. The spelling of place names and the use (or not) of diacritics can connote a bias and have profound implications today. For example, Myropil' (Ukrainian spelling) is now located in independent Ukraine; however, historically the more common spelling of the town, Miropol, is closer to the Russian (Miropol'). One spelling, Miropolye, reflects the Yiddish pronunciation, which was heard prior to the Holocaust and is no longer in use because of the annihilation of the Jewish population there. For the period covered in *The Ravine,* the town of Miropol' was controlled by Russia and within the Soviet Union. German rulers, during the brief but devastating occupation of the town (1941–44), used the spelling Miropol (dropping the Russian accent), but sometimes the Ukrainian spell-

ing, Myropil', appears in wartime documentation. Since this book spans most of the twentieth century and draws on sources in German, Slovakian, Russian, Ukrainian, Yiddish, Hebrew, and Polish, I decided to employ accepted English place names wherever possible, and, for less well known localities, to transliterate them into English based on the most commonly used spelling and diacritics in the documentation of the time.

first seeing the photograph: Holocaust photographs were taken during the Nazi era and the liberation of the camps. Many of these images document persecution, suffering, and crimes; others, such as family photographs, capture the private lives of the victims as they wished to be remembered. The critical analyses of atrocity images spawned a subfield of study, featuring, among others, Susan Sontag, *On Photography* (New York: Farrar, Straus and Giroux, 1977); Barbie Zelizer, "From the Image of Record to the Image of Memory: Holocaust Photography, Then and Now," in *Picturing the Past: Media, History, and Photograph,* ed. Bonnie Brennen and Hanno Hardt (Urbana-Champaign: University of Illinois, 1999); Georges Didi-Huberman, *Images in Spite of All: Four Photographs from Auschwitz* (Chicago: University of Chicago Press, 2012); Marianne Hirsch, *The Generation of Postmemory: Writing and Visual Culture After the Holocaust* (New York: Columbia University Press, 2012); David Shneer, *Through Soviet Jewish Eyes: Photography, War, and the Holocaust* (New Brunswick, NJ: Rutgers University Press, 2010); Daniel Magilow and Lisa Silverman, "The Boy in the Warsaw Ghetto (Photograph, 1943): What Do Iconic Photographs Tell Us About the Holocaust?," in *Holocaust Representations in History: An Introduction* (London: Bloomsbury, 2015), 13–21; Sybil Milton, "The Camera as Weapon: Documentary Photography and the Holocaust," *Simon Wiesenthal Center Annual* 1 (1984): 45–68; Janina Struk, *Photographing the Holocaust: Interpretations of the Evidence* (London: I. B. Tauris, 2004).

4   *These iconic snapshots:* Regarding the display of atrocity photographs, see Andreas Nachama, ed., *Topography of Terror: Gestapo, SS, and Reich Security Main Office on Wilhelm- and Prinz-Albrecht-Strasse,* 2nd ed. (Berlin: Stiftung Topographie des Terrors, 2010); H. Heer, ed., *Verbrechen der Wehrmacht: Dimensionen des Vernichtungskrieges, 1941–1944; Austellungskatalog* (Crimes of the Wehrmacht: Dimensions of the war of annihilation, 1941–1944; exhi-

bition catalog) (Hamburg: Hamburger Institut für Sozialforschung, 2002), 107–20; "the last living seconds of the Jews (Dubno)" appears on page 126 of the catalog. Study of the "last Jew in Vinnytsia" is in Guido Knopp's *Der zweite Weltkrieg: Bilder die wir nie vergessen* (The Second World War: Images that we never forget) (2014) and Erik Boehlke, "Geheime Botschaften in Bildern," in Daniel Sollberger, Jobst Böning, Erik Boehlke, Gerhard Schindler, eds., *Das Geheimnis Psychologische, psychopathologische und künstlerische Ausdrucksformen im Spektrum zwischen Verheimlichen und Geheimnisvollem* (2016).

7   *Fired cartridge casings:* Regarding "bullets not wasted on children," see Schwammberger testimony in "Tale of Nazi Horror Unfurls in Stuttgart Trial," *New York Times,* November 14, 1991, https://www.nytimes.com/1991/11/14/world/tale-of-nazi-horror-unfurls-in-stuttgart-trial.html; statement of the former Einsatzgruppe C member Heinrich Huhn, October 13, 1965, in the trial of Kuno Callsen, BAL, 207 AR-Z 419/62. There is vast testimony recounting the murder of children through suffocation and bludgeoning, revealing the sadism and pragmatism of the killers. See Soviet witness statement by Lev Aleksandrovich Shein, May 5, 1944, in the Heinrich Schmidt/Karl Danner Case, BAL, II 204a/AR-Z 122/68, 300–302; also the statement of Fritz Margenfeld, July 28, 1971, BAL, Stuttgart Staatsanwaltschaft, 84 Js 3.71, I; see also Patricia Heberer, *Children During the Holocaust* (Lanham, MD: Altamira Press, 2011), and another example gleaned from a family photograph: "The Rushkin family poses with their new motorcycle. Photograph," Photograph Number 39620, held at the USHMMA.

12   *Every fourth Jewish victim:* Dieter Pohl, "The Holocaust in Ukraine: History–Historiography–Memory," in *Stalin and Europe: Imitation and Domination, 1928–1953,* ed. Timothy Snyder and Ray Brandon (New York: Oxford University Press, 2014), 190–206.

13   *Was not the murder:* On the critique of the aesthetic versus the evidentiary, see Didi-Huberman, *Images in Spite of All;* Susan Sontag, *Regarding the Pain of Others* (New York: Farrar, Straus and Giroux, 2003); and Jennifer Evans, Stefan-Ludwig Hoffmann, and Paul Betts, eds., *The Ethics of Seeing: Photography and Twentieth-Century German History* (New York: Berghahn, 2018).

14 *Miropol had a local studio:* David Shneer, "Photography," in *YIVO Encyclopedia of Jews in Eastern Europe,* https://yivoencyclopedia.org/article.aspx/Photography.

By 1939, 10 percent: Elizabeth Harvey and Maiken Umbach, "Photography and Twentieth-Century German History," *Central European History* 48 (2015): 287–99. Bernd Boll estimated that 10 percent, or seven million Germans, mostly young men, had cameras. See his essay "Das Adlerauge des Soldaten: Zur Fotopraxis deutscher Amateure im Zweiten Weltkrieg" (The eagle-eye of the soldier: Amateur German photography in World War II), in *Fotogeschichte* 22 (2002): 75–88, and Julia Torrie, "Visible Trophies of War: German Occupiers' Photographic Perceptions of France, 1940–44," in Evans, Hoffmann, and Betts, eds., *The Ethics of Seeing,* 112.

fifteen thousand photojournalists: See Maiken Umbach's study in David Crew, "Photography and Cinema," in *The Oxford Illustrated History of the Third Reich,* ed. Robert Gellately (Oxford, UK: Oxford University Press, 2018), 157–88.

15 *Agfa, Zeiss, and other film and camera manufacturers:* See "Das Gesicht des Krieges" (The face of war), *Deutschen Kamera-Almanach* 31, ed. Karl Weiss (Berlin, 1941); Bernd Hüppauf, *Fotografie im Krieg* (Photography in war) (Paderborn: Wilhelm Fink, 2015); Habbo Knoch, *Die Tat als Bild* (The deed as picture) (Hamburg: Hamburger Edition, 2001); Klaus-Michael Mallmann, Volker Riess, and Wolfram Pyta, eds., *Deutscher Osten, 1939–1945: Die Weltanschauungskrieg in Photos und Texten* (The German east, 1939–1945: The Nazi ideological war in photos and texts (Darmstadt: Academic, 2003).

photographed what they encountered: According to Christopher Browning, by February 1943, about 80 percent of the Jews killed in the Holocaust were dead, the majority in Poland and Ukraine. See his essay "One Day in Jozefow," in *Lessons and Legacies: The Meaning of the Holocaust in a Changing World,* ed. Peter Hayes (Evanston, IL: Northwestern University Press, 1991), 301. Most soldiers' photographs were taken behind the lines in the occupied zones in 1941 and 1942; perhaps they assumed the war would be over quickly and the images would be trophies of victory and history. Peter Jahn and Ulrike Schiegelt, eds., *Foto-Feldpost: Geknipste Kriegserlebnisse, 1939–1945* (Photo field post: Snapshots of war experiences, 1939–1945) (Berlin: Elefanten Press,

2000); Joe Heydecker, "Photographing Behind the Warsaw Ghetto Wall," *Holocaust and Genocide Studies* 1, no. 1 (1986): 63–78.

Images of dead Jews: Peter Jahn, "Bilder im Kopf—Bilder auf dem Papier" (Images in the head—images on paper), in *Foto FeldPost*, 8–12.

16 *this particular commander:* Second Lieutenant Max Täubner's platoon rampaged across Ukraine in 1941 under orders certified by Bernhard Frank.

"shall not be punished": General Field Marshal Gerd von Rundstedt, commander of Army Group South, Intelligence Command, IC/AO, September 24, 1941, stated that Wehrmacht soldiers should not participate in "excesses" (that is, pogroms) and are "also forbidden to watch or take photographs of measures taken by the Sonderkommando," NARA, RG 238, NOKW-541; Ernst Klee, Willi Dressen, and Volker Riess, eds., *"The Good Old Days": The Holocaust as Seen by Its Perpetrators and Bystanders* (New York: Fischer, 1988), xi, and the verdict against the SS officer Max Täubner, May 24, 1943, found guilty of excessive conduct and of photographing mass murder, 202; the Sixth Army order of August 10, 1941, banning the photographing of executions, in Bernd Boll and Hans Safrian, "On the Way to Stalingrad," in *War of Extermination: The German Military in World War II 1941–1944,* ed. Hannes Heer and Klaus Naumann (New York: Berghahn Books, 2000), 249.

the only known German wartime trial: Orders forbade the photographing of executions as of 1940 in Poland; the German Army's April 1941 guidelines for the invasion of the Soviet Union did the same. Another order was circulated on April 16, 1942, and then sent to the western territories of Belgium and France; it was recirculated in April 1944 and May 1944. In a June 1944 order, Himmler stated that "executions are unfortunately necessary in times of war. Photographing them is as tasteless as it is damaging for our Fatherland, since the enemy exploits such photographs in its propaganda." See Staatsarchiv München, STAANW 34865/68. For example, the commander of Army Group South to troops, September 24, 1941, banning the photographing of executions carried out by Sonderkommandos (prisoners forced to assist in the Nazi death-camp killings), reprinted in Heer, *Verbrechen der Wehrmacht,* 122. See Yehoshua Robert Buchler, "'Unworthy Behavior': The Case of SS Officer Max Täubner," *Holocaust and Genocide Studies* 17 (2003): 409–29. Verdict reprinted in Klee, Dressen, and Riess, eds., *"The Good Old Days,"* 196–207. Also see Boll, "Das Adlerauge."

17   *"question of explicit imagery"*: "A Working Response to the Question of Explicit Imagery Including 'the Pornography of Murder,' Nudity and Violence in
a Museum," prepared by Michael Berenbaum, Alice Greenwald, and Shomer
Zwelling on behalf of the Content Team, February 26, 1988, Content Committee Meeting, USHMM, February 29, 1988, Institutional Records of the
USHMM, Accession No. 1997-016.1, folder "Content Committee," RG 01,
USHMMA.

18   *"wears off with repeated"*: Sontag, *On Photography*, 20.
their history and content: Crass and anti-Semitic commercialization of images such as "the last Jew in Vinnytsia" shows that the shock "value" persists
but is exploited for other ends. In 2019, the British website for the mass re-
tailer Amazon sold hoodies, tank tops, and T-shirts printed with this image,
and after highly publicized criticism removed the item. The manufacturer was
a company named Harma Art. See https://www.washingtonexaminer.com/
news/amazon-stops-selling-shirt-showing-nazi-executing-jewish-man.
veracity, probability, and logic: Christopher Browning developed these
tests in his book *Collected Memories: Holocaust History and Post-War Testimony* (Madison: University of Wisconsin Press, 2003).

19   *we should not remain:* Ulrich Baer, *Spectral Evidence: The Photography of
Trauma* (Cambridge, MA: MIT Press, 2005), 94 and 73.

2. Miropol

22   *Polish nobles ruled:* Simon M. Dubnow, *History of the Jews in Russia and
Poland: From the Earliest Times Until the Present Day*, vol. 1, trans. I. Fried-
lander (Philadelphia: Jewish Publication Society, 1916); R. F. Leslie, ed., *The
History of Poland Since 1863* (New York: Cambridge University Press, 1980);
Paul Robert Magosci, *Historical Atlas of East Central Europe* (Seattle: Univer-
sity of Washington Press, 2002).

23   *The Polish ruling class:* Samuel Kassow, "Shtetl," in *YIVO Encyclopedia
of Jews in Eastern Europe,* https://yivoencyclopedia.org/article.aspx/Shtetl;
Dan Shapira, "The First Jews of Ukraine," *Polin: Studies in Polish Jewry* 26
(2014): 65–77; Shaul Stampfer, "Maps of Jewish Settlement in Ukraine in
1648," *Jewish History* 17 (2003): 107–14. Regional rulers invited Jews to their
fiefdoms to develop the economy, and Jews were early settlers in Ukraine, ar-

riving with Greek traders along the Black Sea coastline in ancient times and
then residing in Kiev by the middle of the eighth century as Khazars (Turkic
people who converted to Judaism). See Henry Abramson, "Ukraine," in *YIVO
Encyclopedia of Jews in Eastern Europe,* https://yivoencyclopedia.org/article
.aspx/Ukraine; also Yad Vashem, "Miropol," in *The Untold Stories,* https://
www.yadvashem.org/untoldstories/database/index.asp?cid=1032.

24   *The Jews were critical:* See Yohanan Petrovsky-Shtern, *The Golden-Age
Shtetl: A New History of Jewish Life in East Europe* (Princeton, NJ: Princeton
University Press, 2015), 126. Besides the marketplace, another center of interaction between Jews and Christians was the local tavern. Ukrainians, who fre-
quented Jewish taverns (the Poles had granted distilling licenses to the Jews),
cursed the Jews for profiting from the increasing alcoholism that plagued their
communities. Not far from Miropol was a roadside drive-in saloon, where one
could easily pull up with a horse-drawn cart and load up on grain alcohol.
Another Jewish tavern, at the edge of Miropol, in Kamenka, sold on average
about two thousand buckets of vodka per month, or eight thousand gallons.

Jews and Ukrainians: S. Ansky, *The Dybbuk: Between Two Worlds,* 3rd ed.
(Washington, DC: Regnery, 1980); Jeffrey Veidlinger, *In the Shadow of the
Shtetl: Small-Town Jewish Life in Soviet Ukraine* (Bloomington: Indiana Uni-
versity Press, 2013).

The dorfsgeyer: Later, during the Nazi occupation, the local hierarchy was
turned upside down — Jewish leaders were the first to be murdered, and the
craftsmen and their families were selected to live. As Ludmilla Blekhman, a
survivor of the mass killing, recalled, in 1941 "the tailors were struggling with
the orders the Germans gave them. The shoemakers repaired their heels. The
barbers cut hair." See Blekhman's videotaped testimony, https://www.youtube
.com/watch?v=e02s_G-TjQA; the entire interview (seven VHS tapes, interview code 33782) is available at the Visual History Archive (VHA), USC
Shoah Foundation. The quotation is from tape 3, segment 15:09. Thanks to
Crispin Brooks and Katerina Kan at the VHA for providing English translations of the Russian recording.

The VHA contains eight additional survivor testimonies mentioning
Miropol and its environs, but the survivors were not witnesses to events there
during the Nazi occupation or after the war. Their family names do not appear
on the partial list of victims in Miropol. I uncovered 407 testimonies at the

VHA in which survivors present photos of mass graves or atrocities that are known (mostly published; some are iconic images). Nearly all of the fifty-five thousand testimonies conclude with survivors showing photos of loved ones, since the concluding section of the interview focused on the restoration of life, mostly by establishing a family, in the aftermath of the Holocaust.

25   *turn hostile to Jews:* Mutual feelings of disrespect and scorn existed between the two groups. Robert Edelman, "Rural Proletarians and Peasant Disturbances: The Right Bank Ukraine in the Revolutions of 1905," *Journal of Modern History* 57, no. 2 (June 1985): 248–77. Also, Kassow, "Shtetl," *YIVO Encyclopedia.*

Miropol had been: See Roman Aftanazy, *Dzieje rezydencji na dawnych kresach Rzeczypospolitej* (History of residences in the former borderlands of the Polish-Lithuanian Commonwealth), vol. 5 (Volyn Voivodeship: Zakład Narodowy im. Ossolińskich, 1991).

"sold at the slave markets": Polin: Studies in Polish Jewry, vol. 26, *Jews and Ukrainians,* ed. Yohanan Petrovsky-Shtern and Antony Polonsky (Oxford, UK: Littman Library of Jewish Civilization, 2014), 8.

The imperial government established: The dethroning of the Polish lord, removed from his seat in the castle, was welcomed by his lowliest subjects, the Ukrainian serfs. Alexander II, known as the tsar liberator, emancipated these serfs in 1861. This tsar also introduced provincial ruling councils, or *zemstvos,* but Jews, who formed a majority in many towns in the Pale, nonetheless had minority status there, as non-Christians. No more than a third of the members on a municipal council could be Jews; no Jew could occupy a place on the provincial councils. Jews could not enter the civil service or serve as mayors, policemen, judges, or commissioned officers in the military; strict quotas meant that only a limited number could attend university. The system, including the restricted area of residence assigned to them, was designed to keep Jews down and "in their place."

By means of the new railways, telegraph communication, and other forms of imperial development, metropolitan Moscow slowly took over the rural western provinces, draining their resources and imposing the tsar's absolute authority. The trains were loaded up, taking away the wares and produce that had previously been at the center of the local economy. Jews were removed as well, conscripted into the tsar's army to serve for up to twenty-five years.

Young members of the Jewish community sought to assimilate into emerging urban centers. The social fabric of Ukraine could not be mended, not even by the best of Miropol's Jewish tailors.

A program of Russification: Russian became the official language of government and education in Ukraine. New laws promoted conversion to Orthodox Christianity and punished those loyal to Jewish religious practices. For example, converts to Christianity of either sex were to receive monetary payments of fifteen to thirty rubles; children were granted half the sum. Jews holding divine worship at home without permission of the authorities could be punished by law. Their sacred objects were disrespected: "robberies of articles used in public worship, and of effects appertaining to the synagogue, is not considered as sacrilege." If a Jewish man or woman converted to Christianity but that person's spouse refused to do so, a divorce would be granted. In another assault on Jewish business and culture, heavy taxes were levied for "every animal that is slaughtered kosher," for the purchase of Sabbath candles and Jewish religious apparel, and the wearing of the skullcap (five silver rubles a year). See the Russo-Jewish Committee of London, "An Abridged Summary of Laws, Special and Restrictive, Relating to the Jews in Russia, Brought Down to the Year 1890," reprinted as an appendix in *The Persecution of the Jews in Russia,* Report of the Guildhall Meeting, December 10, 1890 (Philadelphia: Jewish Publication Society of America, 1897).

Industrialization introduced new class hierarchies and economic dislocation, and modernization changed customs of consumption and dress. Many Jewish men opted to leave their caftans at home, and some Jewish women began to style their hair without covering it, apply cosmetics, and adopt other grooming techniques that were antithetical to orthodox practices and notions of beauty and femininity. Younger Jews looking to the future feared being left behind in a backwater of the Russian Empire; the Ukrainian nationalist movement, which sought a Ukraine for Ukrainians, not for Jews, and the rise of Zionism increased interethnic tensions and divisions within the Jewish community. Many wished to continue the time-honored traditions of the synagogue, Sabbath, mikvah, heder, khupa, and the sanctity of the family, rather than assimilate and hide their Jewishness. A myriad of extreme pressures, which sometimes included physical assault, led millions to emigrate, thus upending life in the shtetl.

26 *Among them was S. Ansky:* The change and ambivalence that character-

ized these Jewish communities were captured by the ethnographer S. Ansky (1863–1920), who migrated from the Pale to become part of the assimilated urban intelligentsia in St. Petersburg. He sought to salvage and preserve the vanishing world of the shtetls of the Pale in an expedition there in 1912. He amassed thousands of photographs of old synagogues and other historical Jewish buildings and scenes from daily life. See the photo by Solomon Iudovin titled "Wedding in Polonnoe," which was a town close to Miropol, in *Photographing the Jewish Nation: Pictures from S. An-sky's Ethnographic Expedition,* ed. Eugene Avrutin et al. (Waltham, MA: Brandeis University Press, 2009), 31 and 39; see also the introduction, by Joachim Neugroschel, in S. Ansky, *The Enemy at His Pleasure: A Journey Through the Jewish Pale of Settlement During World War I* (New York: Henry Holt, 2002), xiii.

27   *a gutted civilization:* On the pogroms and Symon Petliura's devastation there, during and in the aftermath of the Great War, see Harry S. Linfield, "Survey of the Year 5682 (June 1921–May 1922)" in *The American Jewish Yearbook,* ed. Harry Schneiderman for the American Jewish Committee, vol. 24 (Philadelphia: Jewish Publication Society of America, 1922), 63. See also Ansky, *The Enemy at His Pleasure,* 29, 15–16. For the demographic revolution caused by the war and genocides, see Frank Lorimer, *The Population of the Soviet Union: History and Prospects* (Geneva: League of Nations, 1946), 42, and Zvi Gitelman, *A Century of Ambivalence: The Jews of Russia and the Soviet Union, 1881 to the Present* (Bloomington: Indiana University Press, 2001).

        the videotaped testimony: Blekhman testimony, VHA, interview code 33782, tape 3, segment 1:00.

28   *the Polish fortress:* It belonged to Count Marian Hutten-Czapski (1816–1875), a descendant of the Radziwills of the grand duchy of Lithuania and Poland. The count's neo-Gothic manor reflected a hybrid aesthetic, combining elements of old and new Europe, Eastern and Western culture. The interior boasted elaborate carved stucco, oak wainscoting, oil paintings, and a library with more than five thousand books. The count's stables housed Arabian and English horses, and his apiary contained a thousand beehives. Hutten-Czapski studied botany and law and wrote books on hippology. He was a passionate Polish nationalist of the poet Adam Mickiewicz's generation of romanticists and liberal democrats; Hutten-Czapski participated in the 1863 uprising to restore the Polish Republic, which the Russians squashed. With

his arrest and deportation to Siberia, the socioeconomic system centered on his Miropol manor collapsed. Despite its rigidly feudal organization, it had sustained a diverse population, including Catholic Poles, Orthodox Jews, Orthodox Christian Russians, Protestant Germans, and pagans, as well as the Orthodox Christian Ukrainians.

31   *One of the few:* The family of Arkady Brazin, surname Maisich, is there. The tree-branch tombstone seems to state the name of the child, Ilya, as the son or daughter of Itzhak Rybolov. The Hebrew calendar date is partially visible: 28 19 36.

3. The *Aktion:* The German Killers

33   *Ivan Demjanjuk:* See Lawrence Douglas, *The Right Wrong Man: John Demjanjuk and the Last Great Nazi War Crimes Trial* (Princeton, NJ: Princeton University Press, 2016). On the discovery and acquisition of the Sobibor photo album, see https://www.ushmm.org/information/press/press-releases/sobibor-perpetrator-collection. Perhaps Demjanjuk's case would have developed differently if the recently discovered photo album of the deputy commandant of Sobibor had been used as evidence to confirm Demjanjuk's identity and his participation as a guard closely interacting with the German SS.

In searching for the possible German killers, I listed all the German units that I knew had passed through or were stationed in and around Miropol in 1941: Einsatzkommando 5; Higher SS and Police Regiment South; Security Division 454 and Infantry Regiment 375, Home Guard Regiment 637, Secret Field Police units 721 and 708, and civilian officials attached to the occupation administration. See Wendy Lower, *Nazi Empire-Building and the Holocaust in Ukraine* (Chapel Hill: University of North Carolina Press, 2005), 56, and West German investigations and trials against Gebietskommissar Paul Blümel and the agricultural leader Konrad Heinemann, BAL, Sta Munich, 35–320 Js 16 839/75, and Kassel, 3 Ks 5/57; BAL 162/7354. Miropol was situated on the train line that ran between Lviv, Chudniv, Berdychiv, and Fastiv. See "Der Generalbezirk Shytomyr" (General district of Shytomyr [Zhytomyr]), RmfdbO, Hauptabteilung 1 Raumplanung, March 15, 1942, ZSA P1151-1-51.

35   *The German policemen:* Christopher Browning, with contributions from Jürgen Matthäus, *The Origins of the Final Solution: The Evolution of Nazi*

Jewish Policy, September 1939–March 1942 (Jerusalem: Yad Vashem, 2004), 231–33.

"For every echelon": "The Kommandostab Revisited," Raul Hilberg's review of Martin Cüppers's *Wegbereiter der Shoah* (Pioneers of the Shoah), in *Yad Vashem Studies* 34 (2006): 359–61. The orders were from the policeman Max Montua and referenced in Raul Hilberg, *Sources of Holocaust Research: An Analysis* (Chicago: Ivan R. Dee, 2001), 59.

One order, dated: Order by Max Montua, July 11, 1941, in Military History Archives, Prague, RF SS 46 (153); see Jürgen Matthäus, Konrad Kwiet, and Jürgen Förster, *Ausbildungsziel Judenmord? "Weltanschauliche Erziehung" von SS, Polizei, und Waffen-SS im Rahmen der "Endlösung"* (Training aim mass murder of the Jews? The "ideological education" of the SS, the police, and the Waffen-SS in the framework of the "Final Solution") (Frankfurt am Main: S. Fischer, 2003).

A witness recalled: The towns listed as crime scenes of Higher SS and Police Regiment South are in 9294/36 *Tatortverzeichnis* (crime scene list). Police Battalion 303, Companies 1 and 3, were in Miropol. Police Battalions 314 and 45 were not. One testimony by the former Orpo 303 member Wulf stated that after Kiev, the unit was sent back to Miropol for more "cleansing" actions. See investigation files held in Amberg Staatsarchiv, Staatsanwaltschaft Regensburg 92941/1: BAND I — Akten in der Strafsache der Strafkammer bei dem Landgericht Regensburg, gegen Rosenbauer, Besser, und Krenze (HSSPF Police Regiment Sud) wegen Mord NSG. Anklageschrift 1978. 4 Js 1495/65.

36 *SS records in Prague:* Dennis Reece, "Mission to Štěchovice: How Americans Took Nazi Documents from Czechoslovakia — and Created a Diplomatic Crisis," *Prologue* 39, no. 4 (US National Archives, Winter 2007); Yehoshua Buchler, "Kommandostab Reichsführer-SS: Himmler's Personal Murder Brigades in 1941," *Holocaust and Genocide Studies* 1, no. 1 (1986); Martin Cüppers, *Wegbereiter der Shoah: Die Waffen-SS, der Kommandostab Reichsführer-SS, und die Judenvernichtung, 1939–1945* (Pioneers of the Shoah: The Waffen-SS, the command staff of the Reichsführer SS, and the extermination of the Jews, 1939–1945) (Darmstadt: Wissenschaftliche Buchgesellschaft, 2005); G. M. Prechtl — *Unsere Ehre Heißt Treue: Kriegstagebuch des Kommandostabes Reichsführer-SS — Tätigkeitsberichte der 1. und 2. SS-Inf. Brigade, der 1. SS-Kav. Brigade, und von Sonderkommandos der SS.* (Our

honor means our loyalty: War diary of the command staff Reichsführer-SS
—Activity reports of the first and second SS infantry brigades, the first SS
cavalry brigade, and the Sonderkommandos of the SS) (Vienna: Europa Verlag, 1984).

37   *their lunch breaks:* Testimony of former member of Order Police Battalion
45, Third Company, in 9294/20 Hilfsakten, Band II, Records of the Staatsanwaltschaft Regensburg 92941, Akten in der Strafsache der Strafkammer bei
dem Landgericht Regensburg, gegen Rosenbauer, Besser, and Krenze (HSSPF
Police Regiment Sud), ASA, 4 Js 1495/65.

Then a colleague: Thanks to Andrej Umansky for bringing this file to my
attention. The myth of a clean customs guard was broken by Thomas Sandkühler's "Von der 'Gegnerabwehr' zum Judenmord: Grenzpolizei und Zollgrenzschutz im NS-Staat" (From "enemy defense" to Jewish murder: Border
police and border protection in the Nazi state), in *Beiträge zur Geschichte des
Nationalsozialismus* 16 (2000): 95–154. However, Sandkühler does not identify a clear case in which customs guards shot Jews in Ukraine, such as in the
town of Miropol.

Kurt Hoffmann: Silesia was a province taken by Prussia during the partitions of Poland by Prussia, Austria-Hungary, and Russia in the late eighteenth
century. It remained in Prussia and then the German Empire until the defeat
of the German monarchy in World War I; Silesia was returned to Poland under the terms of the Treaty of Versailles in 1919.

Hitler's popular demand to nullify the "vindictive" Versailles Treaty in-
cluded a return of historically German-ruled lands within Poland. Silesian
Germans were among the more extremely patriotic and tended to support
Hitler's radically nationalist ideology. They distinguished themselves in the
Nazi Party, the Wehrmacht, and the SS police forces. See Michael Mann,
"Were the Perpetrators of Genocide 'Ordinary Men' or 'Real Nazis'? Results
from Fifteen Hundred Biographies," *Holocaust and Genocide Studies* 14, no. 3
(Winter 2000): 331–66.

39   *sent to Ukraine:* Soviet Ukraine and Nazi-occupied Ukraine were commonly viewed as a region of Russia (referred to as "the Ukraine"), not as a
country or nation in its own right. Although the population of Ukraine (today's borders) was home to a sizable minority of Russians, Ukraine has often been erroneously characterized as "Russia." Paul Magosci, *A History of*

Ukraine: The Land and Its People (Toronto: University of Toronto Press, 2010).

Two of Hoffmann's: Silesia was also annexed by Poland in the interwar period and was home to a large ethnic German population; see previous note concerning Kurt Hoffmann.

40 *"The person who filed":* Kurt Hoffmann case, Vermerk, Polizeihauptmeister Priebe, January 15, 1969, BAL, B162/28709.

41 *"I have never shot":* Hoffmann case, statement of Erich Kuska, Bremen, August 14, 1969, BAL, B162/28709.

42 *"One could see that":* Hoffmann case, statement of Kuska, August 14, 1969, BAL, B162/28709.

He correctly identified: Franziska Bruder, *"Den ukrainischen Staat erkämpfen oder sterben!": Die Organisation ukrainischer Nationalisten (OUN), 1928–1948* ("The Ukrainian state, fight or die!": The organization of Ukrainian Nationalists [OUN], 1928–1948) (Berlin: Metropole, 2006), 113–75; Dieter Pohl, "Ukrainische Hilfskräfte beim Mord an den Juden" (Ukrainian auxiliary police in the murder of the Jews), in *Die Täter der Shoa: Fanatische Nationalisten oder der ganz normale Deutsche?* (The perpetrators of the Shoah: Fanatical nationalists or ordinary Germans?), ed. Gerhard Paul (Göttingen: Wallstein, 2002), 205–7; Martin Dean, *Collaboration in the Holocaust: Crimes of the Local Police in Belorussia and Ukraine, 1941–1944* (New York: Macmillan, 2000); HSSPF Ukraine, report of November 25, 1941, written to the Orpo chief Daluege in Berlin, regarding the personnel in the east: German and local police. In the Gebietskommissariat of Zhytomyr, where Miropol was located, the stationary regional offices were supported by 772 German officers and 5,144 Ukrainian and ethnic German auxiliaries. They earned less than one Reichsmark (about 80 cents) per day and received benefits such as uniforms, boots, and extra rations; Bundesarchiv Koblenz, R 19/122. Thanks to Ray Brandon for assisting with the research on the police.

But in order to observe: Hoffmann case, statement of Kuska, August 14, 1969, BAL, B162/28709. During the questioning of the accused, the prosecutor asked for wartime photos. "I no longer have wartime photos in my possession," replied a former customs guard in Kuska's unit. Statement of Rudolf John, November 24, 1969, BAL, B162/28709. One tried to blame Orpo 303, the unit that had carried out killings in Miropol in the summer and in September. Statement of Stefan Schattauer, November 27, 1969, StA Hanover 90/69, II 204 AR 124/169, BAL, B162/28709.

43 *"How may a historian":* Browning, *Collected Memories,* 39.

German military and the SS: See Lower, *Nazi Empire-Building,* 95–96. According to the reports, two shootings occurred there, one on August 9, 1941, done by Einsatzgruppe C (EK 5), when twenty-four Jews were branded as work shirkers and killed. And an even more obscure record, which the Germans captured from the underground Ukrainian nationalist movement, states that Jews of Miropol were killed in early September by drunken militiamen. Himmler's command staff also received a report on August 6, 1941, about the movement of SS Infantry Regiment 8 through Novy Miropol on July 30, 1941, where they joined members of Infantry Regiment 10 in some security action, which is unclear. Military Historical Institute Archives, Prague.

44 *supporting the resistance:* See the Soviet Extraordinary Commission Report, May 27, 1945, GARF, fond 7021-60-291, p. 545, USHMMA, RG 22.02M, 1995.A.1265. Thanks to Vadim Altskan for assisting with this report. Also see Operational Situation Report #47, Einsatzgruppe C, August 9, 1941, in *Die "Ereignismeldungen UdSSR" 1941: Dokumente der Einsatzgruppen in der Sowjetunion* (The "USSR Event Reports" 1941: Documents of the Einsatzgruppen in the Soviet Union), ed. Klaus-Michael Mallmann, Andrej Angrick, Jürgen Matthäus, and Martin Cüppers (Darmstadt: WBG, 2011), 265.

the summer of 1941: See Blekhman testimony, VHA, interview code 33782, tape 3, segment 00:30–02:00. Blekhman dates the arrival of the Germans to July 4, and then, on July 5, 1941, a "ghetto" was formed; Jews were forced to move into the town center or else face death. And all boys and men (age thirteen and older) had to report for labor assignments.

45 *The 1969 Bremen investigation:* Miropol figured as a crime scene in at least two additional investigations, one related to the Higher SS and Police Regiment South, and the other, the civilian commissariat offices (Paul Blümel, Konrad Heinemann, and other staff in Chudniv, BAL, B162/3263). The statements of the customs guards denounced by Kurt Hoffmann are among the half million testimonies taken between 1958 and 1992, now archived at the Bundesarchiv in Ludwigsburg, the location of the Zentrale Stelle der Landesjustizverwaltungen zur Aufklärung nationalsozialistischer Verbrechen (the Central Office for the Investigation of Nazi War Crimes). There are more

than 750,000 names in the archive database, among them 104,000 individuals who were investigated, which led to 6,478 convictions (7 percent of the cases concerned the murder of Jews).

48   *It kept increasing:* See Lewis Stone et al., "Quantifying the Holocaust: Hyperintense Kill Rates During the Nazi Genocide," *Science Advances* 5 (January 2019); also see Doris Bergen, *War and Genocide: A Concise History of the Holocaust* (Lanham, MD: Rowman and Littlefield, 2016), 237–38. Seventy-five percent of the Jewish victims of the Holocaust were still alive at the beginning of 1942 and had been murdered by early 1943. The peak occurred in the fall of 1942, with an average daily killing rate of just under fifteen thousand Jewish men, women, and children.

the Soviet "paradise": Hitler's October order to the troops, http://www.ibiblio.org/pha/policy/1941/411002a.html.

The world hitherto: Hitler's October order to the troops.

49   *"considered the extermination":* Reichenau's statement about killing "that Jewish brood" appeared in the controversy authorizing the murder of Jewish orphans in Byelaya Tserkov, Ukraine (about 125 miles from Miropol), August 20–21, 1941, and is quoted in Heberer, *Children During the Holocaust*, 88.

To complement this: Reichenau's order, approved by Hitler and distributed to battalion level. See the captured German records collection at NARA, RG 242, T-315, roll 2216, frame 000283. Photograph of soldiers viewing the order on a bulletin board, next to another photo of a dead Jewish civilian, in a private photo album that the Sudhoff family shared with the author. Copies in author's possession.

"architect of genocide": Richard Breitman, *The Architect of Genocide: Heinrich Himmler and the Final Solution* (Waltham, MA: Brandeis University Press, 1992).

"emptied and freed of Jews": Browning, *Origins of the Final Solution,* 412.

Himmler experienced firsthand: Peter Klein, ed., *Die Einsatzgruppen in der besetzten Sowjetunion, 1941/42: Die Tätigkeit und Lageberichte des Chefs der Sicherheitspolizei und des SD* (The task forces [mobile killing units] in the occupied Soviet Union, 1941/42: Activity and situational reports of the chief of the security police and the SD) (Berlin: Haus der Wannsee Konferenz, 1997), 342; Christian Gerlach, *Kalkulierte Morde: Die Deutsche Wirtschafts- und Vernichtungspolitik in Weissrussland, 1941 bis 1944* (Calculated murder: The German economic and extermination policy in Belarus, 1941 to 1944) (Hamburg: Institut für Sozialforschung, 1999), 573–74. Karl Wolff, Himmler's adjutant, gave postwar testimony on witnessing the massacre and the spraying of brains on Himmler's uniform and face; Wolff revealed this in the documentary film series *World at War,* http://www.holocaustresearchproject.org/einsatz/ himmlerinminsk.html. Also see related testimony in the Munich prosecution of Karl Wolff, Staatsarchiv München, STAANW, 34865/44.

50 *In September 1941:* Breitman, *The Architect of Genocide,* 196; Bergen, *War and Genocide,* 241.

"brief twelve-day span": Browning, *Origins of the Final Solution,* 359–60 and 368–69; Christopher Browning, "On My Book *The Origins of the Final Solution:* Some Remarks on Its Background and Its Major Conclusions," in *Holocaust: Historiography in Context: Emergence, Challenges, Polemics, and Achievements,* ed. David Bankier and Dan Michman (New York: Berghahn, 2008), 412–13; Lower, *Nazi Empire-Building,* 226.

at the micro level: Michaela Christ, *Die Dynamik des Tötens: Die Ermordung der Juden in Berditschew, 1941–1944* (The dynamics of killing: The murder of the Jews in Berdychiv, 1941–1944) (Frankfurt: Fischer Verlag, 2011).

51 *Three German SS officers:* They were probably from the Sipo-SD office in Berdychiv; one or more might have been formerly active in Einsatzgruppen C/ EK5. Hoffmann case, statement of John, January 22, 1969, BAL, B162/28709.

The officers set: This compares with a rare detailed account from wartime, penned by the diarist Roman Kravchenko-Beresnoj (1926–2011), which is reprinted as Document 152 in *Die Verfolgung und Ermordung der europäischen Juden durch das nationalsozialistische Deutschland, 1933–1945* (The persecution and murder of European Jews by Nazi Germany, 1933–1945), vol. 8: *Sowjetunion mit annektierten Gebieten II* (The Soviet Union, with annexed areas) (Berlin: De Gruyter, 2016), 360–65; also see Document 155, on the post-massacre hunts for Jews, and Document 160, on the local mayor's call for laborers to assist with the burying of Jews who had been shot, describing the process of German requisition of materials and local laborers. This process occurred in hundreds of other towns in Ukraine. Yahad–In Unum has identified about two thousand sites and has collected testimonies from some four thousand witnesses. The pattern is clear and is summarized in Patrick Desbois, *In Broad Daylight: The Secret Procedures Behind the Holocaust by Bullets* (New York:

Arcade, 2011). For German testimonies, including photographs of the mass shootings, see the valuable collection edited by Andrej Umansky: *La Shoah à l'est: Regards d'Allemands* (The Shoah in the east: Perspectives of the Germans) (Paris: Fayard, 2018).

52 *"about the size":* Ukrainian witnesses and gravediggers said that the pit was about the size of a room, was as deep as the height of a man, and moved for days after the shooting. See Petro G. (b. 1928), interview with the author and Yahad–In Unum, July 19, 2016, interview code 2124; Antoninya C. (b. 1926), interview with the author and Yahad–In Unum, July 19, 2016, interview code 2125; Lydia S. (b. 1926), interview with the author and Yahad–In Unum, July 21, 2016, interview code 2131; all interviews took place in Miropol, Ukraine.

The Jewish men: Jews who did the digging were killed right away to prevent information about the impending action from reaching the Jewish community in town; such information would have sparked resistance, panic, and flight, which the Germans wished to avoid. There would not have been enough German manpower in town to respond immediately and effectively to wide-scale popular resistance. See *Die "Ereignismeldungen UdSSR" 1941,* ed. Mallmann, Angrick, Matthäus, and Cüppers.

The pit was eight by eight: Hoffmann case, statements of Schattauer, November 27, 1969, and Josef Bauer, November 28, 1969, BAL, B162/28709.

The Germans calculated: This follows the pattern identified in massacres and killing sites in Ukraine, Poland, Russia, and Lithuania analyzed by Desbois, *In Broad Daylight,* chapters 1 and 2.

"Why are there still": Customs officials were not routinely deployed, but this is not the only documented case of their ad hoc participation, including their roles as shooters. For a similar case in Marcinkance, Poland, see Christopher Browning, "The Holocaust in Marcinkance in the Light of Two Unusual Documents," in *The Holocaust: The Unique and the Universal, Essays Presented in Honor of Yehuda Bauer,* ed. Shmuel Almog, David Bankier, Daniel Blatman, and Dalia Ofer (Jerusalem: Yad Vashem, 2001), 66–83. Also, Browning, "Marcinkance Revisited in Light of New Evidence," in *Holocaust and Antisemitism: Research and Public Discourse, Essays Presented in Honor of Dina Porat,* ed. Roni Stauber, Aviva Halamish, and Esther Webman (Jerusalem: Yad Vashem, 2015), 53–70. In Palanga, Lithuania, at this same time,

on October 12, 1941, customs guards shot three hundred Jewish women and children; see Desbois, *In Broad Daylight,* vii, case researched by Andrej Umansky.

53 *"I am not entirely":* On Nette and the Skat game, see Hoffmann case, statement of John, November 24, 1969, BAL, B162/28709.

Leaving the Skat game: Hoffmann case, statement of John, November 24, 1969, BAL, B162/28709.

"Who will volunteer": Hoffmann case, statements of Kurt Hoffmann, January 22 and May 19, 1969, BAL, B162/28709.

The volunteers left: Hoffmann case, statements of Hoffmann, January 22, 1969, and John, November 24, 1969, BAL, B162/28709.

She agreed to help: Blekhman testimony, VHA, interview code 33782, tape 3, segment 12:00.

54 *seal off the town:* Testimony of Dmitri Nikiforovich Gnyatuk, reenactment of events, photographed by Makareyvych, YVA, RG TR.18, file no. 273; case against Les'ko, Rybak, and Gnyatuk, started June 5, 1986, ended December 5, 1986, nine vols., SBU, KGB archival no. 32425. Thanks to Liya Kaplinskaya for providing English translations.

Ivan Grigorievich Lesk'o (not related to the Ukrainian shooter Les'ko) recalled that he was ordered to take position at the Polish church (Saint Antonia), to prevent escapees from reaching the other side of town across the river and to seal off the newer part of town, Novy Miropol, on the other side of the river. He was brought there in the early morning and remained until nightfall, armed with a rifle, and was relieved by another guard. This testimony is evasive, seeking distance from the events of the killing. Lesk'o asserted that he did not hear bullets or see murder, and did not know who participated in the killing. He was convicted in February 1946 for having served in the police as a traitor to the homeland and was sentenced to twenty years of hard labor; this was later reduced to ten years. He stated that he was beaten during his incarceration and sustained head trauma, resulting in memory loss.

"Mil'ka, Mil'ka": Vladimir Melamed, "Organized and Unsolicited Collaboration in the Holocaust: The Multifaceted Context," *East European Jewish Affairs* 37 (August 2007): 222.

Others assaulted them: Blekhman testimony, VHA, interview code 33782, tape 4, segment 02:01.

The pogrom had begun: Barbara B. (b. 1930) stated that Jews were rounded up at night. She heard commotion and at dawn heard the shootings. She went to the pit afterward and saw the ground moving. Interview with the author and Yahad–In Unum, July 21, 2016, interview code 2132, Miropol. Tanya D. (b. 1926) stated that there were few Germans in town: "I didn't see many, the Hungarians, the Slovaks were here for a longer time." She worked at a military base and recalled a few Jewish specialists were left in workshops: shoemakers, tailors, a dentist. "We could hear the shootings and the screams. Ukrainian policemen chasing them. The policemen destroyed the Jewish houses. They took the bricks to build their own homes." Interview with the author and Yahad–In Unum, July 20, 2016, interview code 2128, Miropol.

55 *They chased young:* Hoffmann case, statements of Hoffmann, January 22 and May 19, 1969, BAL, B162/28709, corroborated by two Ukrainian witnesses, one living near the marketplace and the other living near the police station. Sofia B. saw the Jews in a column, carrying their belongings. She heard the shootings. And she saw the policeman Roman Kovalyuk chasing a young Jewish girl into the forest. See Sofia B. (b. 1929), interview with the author and Yahad–In Unum, July 22, 2016, interview code 2133, Miropol.

A girl crawled out: Zinaida L. (b. 1934), interview with the author and Yahad–In Unum, July 23, 2016, interview code 2135, Miropol. Zinaida lived at the marketplace; one cold autumn night, she saw a column of Jews; they were crying. Her entire family watched the scene, peering through holes in the house. Later the next day they heard the shootings, firing at once, not a single shot but several killed at once. From their house they also saw Ukrainian police dragging a Jewish grandmother in her bed into the courtyard below their house, where they shot her. One of the Jewish woman's daughters was not there, she ran away, she was about thirty years old, and "we hid her in our cellar for about a week." Zinaida remembered the policeman Ivan Les'ko and thought that he had been killed in 1944.

About two hundred Jews: Statement of Efimovna Feferberg, October 12, 1986, case against Les'ko, Rybak, and Gnyatuk, ended December 5, 1986, SBU, RG TR.18, file no. 273. There are different estimates in the sources, with figures ranging from ninety-six to three hundred for this mass shooting. The total number of Jews killed in Miropol during the Holocaust was about a thousand.

56   *They waited outside:* Fanya T. (b. 1926), interview with the author and Yahad–In Unum, July 20, 2016, interview code 2129, Miropol.

Some tried to bribe: Lydia S., July 21, 2016, interview code 2131.

She was turned away: Liubov P. (b. 1930), interview with the author and
Yahad–In Unum, July 22, 2016, interview code 2134, Miropol. Rukla the seamstress came to their house when the gathering action was underway, pleaded to
be hid, and asked for food, but she was turned away.

Ukrainians were afraid that they would be killed too. This threat was specified in German orders: sheltering Jews would be punished by death. Indeed,
such orders were publicized and achieved what the Germans desired — dis-
suading locals from helping the Jews. The threat was real; there are documented cases in which those who sheltered Jews were murdered. Lower, *Nazi
Empire-Building,* 200; Rubenstein and Altman, eds., *The Unknown Black
Book* (Bloomington: Indiana University Press, 2010), 61, 66, 67, 188.

Between 5 and 6 a.m.: Hoffmann case, statement of Hermann Recke, November 26, 1969, BAL, B162/28709.

Individuals who refused: Liubov P., July 22, 2016, interview code 2134.
She stated, "We saw the column of Jews, women and children. Saw mostly
Ukrainian guards, and people standing around a big hole, perhaps a ravine [. . .] there were many children." As the peasant Antoninya C. began her
day at work in the fields, she heard gunfire coming from the direction of the
fortress and forests; July 19, 2016, interview code 2125. Lydia S. said, "In the
morning we went out to care for cows, we heard the bursts of gunfire"; July 21,
2016, interview code 2131.

a German customs guard: Hoffmann case, statement of Bauer, November
28, 1969, BAL, B162/28709.

57   *The Jewish dentist:* Blekhman testimony, VHA, interview code 33782,
tape 4, segment 10:31.

another customs guard: Hoffmann case, statement of Recke, November 26,
1969, BAL, B162/28709.

Along the path: Hoffmann case, statement of Kuska, August 14, 1969,
BAL, B162/28709.

The executioners gathered: Liubov P., July 22, 2016, interview code 2134.
Slovakian Secret Police investigator Lisý's interrogation of Škrovina, state-

ment of Lubomir Škrovina (b. 1916), June 25, 1943, Ministerstvo Vnútra Slovenskej Republiky Slovenský Národny Archív, file 209.474.63, document 4. I am grateful to Marianna Kramarikova and Dr. Ján Hlavinka for assisting with the translation from Slovak into English.

The pit was not: Hoffmann case, statement of Kuska, August 14, 1969, BAL, B162/28709.

The sound reached: Hoffmann case, statement of John, November 24, 1969: "One could hear shots occurring four hundred meters from our barracks." Zinaida L. (July 23, 2016, interview code 2135) heard a uniform firing, not a single shot but rather several going off at once.

58 *The photographer documented:* For Slovakian testimonies about the photographer, including the statement that bullets were not wasted when the Germans placed a mother's head beside her child's and killed them both with one bullet, see Slovak National Archives, Records of Former Fascist Regime, Police, Bratislava, file 209 474 63; ABS, H-770-folder 3. Also see the 1958 interrogations of Lubomir Škrovina and Škrovina's former commander, Ivan Hrushka, in the archives of the former Soviet Ministry of Interior, Prague, file 595617_MV_1_3_0006–1 and file 595617_MV_3_3_0023–1. Corroborated by Schattauer, the German customs official who went to watch the killing from a distance of about fifty meters and saw that the Jews still had their clothing on; Hoffmann case, statement of Schattauer, November 27, 1969, BAL, B162/28709.

The Ukrainian police: Reenactment by Ukrainian policeman Gnyatuk and report of November 11, 1986, by the senior investigator UKGB, Major Makareyvych, YVA, RG TR.18, file no. 273; case against Les'ko, Rybak, and Gnyatuk, ended December 5, 1986, SBU.

They grabbed small children: Lydia S., July 21, 2016, interview code 2131.

One was a nurse: Liubov P., July 22, 2016, interview code 2134. Liubov lived along the Sluch River and offered this testimony: "We were gathering wood in the forest, we heard the noise, startled, hid behind trees. Saw column of Jews, women and children. Saw mostly Ukrainian guards, and people around a ravine [. . .] there were many children. Many still alive after the policemen left. We looked into the pit. Jews had little bundles. We saw the shooting by accident. Overwhelmed. It was horrible; we saw the Jews crying, mothers holding children, pushed into pit. They faced the pit; shooters had submachine guns. The Jews were shot in their clothes and they had their bundles. Those who were next could see what was happening."

59   *jumped into the pit:* Liubov P., July 22, 2016, interview code 2134. "Entire families were killed first, brought to the pit, then in groups of eight to ten Jews and forced to stand next to one another at edge of pit, shot from behind. I saw this from a distance of twenty meters. Some women jumped into the pit with their small children. And therefore shot in the pit by the killers above." See also Hoffmann case, statement of Bauer, November 28, 1969, BAL, B162/28709.

At noon a German: Hoffmann case, statements of Recke, November 26, 1969, and Schattauer, November 27, 1969, BAL, B162/28709.

shooting for two hours: See Desbois, *In Broad Daylight,* 39. In the provincial massacres, manned by seasoned German death squads, the rate was about 140 persons killed per hour, or 2–3 per minute.

The Ukrainian militia returned: Christ, *Die Dynamik des Tötens.*

Peasants and other locals: Maria R. (b. 1925), interview with the author and Yahad–In Unum, July 23, 2016, interview code 2135, Miropol.

The horse-drawn carts: Maria R., July 23, 2016, interview code 2135.

The popping of bullets: Hoffmann case, statement of Kuska, August 14, 1969, BAL, B162/28709.

Erich Kuska and: Hoffmann case, statement of John, November 24, 1969, BAL, B162/28709. He remarked that Kuska liked to play with explosives and detonate Russian mines in the river to kill fish for lunch and that he "made no secret" of his hatred of the Jews.

60   *She knocked on the door:* Fanya T., July 20, 2016, interview code 2129.

The Ukrainian police ordered: Antoninya C., July 19, 2016, interview code 2125. According to Liubov P., July 22, 2016, interview code 2134, "People from the village were requisitioned to cover the pit. We ran to the village, shaking, and saw our teacher, and asked what is going on, we can hear shooting, we told him. He said, 'Do not tell anyone.'" Ukrainian girls were the lowest in the hierarchy of "forced laborers" tasked with the dirty work of the Holocaust by bullets, and were primary witnesses; we cannot dismiss their statements today as the flawed memories of elderly babushkas. The mass shootings contained a gendered hierarchy of violence — the men as organizers, managers, and calculators of mass-grave size and the number of arms and bullets. Men exerted the power of pulling the trigger, and the female support staff served as diggers, cleaners, menders, and so on.

limbs were visible: Hoffmann case, statement of Hoffmann, May 19, 1969, BAL, B162/28709. Ukrainian witnesses and gravediggers said that days after the shooting, the earth covering the victims was still moving. Petro G., July 19, 2016, interview code 2124; Antoninya C., July 19, 2016, interview code 2125; Lydia S., July 21, 2016, interview code 2131.

61 *"I could not verify":* Hoffmann case, Dr. Hoeffler, Oberstaatsanwalt, to Kurt Hoffmann, Renter in Laatzen, May 27, 1970, BAL, B162/28709.

62 *The testimonies can:* Browning, *Collected Memories,* 11–13.

4. The Photographer

65 *"worked against the New":* Statement of Škrovina, June 25, 1943, Ministerstvo Vnútra Slovenskej Republiky Slovenský Národny Archív, file 209.474.63, document 4.

66 *Lubomir Škrovina:* Statement of Škrovina, June 25, 1943, Ministerstvo Vnútra Slovenskej Republiky Slovenský Národny Archív, file 209.474.63, document 4. On Lisý, see Ján Hlavinka, *The Holocaust in Slovakia: The Story of the Jews of Medzilaborce District* (Bratislava: Avotaynu, 2011).

The Slovaks were allied: Jürgen Förster, "Slowakie" (Slovakia), in *Das Deutsche Reich und der Zweite Weltkrieg: Der Angriff auf di Sowjetunion* (The German Reich and the Second World War: The attack on the Soviet Union), ed. Horst Boog, Jürgen Förster, Joachim Hoffmann et al. (Stuttgart: Deutsche Verlags-Anstalt, 1983); Rolf-Dieter Müller, *An der Seite der Wehrmacht: Hitlers ausländische Helfer beim "Kreuzzug gegen den Bolschewismus," 1941–1945* (At the side of the Wehrmacht: Hitler's foreign helpers in the "crusade against Bolshevism," 1941–1945) (Frankfurt: Fischer Verlag, 2010), 100–106. Müller counted about 18,500 Slovak soldiers, including those in the security detachments in Ukraine and concentrated around Zhytomyr, the district capital near Miropol.

all males of ages: William M. Mahoney, *The History of the Czech Republic and Slovakia* (Westport, CT: Greenwood Publishing Group, 2011).

67 *"In Miropol, Ukraine":* Statement of Škrovina, June 25, 1943, Ministerstvo

Vnútra Slovenskej Republiky Slovenský Národny Archív, file 209.474.63, document 4.

the local train station: Compare the uniforms with the illustrations in the official *Nazi Party Organizational Manual*, plates 47 and 48, which show the different markings and colors of the agencies. *Organisationsbuch der NSDAP*, Edition Zentral Verlag der NSDAP (Munich: Franz Eher, 1943), 7. The presence of customs guards was corroborated by another testimony in the West German investigation of the civilian administration's crimes in the Chudniv district (which includes Miropol). A former German agricultural inspector stationed in Miropol arrived in late 1941 and remembered that the border police were still there. He also refuted his colleagues' assertion that there were no Jews left in Miropol when they arrived because he knew the Jewish dentist, who spoke German well, and he witnessed the January 1942 massacre of the specialists, which was carried out by members of the Sipo-SD office in Berdychiv, with the assistance of the civilian district commissar, Dr. Paul Blümel. See statement of Jakob Feser, February 12, 1965, BAL, B162/7355. Blümel entered the United States illegally, was discovered in Ocala, Florida, and in April 1985 was forced by the US Department of Justice's Office of Special Investigations to return to West Germany. https://www.nytimes.com/1985/04/30/us/2-war-crime-suspects-leave-united-states.html.

68 *Škrovina, who was:* Statement of Škrovina, June 25, 1943, Ministerstvo Vnútra Slovenskej Republiky Slovenský Národny Archív, file 209.474.63, document 4.

69 *other wartime sources:* Captured German Records, Rear Army Group South, SD454, KTB entries on Slovak security units, NARA, RG 242, T315 reel 2216, frames 000190, 000201, 000218–19.

Local witnesses remembered: Author interview with Lubomir Škrovina Jr., September 4, 2017, Banská Bystrica, Slovakia, Museum of the Slovak National Uprising, with Radu Ioanid and Ján Hlavinka. Thanks to Noemi Szekely-Popescu for finding the family and conducting preliminary interviews in July 2017. No additional information turned up in archival or online database searches for Gero, or Gerö, the incomplete name given by Lubomir's son as he recalled his father's Jewish friends during the war who stayed in their home. Ladislav Gotthilf was another name given, and it appears in the database of Jewish physicians from Czechoslovakia prepared as a memorial book for physicians who died during the Holocaust. It was compiled by the Israel Medical Association and the Jerusalem Academy of Medicine by Dr. Shmuel Grünwald and is available online at https://www.jewishgen.org/database.

74 *"persons murdered on their":* Interrogation of Škrovina, September 3, 1958, ABS, H-770, H-1.

75 *Škrovina survived the war:* Author interview with Lubomir Škrovina Jr., September 4, 2017.

76 *"bourgeois nationalist":* Mahoney, *The History of the Czech Republic.*
Slovak autonomy: The Slovak presence in Nazi-occupied Ukraine began with expeditionary groups. To keep apace with the German units advancing east, the Slovaks of the First (Mobile) Infantry Division formed mobile units, called *Schnell* divisions, consisting of about ten thousand men attached to the Seventeenth Army (such as the Brigade Pilfousek). At the end of August 1941, the Slovak Army Group was reorganized into two infantry divisions, the First (Mobile) and Second Infantry Divisions (about forty-two thousand men). The *Schnell* divisions were active in the Zhytomyr region, in the battle for Kiev around the Dnieper, near Rostov and Melitopol, and in coastal patrols in the Crimea. The Second Slovak (Security) Infantry Division (about six to eight thousand men, of the 101st and 102nd Regiments) carried out policing and combat duties against alleged saboteurs, partisans, and other security threats behind the lines, especially concentrating their activity in the northern half of the Zhytomyr region (including Miropol) as of October 1941. At the time, it was not clear if they were involved in anti-Jewish massacres during their security raids of villages.

Besides the broken chronological record, the histories of the Slovak units are tricky to follow because the units underwent several transformations, including assignments that combined regular combat and special security duties. See Wendy Lower, "Axis Collaboration, Operation Barbarossa, and the Holocaust in Ukraine," in *Nazi Policy on the Eastern Front, 1941: Total War, Genocide, and Radicalization,* ed. Alex Kay, Jeff Rutherford, and David Stahel (Rochester, NY: University of Rochester Press, 2012), 186–211. See also Stanislav J. Kirschbaum, *A History of Slovakia: The Struggle for Survival,* 2nd ed. (London: St. Martin's Press, 2005). Kirschbaum's text seems rather apologist, especially regarding Tiso. It stresses the modernization of Slovakia during the war and the temporary haven for Jews there.

The secret police confiscated: "Action Fox" 1955 protocols, ABS, H-7703-3; interrogations and thirty-one photographs, ABS, H-770, part of file Z-10–911; and Postwar Investigations of Slovak Security Divisions in Belarus and Ukraine, 1948–1982, ABS, file a. no. 595617 MV.

77 *The police had taken:* Author interview with the photographer's children, son Lubomir Škrovina Jr. and daughter Jana (b. 1951), September 4–5, 2017. Thanks to Ján Hlavinka for interpreting. Filmed interview has been donated to the USHMMA.

"As far as I know": Interrogation of Škrovina, September 3, 1958, ABS, H-770, H-1.

Prosecutor: "Tell us": Monday, October 13, 1941, according to Alexander Kruglov. See his entry "Miropol" in *Encyclopedia of Camps and Ghettos,* vol. 2, *Ghettos in German-Occupied Eastern Europe,* ed. Martin Dean (Bloomington: Indiana University Press, published in association with the USHMM); Soviet Extraordinary Commission report on Miropol, GARF, 7021–60–291, 5. Thanks to Alexander Kruglov for sharing his 1992 correspondence with the Office of the Security Services of Ukraine, Zhytomyr district.

79 *onlooker and photographer:* Interrogation of Škrovina, September 3, 1958, ABS, H-770-3, p. 3.

"I must say that he": File 595617_MV_3_3_0016–1, 3rd file, dated June 9, 1959, former Soviet Czech Ministry of Interior, ABS.

had kept the photographs: Author interview with Lubomir Škrovina Jr., September 4, 2017. During the Slovak National Uprising in 1944, American forces arrived in Banská Bystrica to lend their support. At this time, Škrovina testified, he had tried to give the prints to the American military, hoping they would reach the Czech government-in-exile in London. Lubomir Škrovina's son repeated this story recently and added that his father used his radio skills to support the resistance, the uprising, and communications with London. In fact, Škrovina was later awarded a medal for bravery for having supported the Slovak resistance movement.

Among his private papers is a commemorative medal issued by the president of the Czechoslovak Socialist Republic, which was given to Lubomir Škrovina Sr. on August 29, 1964, in memory of the fight against fascism twenty years after the Slovak National Uprising. In December 1964 another medal was awarded to him at the Museum of the Slovak National Uprising (where we interviewed his son), recognizing the Free Slovak Transmitter (radio).

An affidavit of 1971 also testified to Lubomir Škrovina's participation in the uprising, from March 1943 to May 1945, as an employee of the Free Slovak Transmitter, as a courier and supplier, and as a technician, keeping the radio waves open across Slovakia. During this time, the Germans destroyed his radio shop and took materials from it. Affidavit of Anton Holly, Bratislava, July 16, 1971. Private family papers shared with author.

82 *my own portrait of Škrovina:* In letters to his wife from 1941, and family papers. Thanks to Jana Škrovina for sharing facsimiles of the letters, and to Michael Kraus, J. Luke Ryder, and Gabriela Hlavova for assisting with deciphering the handwriting and translating the Slovak into English.

83 *"in the past nor in":* File 209.474.63, pp. 5, 27, dated June 25, 1943, Slovak National Archives, Bratislava.

84 *"If we are to determine":* James Curtis, "Making Sense of Documentary Photography," *History Matters: The U.S. Survey Course on the Web* (George Mason University, June 2003), http://historymatters.gmu.edu/mse/photos/.

86 *become free of Jews:* Apparently Tiso was so anxious to rid his country of Jews that he paid the Germans five hundred Reichsmarks for each one deported; entries for October 20–21, 1941, in *Der Dienstkalender Heinrich Himmlers, 1941/42* (Heinrich Himmler's official calendar, 1941–42), ed. Peter Witte, Michael Wildt, Martina Voigt et al. (Hamburg: Christians, 1999), 241. Tiso also toured Ukraine in November 1941 and claimed after the war that he had objected to Slovak forces' participation in mass shootings of Jews. See James Mace Ward, *Priest, Politician, Collaborator: Jozef Tiso and the Making of Fascist Slovakia* (Ithaca, NY: Cornell University Press, 2013).

"Dear Bobanku": The Škrovina family donated the wartime letters of Lubomir Škrovina to the USHMM in 2017.

88 *Slovakia stood in:* Thanks to the Škrovina family for sharing this information, to Ján Hlavinka for finding Slovak sources to corroborate the family's stories, to Marianna Kramarikova for translating the Slovak records, and to J. Luke Ryder for sharing his dissertation and expertise on the Slovak National Uprising: "Slovak Society, the Second World War, and the Search for Slovak 'Stateness'" (PhD diss., McGill University, 2017). The other doctor who was

hidden in Škrovina's attic was Dr. Eugen Just (1906–1995), who joined the
Soviet partisans, Yegerov Brigade, and continued to practice medicine after
the war. Josef Sulaček, *Biele Pláště: Tragické Osudy Židovských Lekárov na
Slovensku v Období Druhej Svetovej Vojny 2. Cast* (Bratislava: SNM-Múzeum
Židovskej Kultúry, 2006), 38 and 49.

Slovak National Uprising: Gerhard Weinberg, *The Foreign Policy of Hitler's Germany: Starting World War II, 1937–1939* (Amherst, NY: Prometheus,
1994). Slovakia was a newly independent state and had Germany to thank for
its autonomy; the breakup of Czechoslovakia had been orchestrated by Hitler
through the Munich Pact, in 1938–39. German-Slovak relations were formal-
ized in March 1939 under the terms of a "protective treaty," which gave Germany the upper hand in Slovakia's foreign, military, and economic policies.

89 *"every police station":* Benjamin Frommer, *National Cleansing: Retribution
Against Nazi Collaborators in Postwar Czechoslovakia* (Cambridge, UK: Cambridge University Press, 2005), 53.

"Jewish civilians executed": Letter shared with author, Škrovina family collection.

90 *guards at gassing centers:* On Ukrainian collaborators as "the worst" and
their role as Trawniki guards, see Frank Golczewski, "Shades of Grey: Reflec-
tions on Jewish-Ukrainian and German-Ukrainian Relations in Galicia," in
The Shoah in Ukraine, ed. Ray Brandon and Wendy Lower (Bloomington:
Indiana University Press, 2008), 114–55.

As an independent scholar: Pavol Mestan to Lubomir Škrovina, July 10, 1997,
Slovak National Museum, Bratislava. Letter in possession of Jana Škrovina and
shared with the author. I received outstanding assistance at the Security Services Archive (ABS) from Jitka Bilkova, who provided scans of records that I
had not requested and pointed me to leads in other Slovak archives.

91 On Photography *(1973):* Sontag, *On Photography,* 3–6, 10–18, 105, and 115–32.
"Photographing is essentially": Sontag, *On Photography,* 11.
"material vestige": Sontag, *On Photography,* 154.

92 *"instant of truth":* Arendt, quoted and analyzed in Didi-Huberman, *Images
in Spite of All,* 30. Also see Sharon Sliwinski, *Human Rights in Camera* (Chicago: University of Chicago Press, 2011).
"in the eye of history": Didi-Huberman, *Images in Spite of All,* 39.

5. The Search for the Family

96 *"couple was like a tree"*: Ansky, *The Enemy at His Pleasure,* 23.

there in plain sight: Joanna Beata Michlic, ed., *Jewish Families in Europe, 1939–Present: History, Representations, Memory* (Waltham, MA: Brandeis University Press, 2017). See Lenore Weitzman's essay in this volume: "Resistance in Everyday Life: Family Strategies, Role Reversals, and Role Sharing in the Holocaust," 46–66.

diarist named Samek: Wendy Lower, *The Diary of Samuel Golfard and the Holocaust in Galicia* (Lanham, MD: AltaMira Press and the USHMM, 2011).

97 *"They wouldn't admit"*: Piotr Rawicz, *Blood from the Sky,* excerpted in Eric J. Sundquist, ed., *Writing in Witness: A Holocaust Reader* (New York: SUNY Press, 2018), 171.

98 *The commission's final report:* Soviet Extraordinary Commission Report, May 1945, GARF, fond 7021, opis 60, delo 291, USHMMA.

99 *"no items found"*: Jan Lambertz, "Early Post-war Holocaust Knowledge and the Search for Europe's Missing Jews," in *Patterns of Prejudice* 53, no. 1 (2019): 63.

most of them were children: Pages of Testimony Collection, Yad Vashem, Jerusalem, 1954–2004: United Nations Educational, Scientific, and Cultural Organization," Memory of the World (UNESCO, 2013), http://www.unesco.org/new/en/communication-and-information/memory-of-the-world/register/full-list-of-registered-heritage/registered-heritage-page-7/pages-of-testimony-collection-yad-vashem-jerusalem-1954–2004/.

101 *this family photograph:* Names of those in the photograph:

Standing, from left to right:

Sheira, Eda, Boris Fila Sandler (boy), Roman Vaselyuk (boy), Khiva Brontzovskaya Vaselyuk (mother of Roman)

Seated, from left to right: Shuva Sandler, Adela Sandler

In the Miropol list of victims from 1944, more Sandlers are listed: Vasya Mortkovna Sandler (b. 1902), Sonya Yankelevna Sandler (b. 1924), and Boris Yankelevich Sandler (b. 1938).

103 *"The family was the nucleus"*: Petrovsky-Shtern, *The Golden-Age Shtetl,* 231.

104 "Eshet chayil": A Woman of Valor, Proverbs 31:10–31, Hebrew Bible.

Fathers taught sons: Dalia Ofer, "Parenthood in the Shadow of the Holocaust," in *Jewish Families in Europe, 1939–Present,* 5; Stevan Weine et al., "A Family Survives Genocide," *Psychiatry* 60, no. 1 (1997): 24–39.

105 *If she could avoid:* Blekhman testimony, VHA, interview code 33782, tape 3, segment 04:00.

"We were raised to make": Blekhman, VHA, interview code 33782, tape 3, segment 04:00.

weight of this tradition: Fathers like Blekhman's offered protection in other ways, such as planning and organizing community resistance actions with the support of spouses, girlfriends, or other women. At the mass shooting in Miropol, Ludmilla hid among the adults as each family unit was forced to step forward. Blekhman testimony, VHA, interview code 33782, tapes 4 and 5. At Dubno, a German businessman watched as a father held the hand of his ten-year-old son, "speaking to him softly; the boy was fighting tears. The father pointed to the sky, stroked his head, and seemed to explain something to him." At this point, the family was ordered by the SS commander to the execution site, which was behind an earthen mound. Testimony of Hermann Graebe at Nuremberg, November 10, 1945, Document PS-2992, RG 238, NARA.

They cared for the remaining: Heberer, *Children During the Holocaust;* Debórah Dwork, *Children with a Yellow Star: Jewish Youth in Nazi Europe* (New Haven, CT: Yale University Press, 1991). See also Esther Hertzog, "Subjugated Motherhood and the Holocaust," *Dapim: Studies of the Holocaust* 30, no. 1 (February 2016): 16–34.

106 *Mothers comforted children:* Renate Bridenthal, Atina Grossman, and Marion Kaplan, eds., *When Biology Became Destiny: Women in Weimar and Nazi Germany* (New York: Monthly Review Press, 1984); *Women in the Holocaust,* ed. Dalia Ofer and Lenore J. Weitzman (New Haven, CT: Yale University Press, 1998). Disproportionate numbers of women and children were killed because they were deemed "useless eaters" and represented the future of the "race." Another expression of a mother's experience appears in the following excerpt from an essay (reprinted in Sundquist, ed., *Writing in Witness,* 58), which was written by Abraham Levite, from Galicia, Ukraine, who was deported in 1942:

> The mother sits inside. She holds her head between her hands. Her face
> is gloomy, and her heart beats strangely. Pictures of an entire life pass

before her eyes: childhood, youth, and the short period of the family's happiness. Home, husband, the parents' house, the village, fields, forests, gardens, all rush by, shuffled together like playing cards, one image driving out the next, all of it bordered in black, the shattered house, wantonly abandoned, in ruins, the family's nest destroyed: doors and windows torn open, cabinets ripped apart, broken dishes, clothes torn about and trampled, everything left a mess. And now, for heaven's sake, where are they headed?

107 *western aesthetic:* Michael Burleigh and Wolfgang Wippermann, *The Racial State: Germany, 1933–1945* (Cambridge, UK: Cambridge University Press, 1993); George L. Mosse, *Nazi Culture: Intellectual, Cultural, and Social Life in the Third Reich* (Madison: University of Wisconsin Press, 1966); Lisa Pine, *Education in Nazi Germany* (Oxford, UK: Berg, 2010); Paul Ginsbourg, *Family Politics: Domestic Life, Devastation, and Survival, 1900–1950* (New Haven, CT: Yale University Press, 2014).

Nazi policy was two-pronged: Lisa Pine, "Family and Private Life," in *A Companion to Nazi Germany,* ed. Shelley Baranowski, Armin Nolzen, and Claus-Christian W. Szejnmann (Hoboken, NJ: Wiley-Blackwell, 2018), 365.

108 *"We stand or die":* Proceedings of the Trial of War Criminals Before the Nürnberg Military Tribunal, *United States of America vs. Greifelt et al.,* "RuSHA Case no. 8," vol. 4 (Washington, DC: US Government Printing Office, 1946–49), 635.

109 *"the men of a guilty":* Translation of document NO-2400, Prosecution Exhibit 263, Teletype from General Krüger to Himmler, November 9, 1942, Proceedings of the Trial of War Criminals Before the Nürnberg Military Tribunal, *United States of America vs. Greifelt et al.,* "RuSHA Case no. 8," vol. 5, 914.

"should be sterilized": YVA, 0–18/245, in *Documents on the Holocaust,* ed. Yitzhak Arad, Yisrael Gutman, and Abraham Margaliot (Lincoln: University of Nebraska Press, 1999), 400.

Police escorted women: Heberer, *Children During the Holocaust,* 141–42; Raphael Lemkin, *Axis Rule in Occupied Europe* (Washington, DC: Carnegie Endowment for International Peace, 1944), 86–87.

"engaged in a battle": Quoting a thesis on the destruction of the family as a life-force atrocity that is potentially genocidal, presented by Elisa von Jo-

eden-Forgey in "The Devil in the Details: 'Life Force Atrocities' and the Assault on the Family in Times of Conflict," *Genocide Studies and Prevention* 5, no. 1 (April 2010): 1–19. See also Lemkin, *Axis Rule*, 82–87, section on biological genocide. Also see Lemkin's treatment of the Nazi violation of The Hague Convention Article 46, on the right to family honor, violated on a massive scale when families were separated during deportations and in the camps. By contrast, among Germans the promotion of family honor was practiced by elevating one's ancestry, researching names, and changing them to German ones (Lemkin, 77). Thanks to Lauren Fedewa and Henry Schulz for their research assistance on the history of the family.

110 *"if any State for"*: In the original German: "den wenn auch nur ein Staat aus irgendwelchen Gründen eine jüdische Familie bei sich dulde, so würde diese der Bazillusherd für eine neue Zersetzung werden." Hitler to Kvaternik, as noted by Hewel, 383, in *Akten zur Deutschen Auswaertigen Politik, 1918–1945, Serie D: 1937–1941, Band XIII.1, Die Kriegsjahre, Sechster Band, Erster Halbband, 23. Juni bis 14. September 1941* (Files on German foreign policy, 1918–1945, series D: 1937–1941, band XIII.1, the war years, sixth volume, first half, June 23–September 14, 1941) (Göttingen: Vandenhoeck and Ruprecht, 1970). Thanks to Elliott Wrenn, the librarian at the USHMM, for assistance.
Married and the father: For the Himmler family photo albums, see the collections of the USHMM, https://collections.ushmm.org/search/catalog/pa1151335, and the daughter Gudrun's obituary in the *New York Times,* https://www.nytimes.com/2018/07/06/obituaries/gudrun-burwitz-ever-loyal-daughter-of-himmler-is-dead-at-88.html.
"and they winced": Proceedings on April 8, 1948, of the Trial of War Criminals Before the Nürnberg Military Tribunal, *United States of America vs. Ohlendorf et al., "Einsatzgruppen Case no. 9"* (Washington, DC: US Government Printing Office, 1946–49); "Military Tribunal II Case 9: Methods of Execution," 42.
"Jews are free game": Proceedings on April 8, 1948, of the Trial of War Criminals Before the Nürnberg Military Tribunal, *United States of America vs. Ohlendorf et al., "Einsatzgruppen Case no. 9"*; "Military Tribunal II Case 9: Methods of Execution," 42.

111 *more humane and orderly*: Recollections of Kotlova, Kiev, January 13, 1945,

GARF, fond 8114, opis 1, delo 960.II, excerpted in Joshua Rubenstein and Ilya Altman, eds., *The Unknown Black Book: The Holocaust in the German-Occupied Soviet Territories* (Bloomington: Indiana University Press, 2010), 76. This Jewish survivor near Kiev testified that the "bandits" liked to kill children in the presence of their mothers: "Oh, how hard the suffering of a mother is when she sees her children killed."

Former policemen assigned to Order Police Battalions 303 and 45, who swept through Miropol in the summer of 1941, recollected the excessive horrors inflicted upon the Jewish children: they were ripped from their mothers' arms and murdered while their mothers were forced to watch, or killed in their mothers' arms in the pits during the massacres at Vinnytsia, Berdychiv, and Zviahel. These officers also mentioned the incinerating and drowning of entire families. See statements of Willi Herrmann, November 21, 1966, Karl Müller, February 12, 1967, and Karl Habich, handwritten testimony completed in Soviet captivity, June 4, 1946, held in the records of the Staatsanwaltschaft Regensburg 92941/Volume I, Akten in der Strafsache der Strafkammer bei dem Landgericht Regensburg, gegen Rosenbauer, Besser, and Krenze (HSSPF Police Regiment Sud), ASA, 4 Js 1495/65.

"the place where sadistic": *Encyclopedia of Camps and Ghettos, 1933–1945*, vol. 3, *Camps and Ghettos Under European Regimes Aligned with Nazi Germany*, ed. Geoffrey Megargee, Joseph White, and Mel Hecker (Bloomington: University of Indiana Press in association with the USHMM, 2018), 308.

"Go to the right": Max Eisen, *By Chance Alone: A Remarkably True Story of Courage and Survival at Auschwitz* (New York: HarperCollins, 2017). At the National Policy Conference on Holocaust Education, January 27, 2018, in Toronto, Eisen explained that "I was told the next day that they went up the chimney. Mother was taken to gas chambers with my baby sister 8-month-old Judit. My brother and father and I registered for labor, I was 15 years old. I was the only one to survive."

112   *this brief report:* Report of Meister d. Gen. u Postenführer Mayrhofer to Koziatyn SS and police district leader, May 13, 1943, ZSA, Captured German Records, P1182-1-6.

"Pohrebysche": Lower, *Nazi Empire-Building*, 133–34.

No names are: Natalia Aleksiun, "Daily Survival: Social History of Jews in Family Bunkers in Eastern Galicia," in *Lessons and Legacies XII: New Directions in Holocaust Research and Education,* ed. Wendy Lower and Lauren Faulkner Rossi (Evanston, IL: Northwestern University Press, 2017). The culture of denunciation, bridging the prewar period and wartime, has been stressed by Karel Berkhoff in his study of Ukrainian society in the Reichskommissariat, "Was There a Religious Revival in Soviet Ukraine Under the Nazi Regime?," *Slavonic and East European Review* 78, no. 3 (July 2000): 536–67, and comparatively in the work of Robert Gellately and Sheila Fitzpatrick, "Practices of Denunciation in Modern European History," *Journal of Modern History* 68 (December 1996).

hunted Jewish families: Prior to the war, Nazi leaders targeted families by removing heads of household (for example, Jewish fathers) from their occupations, expelling Jewish children from schools, banning Jewish rituals of food preparation, forbidding marriages between Jews and "Aryans" in order to "protect German blood" (according to the Nuremberg Laws of 1935), and arresting thousands of Jewish men during the November 1938 pogrom. This pattern continued in the way that deportations were organized by family unit and in the final destruction of life, during which families were forced to experience death together, witnessing one another's suffering. Jewish children born after 1930 had a survival rate of less than 2 percent in Nazi-occupied Europe. See Joseph Walk, ed., *Das Sonderrecht für die Juden im NS-Staat: Eine Sammlung der gesetzlichen Massnahmen und Richtlinien — Inhalt und Bedeutung* (The special laws for the Jews in the Nazi state: A collection of the legal measures and guidelines — Contents and meaning) (Heidelberg: Joseph Müller Verlag, 1981); Heberer, *Children During the Holocaust.*

"ostensibly honoring natural": Ward, *Priest, Politician, Collaborator,* 230.

113 *She never saw her:* Jürgen Matthäus, ed., *Approaching an Auschwitz Survivor: Holocaust Testimony and Its Transformations* (New York: Oxford University Press, 2010).

"like fish in a barrel": Hoffmann case, statement of Kuska, August 14, 1969, BAL, B162/28709.

114 *"hearing the screams":* Eric J. Sundquist, introduction to *Writing in Witness.* On the choiceless choices, also see the testimony of those who saw babies abandoned in carriages on the streets — "there was no place for them [. . .]

fear they would cry and lead to discovery" — in Nechama Tec's introduction
to Heberer, *Children During the Holocaust*. And this testimony from a mass
shooting in Zagrodski, near Pinsk in Belarus on August 15, 1942: "It was difficult to hold the children, they were shaking. We took turns. Parents took
the children, took other people's children. This was to help us get through it
all; to get it over with, and not let the children suffer. Mothers took leave of
their children, the mothers, the parents [...] We stood there facing the ditch.
I turned my head. [The gunman] asked, 'Whom do I shoot first?' I didn't
answer. He tore the child away from me. I heard her last cry and he shot her."
Statement of Rivka Yoselewska, May 8, 1961, at the Eichmann trial, reprinted
in Heberer, *Children During the Holocaust*, 83–86.

At war's end no Jewish: "The quest for preserving the family in situations
that did not allow such preservation," in Dalia Ofer, "Motherhood Under
Siege," in *Life, Death, and Sacrifice: Women and Family in the Holocaust,* ed.
Esther Herzog (Jerusalem: Gefen Publishing House, 2008), 23, 3–25.

these child survivors: Over time, how did the family unit respond to the
extreme pressure and assaults that led to separation and eventually murder?
There are traceable patterns. Families tried to survive together, but the stress
also caused resentments and rifts and precipitated divorces. The German intellectual Mohr left for Shanghai in the 1930s, not looking back nor securing
transit for his gentile wife. The survivor Henry F. had few fond memories of
his parents' marriage, and he suspected that his father had been unfaithful to
his mother before the war, which drew Henry closer to her. Henry's recollections of the Holocaust are mostly of his mother. He remembers her shield-
ing his eyes as they walked through the horrible scenes of the Lodz ghetto.
When they were deported from the ghetto to Auschwitz-Birkenau, Henry
was separated from his mother at the selection ramp. Through the communications network among prisoners he soon learned that his mother was ill,
perhaps with tuberculosis. Henry feared that she would be sent to the infir-
mary, deemed too sick to work, and brought to the gas chambers. Assuming
the worst, he managed to obtain a sweater from the Kanada barracks (where
belongings of Jewish deportees were stored) and arranged to meet his mother
at the fence dividing the men's and women's camps. He wrapped the sweater
around his torso and hid it under his camp uniform. As he approached his

mother, he spotted a guard looking at him. He therefore could not stop, remove the sweater, and hand it to her. As he walked, he hesitated and had one
final, loving exchange with his mother.

In 2008 Henry shared this last memory. Teary-eyed and still regretful, he
lamented, "If only I had given her that sweater, then she might have survived."
I surmised, "Maybe your mother would not have kept the sweater. She knew
it was a dangerous exchange and would want you to have it to survive; she
was probably relieved to see you." Henry's father survived, but Henry did not
remain with him after the war, choosing instead to immigrate to America as
a youth. Author interview with Henry F., October 2008, Washington, DC.
Also see Doris L. Bergen, introduction to *War and Genocide*, and Frederick
Reuss, *Mohr* (Denver: Unbridled Books, 2006).

In more stable families, when the head of household — the father — emigrated or was deported or murdered, mothers and children were left to fend
for themselves. George Schwalb's mother saved him through her resourceful-
ness. Though suffering intense grief over the violent murder of her husband,
she resolved to protect her two sons at any cost. By means of social connections and by using jewelry and other valuables, she negotiated hiding places
for them during mass shootings. She and her ten-year-old George did survive,
but barely. George recalled that in moments of starvation, alone and suffering,
he could not understand Nazism and the wider world. Instead, he became angry at his mother. Why couldn't she protect him; isn't that what parents do?
Interview with author, Liepāja, Latvia, July 6, 2017.

the family photograph: This finding is based on an inventory of more than
thirty thousand unclaimed personal effects of Jews deported to the camps; the
items are archived at the International Tracing Service in Bad Arolsen, Germany. USHMM presentation "Material Culture from Textual Sources: Documentary Archaeology in Medieval Marseille and Beyond," December 2017, by
Gabriel Pizzorno. Robert M. Ehrenreich and Jane Klinger, "War in Context:
Let the Artifacts Speak," in *Does War Belong in Museums? The Representation
of Violence in Exhibitions,* ed. Wolfgang Muchitsch (Bielefeld: Transcript Verlag, 2014), 145–54.

115 *Legal scholars:* William Schabas, *Genocide in International Law: The Crime
of Crimes* (New York: Cambridge University Press, 2009). Only recently has
genocide studies become a distinct academic field, freeing the concept of geno-

cide from a narrow legal definition and enabling exploration of concepts such as the victim group as a family unit. In 2015, the theorist Mohammed Abed published an essay about what happens to a group experiencing extinction intentionally imposed by others. When the group is being destroyed, "family life, a locus of socialization and cultural reproduction, will often be seriously disrupted. In some cases, families will be destroyed" (353). Mohammed Abed, "The Concept of Genocide Reconsidered" in *Social Theory and Practice* 41 (April 2015): 328–56. In the 1990s, Rwanda and Bosnia cast a glaring light on acts of mass rape and sexual violence as aspects of genocide. The deliberate violation and impregnation of women, along with infecting them with diseases such as HIV/AIDS, were intended to destroy victim families and communities. As scholars investigate premodern cases of genocide, they are finding that the slavery system, which separated men from women, first destroyed the family unit and then the community, leading over time to the disappearance of a particular people, such as the Inca in Peru, who were destroyed by Spanish colonizers. See Adam Jones, *Genocide: A Comprehensive Introduction*, 3rd ed. (New York: Routledge, 2017), 150–63 and 625–46; Carol Rittner and John K. Roth, eds., *Rape: Weapon of War and Genocide* (St. Paul: Paragon, 2012).

In Lemkin's explanation: Raphael Lemkin, "Genocide as a Crime Under International Law," *American Journal of International Law* 4, no. 1 (January 1947): 147.

to end procreation: Totally Unofficial: The Autobiography of Raphael Lemkin, ed. Donna-Lee Frieze (New Haven: Yale University Press, 2013).

"any injury done": See American Military Tribunals at Nürnberg, Green Series, vol. 4/5, "The Einsatzgruppen Case" and "The RuSHA Case" (Washington, DC: US Government Printing Office, 1949), "The Nature of the Charges," Count One, Report of the VII Conference for the Unification of Penal Law, July 11, 1947, in vol. 4, 48, and Judgment in vol. 5, 102–52.

116 *"The number of deaths":* See American Military Tribunals at Nürnberg, Green Series, vol. 4, "The Einsatzgruppen Case," Trial 9, "XI. Opinion and Judgment," 413.

Lemkin and other legal scholars: Dagmar Herzog, *Unlearning Eugenics: Sexuality, Reproduction, and Disability in Post-Nazi Europe* (Madison, WI: University of Wisconsin Press, 2018).

117 *This is surprising:* They had to respond to what happened during the war. The death rates for children were higher than ever before in history. In eastern Europe babies and toddlers had less than a 1 percent chance of survival. Countless perished due to malnutrition and illness, and more than a million Jewish kids were shot, gassed, and killed by other means in the Holocaust. Hundreds of thousands were orphaned, creating a humanitarian crisis that prompted the establishment of UNICEF. Nations whose populations had been decimated by the war claimed these orphans as citizens. Still, despite the downfall of the Third Reich, some ideas from the eugenics movement remained prevalent, and often American and European welfare workers and doctors evaluated the orphans based on race, deciding which were fit for "good" homes. Aid workers and psychologists feared that angry, forlorn children might act out or seek revenge. One aid worker described the child survivors of the camps and wartorn Europe as "tired, wan, broken little old men and women," who struggled "to learn to play again." Marija Platace Futchs Fine, *Wide Eyes: A War Orphan Unlocks the Mystery of Her Latvian Roots After Seventy Years* (Bloomington, IN: Xlibris, 2016); also see Tara Zahra, *The Lost Children: Reconstructing Europe's Families After World War II* (Cambridge, MA: Harvard University Press, 2015), 9, and Dwork, *Children with a Yellow Star.*

"The family is the national": This was an expanded version of the existing Hague Convention on Land Warfare, Article 46, which states that the international community must respect family honor and rights.

6. Excavating History

119 *"Every village and town":* Lower, *The Diary of Samuel Golfard.*

120 *list of 1,500 cemeteries:* "Jewish Cemeteries, Synagogues, and Mass Graves in Ukraine: Final Report, 2005," JewishGen (The United States Commission for the Preservation of America's Heritage Abroad), accessed February 10, 2020, https://www.jewishgen.org/bessarabia/files/JewishHistory/survey _ukraine_2005.pdf.

It often involves: Konrad Kwiet, "A Historian's View: The War Crimes Debate Down Under," *Dapim: Studies on the Holocaust* 24, no. 1 (2010): 319–39. The excavation of a mass grave in Serniki, Ukraine, uncovered personal belongings and bullet fragments. The archaeologists' evidence informed a Nazi-war-crimes trial in New South Wales, Australia, in the early 1990s.

buried objects that tell: Ehrenreich and Klinger, "War in Context." Also see Ian Woodward, *Understanding Material Culture* (Los Angeles: Sage Publications, 2014).

This scarred landscape: Presentation by Kathryn Brown, Anthropocene Plenary Panel, American Historical Association Annual Conference, New York City, January 3, 2020.

"The Holocaust sits between": Caroline Sturdy Colls, *Holocaust Archaeologies: Approaches and Future Directions* (New York: Springer, 2015), 57.

121 *spectacles of barbarism:* Maria R. (b. 1925), interview with the author and Yahad–In Unum, July 23, 2016, interview code 2135, Miropol. See also similar accounts by survivors reprinted in Rubenstein and Altman, eds., *The Unknown Black Book.*

122 *Here I could test:* Colls, *Holocaust Archaeologies,* 11.

In most cases of homicide: Jennifer L. Truman and Lynn Langton, "Criminal Victimization, 2014," Bureau of Justice Statistics (Washington, DC: US Department of Justice, Office of Justice Programs, September 29, 2015), https://www.bjs.gov/content/pub/pdf/cv14.pdf.

123 *Such reports were routinely:* The Einsatzgruppen reports were captured in the two tons of documentation that the Allies found in the former Gestapo offices in Berlin in 1945. They were among the sixteen hundred tons of documents that were processed and used in the American Military Tribunal at Nuremberg. On the files, see Ronald Headland, *Messages of Murder: A Study of the Reports of the Einsatzgruppen of the Security Police and the Security Service, 1941–1943* (Cranbury, NJ: Associated University Presses, 1992), 14 and 46–47.

"ghastly mass murders": Wolfram Wette, *The Wehrmacht: History, Myth, Reality* (Cambridge, MA: Harvard University Press, 2006), 121.

Each site contains: Colls, *Holocaust Archaeologies,* 205.

124 *eminent Catholic priest:* We met in Paris to prepare for the trip. Yahad–In Unum had just moved its headquarters to the exurbs, to a building that could accommodate the expanded staff, and it was outfitted with gated security. At the time, May 2016, French TV broadcasted the advance of Daesh (the Islamic

State) on Fallujah in Iraq. Father Desbois, embroiled with the French government in the war against ISIS, had received death threats. He was collecting testimonies from Yazidi girls and boys who had escaped sexual slavery and forced mobilization in terror camps. These child members of a Kurdish-speaking minority group, Desbois explained, were so ashamed and fearful that they would not speak in the presence of family members. Their stories of suffering sadistic violence had gotten to Father Desbois. Yazidi children were "broken in" by being severed from their families and kept in the constant company of jihadists. Seven-year-old boys were placed in training to become suicide bombers and were forced to witness and carry out beheadings and immolations. Desbois had listened to hundreds of Ukrainian witnesses to the Holocaust. Now, in northern Iraq, he was working in the present, the stories were being told in real time by child victims, and they demanded immediate attention and response. When we left France for Ukraine, CNN headlines stated that ISIS was using Yazidi families as human shields in the battle over Fallujah. Again, I was struck by the fate of the family in this latest case of genocide.

127 *In moist environments:* Katherine J. Powell, "Methods Used by Australian Police Services to Locate Buried Bodies," in *The Detection of Buried Human Skeletal Remains in the Australian Environment* (PhD diss., University of Adelaide, 2006). Also see the report of the Search and Rescue Tracking Institute in Virginia: http://ww.sarti.us/sarti/files/SearchForHumanRemains.pdf.
victims were clothed: Powell, *The Detection of Buried Human Skeletal Remains,* 77; Marcella H. Sorg and William D. Haglund, *Forensic Taphonomy: The Postmortem Fate of Human Remains* (New York: CRC Press, 2017).
Decomposition begins: Sorg and Haglund, *Forensic Taphonomy.*
While he denied: Statement of Heinrich Barth (b. 1901), March 2, 1977, files of the prosecutor of the Munich Landesgericht, 35–320 JS 16 839/75, BAL, B162/76355. Barth was an engineer assigned to the civilian occupation administration in the neighboring district capital of Chudniv (Tschudnow), Ukraine. He recalled that "in Chudniv there was a butcher, who was named Pereguda. After the war he explained to me that one time he slaughtered a pig that shortly before had eaten the arm of a body of the dead from Oelberg [the massacre site outside of town]. The meat of the pig he delivered to the German Kasino." The Kasino was the Germans-only canteen. This statement

appears in the case against Dr. Blümel, a former mayor in Germany and district commissar in Chudniv.

128 *a unique configuration:* Kiho Im and P. Ellen Grant, "Sulcal Pits and Patterns in Developing Human Brains," *NeuroImage* 185 (January 15, 2018): 881–90.

129 *"Szepetowka, in forest":* See document 282, dated March 11, 1944, "Radio Moskau verliest erbeutete deutsche Dokument, darunter solche über die Beseitigung der Leichen ermordeter Juden" (Radio Moscow reads captured German documents, including those about the removal of the corpses of murdered Jews), in Bert Hoppe and Romina Becker, eds., *Die Verfolgung und Ermordung der europäischen Juden durch das nationalsozialistische Deutschland, 1933–1945: Sowjetunion mit annektierten Gebieten II, Band 8* (The persecution and murder of European Jews by National Socialist Germany, 1933–1945: Soviet Union with annexed areas, vol. 8) (Oldenbourg: De Gruyter, 2016), 684–89. Only part of the list was read over the radio. The full list is not reprinted or cited in this document collection, though the radio broadcaster referred to a German document that was found by Soviets in the Gestapo office in Rowno, which contained this list as a response to Blobel's request of August 3, 1943.

130 *holding hands by candlelight:* Maria R., July 23, 2016, interview code 2135.

extraordinary memories: If a witness seemed to have a good memory and to be knowledgeable about the massacres, the Jewish history, and the Ukrainian police, we would arrange a formal interview session to be filmed over two days. Dozens of people were questioned, but we ended up filming just fourteen who had witnessed the massacre, interacted with Jews who were killed, knew the Ukrainian policemen, or had participated in the postwar investigation and exhumation.

"Do not go into the woods!": Leonid U. (b. 1930), interview with the author and Yahad–In Unum, July 20, 2016, interview code 2127, Miropol.

131 *had to be prepared:* On the debate over displaying human remains, see Edward Tabor Linenthal, *Preserving Memory: The Struggle to Create America's Holocaust Museum* (New York: Columbia University Press, 2001).

The local non-Jewish: Author interviews with Andrej Umansky and Nikolayenko Leonid Fedorovich (b. 1940), former mayor of Miropol, July 19 and 22, 2016, interview code 2126, Miropol. Thanks to Kateryna Duzenko for interpreting. Ludmilla Blekhman referred to Soviet POWs shot in smaller pits in the woods; VHA, interview code 33782, tape 3, segment 17:00.

132 *They rejected it:* Umansky and Fedorovich, July 19, 2016, interview code 2126. When I asked why the exhumation in the Miropol Park started in the mid-1980s, the mayor replied, "I don't know why it was started then, perhaps because of the strong Jewish community in Israel or somewhere else; they decided to rebury the bodies."

the 1980s exhumations: Makareyvych's petition, dated September 16, 1986, to extend the detention of the accused and recommend further steps, which included finding more witnesses, carrying out psychiatric examinations of the accused, and identifying the relatives of the victims, YVA, TR.18/273.1.

investigation was reopened: KGB Department of the Ukrainian SSR Zhytomyr region, Criminal Case No. 40, charged Les'ko, Rybak, and Gnyatuk of committing crimes under Part 1 of Article 56 of the Criminal Code of the Ukrainian SSR. Started June 5, 1986, finished December 1, 1986, YVA, folder 1, file 32425, TR.18/273.1.

locals were requisitioned: The Excomm, or Extraordinary State Commission for Ascertaining and Investigating Crimes Perpetrated by the German-Fascist Invaders and Their Accomplices, had been formed at the end of 1942, to document the murder of peaceful citizens and the rapacious theft and destruction of state property for reparations claims. See Kiril Feferman, "Soviet Investigation of Nazi Crimes in the USSR: Documenting the Holocaust," *Journal of Genocide Research* 5 (2003): 587–602.

133 *He brushed away:* Bitman's photographs of bones, evidence in trial, photographs of October reenactments, and exhumation photos of October 1986: YVA, photographs 11, 13, 14, TR.18/273.7.

134 *In our 2016 interview:* In the prosecutor's speech after the trial on January 4, 1987, he described being present at the exhumation, seeing the skulls with bullet holes, the hand bones twisted with barbed wire, and children's skulls with dents from rifle butts and trees. Thanks to Natalya Lazar for assisting with the translation of the speech, from the private collection of the mayor, copy provided to the author. Speech and translation now deposited in the USHMMA.

"I remember that": Former police guard (b. 1947) in Miropol forest, interview with the author and Yahad–In Unum, July 23, 2016, interview code

2136. We see in the court records the same killers, now elderly, standing at the sites in the forest, pointing to the graves, and speaking about the policemen's violent actions against their Jewish neighbors' former classmates. YVA, TR.18/273.7, 17–18.

135   *among the remains:* Fedorovich, July 22, 2016, interview code 2126.

136   *Besides, I was told:* Telephone call with representative of the German Memorial to the Murdered Jews of Europe, August 15, 2016, while she surveyed the site in Miropol. Today the memorial stands in the park, near the ravine. According to the entry on Miropol in Yad Vashem's *Untold Stories,* "In 1983 the town erected a monument for its civilian war victims. Representatives of the Jewish community in the Zhitomir District and the regional administration initiated the monument. The monument was erected on the bank of the Sluch River, where there was a memorial for 50 soldiers of the Red Army who had been killed by the Germans in 1941. The inscription, in Ukrainian in golden letters, says: 'May the memory be bright of the civilian citizens of Miropol who were shot by the German fascists.'

"In 1986 the Ukrainian KGB used the graves next to the monument as evidence in a trial of Ukrainian collaborators. The defendants included three Ukrainian policemen who were involved in the mass shooting in Miropol. During the trial the collaborators pointed out the spot where the Jews had been killed. Then the mass grave in the municipal park was excavated, and the victims' bodies were exhumed. The bones of approximately 300 Jews were reburied in a grave near the monument. The rest of the remains still lie in the former municipal park." https://www.yadvashem.org/untoldstories/database/commemoration.asp?cid=1032.

7. The Missing Missing

137   *recall the past:* Zelizer, "From the Image of Record."

When I researched photographs: I did this as the 2015 Yom HaShoah scholar at USC's Visual History Archive. In one of many memorable accounts, the survivor Abraham Mahler (interview code 2894, segment 164) presented three atrocity photographs and explained how he got them. After the war he and friends visited Berchtesgaden and in a restaurant recognized a former SS man. They chased him to a spot under a bridge, forced him to show his SS tattoo, took his wallet, and found the atrocity photographs of a hanging. Among the more outstanding of the many testimonies featuring atrocity photographs are those of Lawrence Rhee (interview code 13981, segment 166), Zysman Unger (interview code 36040, segments 63, 64), Anton Winter (interview code 32160, segment 107), Bertram Wyle (interview code 7262), Zrubawel Werba (interview code 51744, segment 75), and Joyce Lipper (interview code 22086, segment 120). See Hirsch, *Generation of Postmemory;* also Marianne Hirsch, "Surviving Images: Holocaust Photographs and the Work of Postmemory," in *Visual Culture and the Holocaust,* ed. Barbie Zelizer (New Brunswick, NJ: Rutgers University Press, 2001), 215–46.

138 *relief and rehabilitation programs:* Daniel Cohen, "The 'Human Rights Revolution' at Work: Displaced Persons in Post-War Europe," in *Human Rights in the Twentieth Century,* ed. Stefan-Ludwig Hoffmann (New York: Cambridge University Press, 2011). Herbert Hoover led important famine-relief campaigns during the Great War and its aftermath in Belgium and Ukraine and after World War II, and the League of Nations sought to protect minorities and the stateless. Efforts like these have expanded with the rise of mass migration and displacement of peoples fleeing conflict, natural disasters, and other deprivations, surpassing the number affected during the World War II era. Bruno Cabanes, *The Great War and the Origins of Humanitarianism* (Cambridge, UK: Cambridge University Press, 2014).

orphaned children: Zorach Wahrhaftig, *Uprooted: Jewish Refugees and Displaced Persons After Liberation* (New York: Institute of Jewish Affairs of the American Jewish Congress and World Jewish Congress, 1946); Zahra, *The Lost Children,* 11.

139 *"I am what is left":* Perla Sneh, *"Khurbn Yiddish:* An Absent Absence," in *Lessons and Legacies XII,* ed. Lower and Rossi, 215.

As Levin described: Meyer Levin, *In Search: An Autobiography* (Paris: Author's Press, 1950). Levin wrote the first play based on the diary of Anne Frank, with the Frank family's approval.

140 *"Dear Uncle Ilya":* Ludmilla Blekhman, letter to Moscow relatives, 1944, YVA, XX1234.

"You betrayed us!": Blekhman testimony, Yad Vashem, "Mass murder of the Jews of Miropol," https://www.youtube.com/watch?v=e02s_G-TjQA.

As survivors gradually: Dalia Ofer, Françoise S. Ouzon, and Judy Tydor

Baumel-Schwarz, eds., *Holocaust Survivors: Resettlement, Memories, Identities* (New York: Berghahn, 2011).

The German radio: "Potential Use of ITS in the Context of Restitution Claims, Referring to the Film *Deutschland: 10 Millionen Menschen suchen sich, Welt im Film,*" presentation by Jo-Ellyn Decker, July 31, 2013, USHMM. Also see Child Tracing Division Records, ITS 82485874#1 (6.1.2/0001/0007–10), USHMMA.

141 *"Jews and various":* "Historical Survey of Central Tracing Activity in Germany, 1945–1951: The Tracing of Missing Persons in Germany on an International Scale with Particular Reference to the problem of U.N.R.R.A. [United Nations Relief and Rehabilitation Administration]," prepared for the personal information of the chief of operations for Germany, ITSA, 6.1.1/0001/006/, USHMMA, doc no. 82492856. Thanks to Jo-Ellyn Decker for assistance in the ITS records. As of May 1946, most displaced persons had returned to their homes and were reunited with a relative, or forcibly repatriated under the terms of the Yalta Agreement, but 3.585 million were still registered as missing. During the war, the International Committee of the Red Cross had established information bureaus and tracing services for the families of soldiers who inquired as to whether a relative had been killed in combat or in enemy hands. This service had in fact started in the 1870s and was expanded as modern warfare, during the Great War and World War II, led to larger numbers of civilian deaths and casualties; https://www.icrc.org/en/doc/resources/documents/misc/57jqrj.htm.

"the tracing problem": "The Tracing of Missing Persons in Germany," 9. The ITS has digitized about 85 percent of its collection of more than thirty million records, and it receives about a thousand inquiries each month from descendants looking for information about relatives involved in or affected by World War II. See Dan Stone, "The Memory of the Archive: The International Tracing Service and the Construction of the Past as History," *Dapim: Studies on the Holocaust* 31, no. 2 (2017): 72 and 74.

"to establish the fate": Suzanne Brown-Fleming, *Nazi Persecution and Postwar Repercussions: The International Tracing Service Archives and Holocaust Research* (Lanham, MD: Rowman and Littlefield, in association with the USHMM, 2016), 170. Stone, "The Memory of the Archive," 69–88.

142 *"the thoroughness and":* "Historical Survey of Central Tracing Activity in

Germany, 1945–1951." The International Tracing Service registered 17.5 million persons persecuted by the Nazis and their collaborators. Fourteen million pages related to them are available online: https://arolsen-archives.org/en/.

their missing relatives: Encyclopedia of Camps and Ghettos, 1933–1945, vol. 3, *Camps and Ghettos Under European Regimes Aligned with Nazi Germany*, Megargee, White, and Hecker, eds., 375.

144 *make Europe* Judenrein: Instead, Nazi ethnographers, anthropologists, and museologists curated Jewish remains and photographed the living as if they were specimens and subjects for a museum display intended to educate future Europeans about the extinct Jewish race. See Dirk Rupnow, "*'Ihr müßt sein, auch wenn ihr nicht mehr seid'* ('You have to be, even if you are no longer'): The Jewish Central Museum in Prague and Historical Memory in the Third Reich," *Holocaust and Genocide Studies* 16 (Spring 2002): 23–53.

"Several days later": Testimony of Samuel Rajzman, in *The Proceedings of the International Military Tribunal at Nuremberg*, vol. 8 (Blue Series), 328. Full testimony available at YVA, 0.3 folder 561.

145 *between 10 and 20 percent:* See Beth Cohen, *Case Closed: Holocaust Survivors in Postwar America* (New Brunswick, NJ: Rutgers University Press, 2007), and Sheila Fitzpatrick, "The Motherland Calls: 'Soft' Repatriation of Soviet Citizens from Europe, 1945–1953," *Journal of Modern History* (June 2018): 323–50. Families were reunited in part, and birth rates soared among this first generation of surviving Jews, especially in the Jewish displaced persons camps in the American zone at Feldafing and Föhrenwald. President Truman signed the Displaced Persons Act in 1948, which was expanded in 1950 to bring more European Jewish refugees to the United States to start a new life. The International Red Cross helped reunite 700,000 people with their families. Some seven million Soviet citizens were forcibly repatriated to their countries, and the last Jewish DP camps were closed in the '50s, as Jews made their way to Israel and immigration quotas were expanded and filled in America and other countries. About 140,000 Jewish survivors came to America.

"died the martyr's death": Jan Lambertz, "Early Post-war Holocaust Knowledge and the Search for Europe's Missing Jews," *Patterns of Prejudice* 53, no. 1 (2019): 61.

"When did the 'missing'": Lambertz, "Early Post-war Holocaust Knowledge," 71.

As refugees and deported: Atina Grossmann, "Remapping Relief and Rescue: Flight, Displacement, and International Aid for Jewish Refugees During World War II," *New German Critique* 117 (Fall 2012): 61–79.

147   *"At that time, during":* Zinaida L., July 23, 2016, interview code 2135.

148   *Detroit, Michigan:* Present at the interview were Svetlana's son, daughter-in-law, and her two grandchildren.

149   *the clear covers:* These albums were a craze in the 1980s and were featured in a *New York Times* article, which warned readers that the photographic heritage of the nation's sixty-four million families was in danger of being lost: "The plastic covering can be harmful not only because it completely seals the photograph in with cardboard, but because the plastic gives off gases that attack photographic images." Glenn Collins, "Fading Memories: Albums Damage Photos," *New York Times,* October 3, 1987.

150   *Svetlana's mother's father:* Author interview with Svetlana Budnitskaya, August 22, 2016, Southfield, MI.

151   *are barely visible:* Through photographs that are handed down over generations, a family constructs and preserves a collective "portrait chronicle of itself" (Sontag, *On Photography,* 8). As Susan Sontag observed (*On Photography,* 8–9), photography became a "rite of family life just when, in the industrializing countries of Europe and America, the very institution of family [underwent] radical surgery," being reduced to a nuclear unit, disaggregated from the larger human community. Photography fought against the "imperiled continuity and vanishing extendedness of family life. Those ghostly traces, photographs supply the token presence of the dispersed relatives. A family's photograph album is generally about the extended family — and, often, is all that remains of it."

meals and treats: Author and Yahad–In Unum interviews with witnesses, interview codes 2125–2137, July 19–22, 2016, Miropol. One witness recognized a Jewish woman in the family photo of the Vaselyuks and Brontzovskayas; she remembered seeing her in town. She asked herself, "Wasn't it near the marketplace behind the soda fountain and tailor's shop, not far from the former Jewish school?" Others in this generation of witnesses whose lives spanned the era of the Soviet Union continued to refer to all citizens as brothers and sisters and comrades, and a few openly displayed their anti-Semitism, scoffing at the rich Jews and the Bolshevik Jews from those days.

8. Justice

153   *lower-level German perpetrators*: See Peter Hayes's astute analysis, which shows that by 1950 the former camp commandants and the commanders of the Einsatzgruppen were mostly dead or behind bars: *Why? Explaining the Holocaust* (New York: Norton, 2017), 307–10. By contrast, the lower-level killers in the police battalions were mostly not indicted and the few brought to trial were not convicted; see Christopher Browning, *Ordinary Men: Reserve Police Battalion 101 and the Final Solution in Poland* (New York: HarperCollins, [1992] 2017), 143–46.

154   *They took on new*: See Sheila Fitzpatrick, *"Tear off the Masks!": Identity and Imposture in Twentieth-Century Russia* (Princeton, NJ: Princeton University Press, 2005). See the forthcoming book by Seth Bernstein, *Return to the Motherland: The Repatriation of Soviet Citizens after World War II.*

    "traitors to the homeland": Leonid U., July 20, 2016, interview code 2127.

    Decades later she described: Lydia S., July 21, 2016, interview code 2131. A similar account was given by Barbara B., July 21, 2016, interview code 2132.

155   *their corpses were exiled*: Barbara B., July 21, 2016, interview code 2132. Among them, Zavlyny became notorious for dragging a Jewish boy through town, tied to a bike. Later a rumor arose that the wife and daughters of Zavlyny had exhumed his body and reburied him in the Orthodox Christian cemetery.

    deportation and hard labor: Lydia S. and Fanya T., July 20, 2016, and July 21, 2016, interview codes 2129 and 2131. These interviewees had lived near the paper factory, among Jews. They named some former schoolmates, whose surnames appear on the list of those murdered in 1941: Rosa Maisich, Rachel Rapaport, Conya Chavit, Mendel and Khais Dohlinski and their daughter Fanya, and others vaguely recalled as a friend: Froika, Krypnyk who worked in the granary, and Bysharynka [?] who sold drinks at the soda fountain.

    erasure of their crimes: "On the punishment of the persons guilty in the crimes against peace and humanity and war crimes, regardless the time of the commission of the crime," Decision of the Chairman of the Presidium of the Supreme Soviet of the USSR, A. Mikoyan and the Secretary of the Presidium,

A. Georgadze, Moscow, Kremlin, March 4, 1985, in the files of KGB prosecutor, Miropol Case, p. 25. YVA, RG TR. 18, file no. 273.1.

156 *a Ukrainian nationalist:* Tarik Amar, *The Paradox of Ukrainian Lviv: A Borderland City Between Stalinists, Nazis, and Nationalists* (Ithaca, NY: Cornell University Press, 2015); Amir Weiner, "War Crimes Trials and Public Justice Soviet Style: Western Ukraine, 1940s–1980s," paper presented at the USHMM, Washington, DC, June 2005, shared with author; Franziska Exeler, "The Ambivalent State: Determining Guilt in the Post–World War II Soviet Union," *Slavic Review* 75 (2016): 606–29.

power of the Soviet system: See *Slavic Review* (Winter 2005) for a collection of essays on how collaboration was dealt with in Soviet Russia, Ukraine, and Poland. Also see Alexander Prusin, "'Fascist Criminals to the Gallows!': The Holocaust and Soviet War Crimes Trials, December 1945–February 1946," *Holocaust and Genocide Studies* 17 (Spring 2003): 1–30, and Tanja Penter, "Local Collaborators on Trial: Soviet War Crimes Trials Under Stalin (1943–1953)," *Cahiers du Monde Russe* 49, nos. 2–3 (April–September 2008): 16.

the wrong Ivan: Douglas, *The Right Wrong Man*. The Office of Special Investigations had opened within the Department of Justice in 1976, tasked with tracking down Nazi war criminals in the United States who had lied in their entry visa applications. Its first case, and among its last, was the one against Ivan Demjanjuk, a Ukrainian camp guard (Trawniki man) who was deported twice from the United States, first to stand trial in Israel as Ivan the Terrible at Treblinka, which turned out to be a case of mistaken identity. This Ivan was in fact a terrible guard, but not at Treblinka; he was instead a guard at Sobibor. Stripped of his American citizenship, he was deported again, this time to Germany, where he was convicted by a Munich court in 2011. The recent discovery of a rare wartime photo album from Sobibor includes an image of Demjanjuk.

Former collaborators tried in every way to escape punishment and mostly denied their crimes. Also see the case of Ivan Borisenko, from the Mirgorod police, who took on a false identity in Germany: USHMMA, RG 31.018m, reel 48, file 198897, frame 1738.

Major Mikola Makareyvych: In 1986, the same year that Makareyvych arrested the Ukrainian policemen who shot Jews in Miropol, Soviet Ukrainian filmmakers released the documentary *From Memory to Retribution*, which claims that thousands of Ukrainian war criminals are at large in the United States. The focus is on the mass shootings across Ukraine. Critical of western approaches, which are considered "too drawn out," the film calls for these criminals to be extradited to the Soviet Union, where, it is argued, war criminals are brought to justice professionally, expeditiously, and in earnest: https://collections.ushmm.org/search/catalog/irn1003160.

157 *"Over there, that is":* Sofia B., July 22, 2016, interview code 2133. The address of Kovalyuk matched that of the Soviet investigation of the police in 1944–45.

159 *Les'ko, whose street name:* Testimony of another policeman, Ivan Grigorievich Les'ko (not related to the defendant), November 4, 1986, YVA, RG TR.18, file 273.

During the war: Testimony of the former female Ukrainian laborer Varvara Evseevna Lysko, October 15, 1986, YVA, RG TR.18, file 273.2. During the war she was arrested by the defendant Les'ko, who placed her in a cell for two days before she was shipped to Breslau, Germany, and liberated by Americans. She also testified against Rybak in his presence, to resolve contradictions; Varvara saw him with a rifle. Statement of August 20, 1986, YVA, RG TR.18, file 273.2.

"Who are the craftsmen?": Blekhman testimony, VHA, interview code 33782, tape 4, segment 06:10.

The German authorities: Statement of Les'ko's sister, Alexandra Stepanova, June 21, 1986, YVA, RG TR.18, files 273.5 and 273.6.

When he was arrested: Arrest documents dated July 22, 1986, YVA, RG TR.18, file no. 273.1.

Gnyatuk, the son: Testimony of neighbor Mariya Tronchuk (b. 1910), and N. Gubernatorva (b. 1929). Gubernatorva stated that her friends were killed in the shootings — Sonya Shteybukh, along with her parents; Ida Gleyzer; and Nysya Vaysburg and her family. YVA, RG TR.18, file no. 273.6.

160 *Now in 1986:* Judicial Board, Criminal Case Zhitomir Regional Court, January 5, 1987, sentencing of Gnyatuk, YVA, RG TR.18, file no. 273.9.

161 *He had signed up for:* Testimony about Rybak's admirer, YVA, RG TR.18, file no. 273.2.

She explained to Makareyvych: Witness N. Gubernatorva and witness K. Yanko (b. 1920), YVA, RG TR.18, file no. 273.6.

These three defendants: Zhytomyr report on Ukrainian and ethnic German police, tabulating 10,504 in stationary and mobile units, in Captured German Records, ZSA, P1151-1-383.

162 *average ratio was 1:18:* This ratio, one German gendarme leader to eighteen Ukrainian stationary police, existed in 1942 in this region. As the war continued, the proportion of German policemen became even smaller: about one German to a hundred non-German auxiliary stationary police. In November 1941, the Higher SS and Police Leader for Ukraine reported to Berlin that in the region of Zhytomyr, where Miropol was located, the stationary regional offices in the rural areas contained a total of 772 German officers supported by 5,144 Ukrainians. These figures did not include the mobile battalions of German Order Police (such as Orpo 303 and 45) deployed in mass shootings, such as the one at Babi Yar. See the report of November 25, 1941, Bundesarchiv Koblenz, R 19/122/. Thanks to Ray Brandon for providing this document.

surrender of weapons: Himmler's order of July 25, 1941, II 208 AR-Z 25/64, in which he explains that "the tasks of the police in the occupied eastern territories cannot be fulfilled solely by the German SS and police units. We need to rely on local helpers. Already the Einsatzgruppen have done this, we can draw from Ukrainians, Baltics, Belorussians and from the non-communist POWs." And Himmler's subsequent order of July 31, 1941, delineated how to select and outfit these forces; Red Army coats could be repurposed, but with an armband showing a police officer's identification number and location. The men were officially issued rubber or wooden batons but could also use a rifle or a pistol. Later, in 1942, the formal call for police added more requirements and perks. The enlistees were to be eighteen to forty-five years old, physically fit, and a minimum 1.65 meters in height. They were supposed to be well regarded by local citizens. Compensation for service was welfare, such as lodging, food, tobacco, and soap, plus free medical treatment and free uniforms. ZSA, P1151-1-147a, microfilmed copy at the USHMM, 1996 A 0269, roll 2. The age restriction was not followed for Rybak, who was seventeen years old. Much older policemen, such as a sixty-two-year-old in Melitopol, also served; Bundesarchiv Koblenz, MA RH 36/300.

drunken militiamen: See Lower, *Nazi Empire-Building,* 42–52 and 96.

163 *reenact what happened:* Yahad–In Unum report on the trip to Miropol
and excerpts of testimony from Soviet, German, and local witnesses and records, created for the author:

> Accused G. shows the approximate location without giving the dimen-
> sions. "The policemen from Miropol brought the column of citizens
> of Jewish nationality here and made them stop about 15 meters away
> from the pit. Two Germans, whom I did not know, and a Deputy Po-
> lice Commander K. stood close to the pit. Z. ordered all the citizens
> of Jewish heritage to undress to their underwear, and after, he pointed
> to a policeman who would conduct the shooting. Among the police-
> men, there was B., P., Ivan L., T., G., and I. There were others too, but
> I forgot their names. Other policemen stayed to guard the citizens of
> Jewish nationality. The policemen who had been called by Z. had to
> line up about 5 meters away from the pit. I was at the left side of the
> pit, and L. was in the middle. Then, the policemen who were guarding
> the column, started to bring the Jews in groups of tens to the pit where
> they lined up facing the ditch. Then, all the policemen that were at
> the edge of the pit raised their rifles and fired at the people standing at
> the edge of the pit. We shot dead 6 groups of ten people of Jewish na-
> tionality each using this method. The policemen fired with rifles and
> Z. shot with a gun. When the 7th group was brought to the pit, I hurt
> myself with a breach of my weapon and Z. sent me home. Thus, during
> this execution, I personally shot dead six people of Jewish nationality.
> I do not know how the shooting was conducted after I left. I do not
> know how many people were shot in the park that day."

October 4, 1986, SBU, record group 35425, file 3, pp. 273–84. Thanks to
Yahad–In Unum for this translation, published here: https://yahadmap.org/
#village/myropil-miropol-zhytomyr-ukraine.1306.

164 *murderers of her family:* Blekhman testimony, VHA, interview code 33782,
tape 4, segment 13:130; YVA, Blekhman papers, RG .33, file no. 3037.

Ukrainian women told: Statement of Feferberg, October 12, 1986, YVA,
RG TR.18/ file no. 273.6. She stated that there were about a thousand Jews in
Miropol when she was evacuated in the summer of 1941.

"kind of hunting": YVA, from the KGB trial record, TR 18/273. Rybak
confessed, stating:

In the autumn of 1941, at the beginning of October or at the end of September, the police of Miropol started the mass shooting of the Jewish population in Miropol, including children, women and men of all ages. The shooting was carried out at the municipal park of Miropol. Approximately one kilometer from the police station of Miropol [. . .]

On the next morning, after the arrival of several police officers from the surrounding areas, all of them armed with rifles, I was given a rifle and 20 bullets. We were responsible for preventing the escape of the Jews [. . .] more than 12 to 15 police officers guarded 100 Jewish civilians. I did not know any of the Jews [. . .] Among them were people of all ages, and some of them carried little babies. I remember that each police officer shot about 15 Jewish civilians, but I cannot remember if the Jewish citizens had to take of[f] their clothes or not.

Translated excerpt published by Yad Vashem, https://www.yadvashem.org/untoldstories/database/sovietReports.asp?cid=1032&site_id=1467.

"I will not state": Umansky and Fedorovich, July 19 and 22, 2016, interview code 2126.

165 *regardless of nationality*: Prosecutor's Speech at the Trial of the Homeland Traitors, Gnyatuk, Les'ko, and Rybak, January 4, 1987, Town of Dzerzhinsk. Thank you to Natalya Lazar for translating this speech, which is deposited in the USHMMA.

166 *They did not need*: David Shneer, "Is Seeing Believing? Photographs, Eyewitness Testimony, and Evidence of the Holocaust," in *The Holocaust: Memories and History,* ed. Victoria Khiterer, Ryan Barrick, and David Misal (Newcastle, UK: Cambridge Scholars Publishing, 2014), 64–85. Shneer's work on Jewish photographers in the Red Army goes beyond the reportage and evidentiary form of the photograph to a deeper analysis of the image as a form of testimony, arguing that rather than viewing photographs as uncontested bearers of truth, we must conceptualize them as "witnesses that give testimony under interrogation [. . .] and help make people believe."

167 *"The things I saw"*: Eisenhower to Marshall, April 15, 1945, Dwight D. Eisenhower Presidential Library, Abilene, Kansas, Dwight D. Eisenhower's Pre-Presidential Papers, principal file, box 8, Marshall George C. (6); NAID #1200571.

"There was an air": Margaret Bourke-White, *"Dear Fatherland, Rest Quietly": A Report on the Collapse of Hitler's "Thousand Years"* (New York: Simon and Schuster, 1946), 73.

Eisenhower ordered: Telegram from SHAEF Supreme Commander to AGWAR, April 19, 1945, requesting official visits to the concentration camps, Dwight D. Eisenhower Presidential Library, Abilene, Kansas, Dwight D. Eisenhower's Pre-Presidential Papers, principal file, box 134, Cables Off: NAID #12007738. Also see exhibition catalog, *Liberation 1945: Days of Remembrance* (Washington, DC: USHMM, 1995).

168 *"The Pictures Don't Lie":* "The Pictures Don't Lie," *Stars and Stripes,* April 26, 1945; "Holding the Mirror up to the Huns," *Daily Mirror,* April 30, 1945. On liberation photography, see *Visual Culture and the Holocaust,* ed. Zelizer, and Janina Struk, "Liberations," in *Photographing the Holocaust,* 124–50.

Oskar Waltke: On Waltke and Lviv, see Dieter Pohl, *Nationalsozialistische Judenverfolgung Ostgalizien* (National Socialist persecution of Jews in eastern Galicia) (Berlin: De Gruyter, 1997), 422, and Eliyahu Yones, *Smoke in the Sand: The Jews of Lvov in the War Years, 1939–1944* (Jerusalem: Gefen Books, 2004), 359. Survivor Dr. Anton Winter recalled the hanging in the Lemberg ghetto in his testimony (segment 21) in the VHA.

170 *"Maybe he had shot":* Nadine Fresco, *La mort des juifs* (Paris: Éditions du Seuil, 2008). The Epstein photos are in the extensive 1944 Soviet Extraordinary Commission report, fond 7021–93–2418–2427, USHMMA. Thanks to Daniel Newman for sharing this report with me. Author interview with Zivcon's daughter, Ilana Ivanova, Liepāja, Latvia, July 5–6, 2017, with survivor witness George Schwab, who was from Liepāja. See Liepāja entry in *Encyclopedia of Camps and Ghettos, 1933–1945,* vol. 2, *Ghettos in German-Occupied Eastern Europe,* ed. Dean, 1013. For the case of the German woman in Hanover, see excerpts in Dieter Reifarth and Viktoria Schmidt-Linsenhoff, *"Die Kamera der Henker: Fotografische Selbstzeugnisse des Naziterrors in Osteuropa"* (The executioner's camera: Photographic testimonies of the Nazi terror in eastern Europe), *Fotogeschichte* 3, no. 7 (1983): 57–71. The story of Frau "Keller" (anonymized) was told to Simon Wiesenthal, who was unable to track down the killer from Vinnytsia, in Wiesenthal's *Murderers Among Us: The Simon Wiesenthal Memoirs* (New York: Bantam, 1968), 195–200.

171 *choose to look:* This position contrasts with the argument to not look presented by Susan Crane and others. See Crane's "Choosing Not to Look: Representation, Repatriation, and Holocaust Atrocity Photography," *History and Theory* 47 (October 2008), 309–30.

Epilogue: The Shoes

173 *experience into words:* See John Berger, *Ways of Seeing* (New York: Viking, 1973), and Sharon Sliwinski's excellent analysis of this phenomenon, drawing from the ideas of Kant, Arendt, and Caruth, in *Human Rights in Camera,* 95–100.

victims whom we cannot see: See Cindy Ott and Neal Maher's work on YouTube (https://www.youtube.com/watch?v=6N-xEtpyFOw) and in a forthcoming guidebook on how to deconstruct a photograph as a source. The process involves considering these features:

(1) composition, colors, scale, spatial relationships, lighting, contrast, cropping, framing;

(2) aesthetics and objects of the time, iconography, and tropes inherited culturally (polka-dot fabric, shoes, army coats, uniforms with insignias);

(3) the direction of movement, the flow of power in the action shot, from the viewfinder to the central object;

(4) the central focal point, where our eyes land first and remain;

(5) visual allegories, the family, evil, violence, humanity, witnessing, suffering in nature;

(6) materiality, such as the print, the negative, the camera model, the shutter speed, type of lens and film, the number of exposures;

(7) the viewer's distance from the subject — the closer the viewer is, the shallower the depth of field, preventing the viewer from grasping the event as a whole and its many dimensions; and

(8) the life of the image, provenance, archives, its private and public dimensions, such as its role in criminal trials, its publication in books, its display in museums, and its changing meanings and context.

174 *As historical sources:* For example, Van Gogh's images of shoes, the boots in Remarque's *All Quiet on the Western Front,* and the recurring muddy boots in

liberation photos at Dachau. For a deeper discussion of shoes as an ontological paradigm, specifically in Van Gogh's work and Heidegger's, see https://plato.stanford.edu/entries/heidegger-aesthetics. For shoes in representations of the Holocaust, see Oren Stier, *Holocaust Icons: Symbolizing the Shoah in History and Memory* (New Brunswick, NJ: Rutgers University Press, 2015), 15–16; and https://encyclopedia.ushmm.org/tags/en/tag/shoes.

"The feet from these": Abraham Sutzkever, "A Load of Shoes," trans. C. K. Williams, reprinted in Eric Sundquist's *Writing in Witness,* 98–99.

175 *behind glass in Birkenau:* The artifact collections are vast and include many personal effects, which specialists in material culture and conservators are interpreting in new ways. See Leora Auslander and Tara Zahra, *Objects of War: The Material Culture of Conflict and Displacement* (Ithaca, NY: Cornell University Press, 2018). When Vassily Grosmann liberated towns and Nazi camps in Poland and Ukraine as a journalist with the Red Army, he immediately grasped the meaning of these objects, the bric-a-brac of bones mixed with the materials that make us human, including the photographs found among the "rotting" dead. He wrote this about Treblinka, a camp that he liberated, in "Treblinka" (1944):

> The earth ejects from itself crushed bones, teeth, various objects, bits of paper; it does not want to keep the secret.
>
> These things ooze from the earth's unhealed wounds. They lie there: the half-rotten shirts that belonged to the ones murdered, their trousers and slippers, moldy cigarette cases, cogwheels from watches, penknives, shaving kits, candlesticks, children's shoes with red tassels, towels with Ukrainian embroidery, lace underwear, scissors, thimbles, corsets and trusses [...] Further on — as if someone's hand had forced them from the depths of the bottomless, swollen earth up into the light — are half-rotten Soviet passports, notebooks with Bulgarian writing, photographs of children from Warsaw and Vienna, letters scribbled by children, books of poetry, a prayer jotted down on a yellow slip of paper, food ration cards from Germany [...] Hovering over everything is the horrible stench of decay; nothing can overcome it, neither fire nor sun nor rain or snow and wind. And hundreds of tiny forest flies swarm around the rotting objects, the bits of paper, the photographs.

176 *Holocaust photographs:* In genocide studies an entire subfield has developed on atrocity prevention. Among its least appreciated tools is the camera. Over a century ago, while millions of Congolese were being enslaved, tortured, and killed under the brutal rubber-extracting regime of King Leopold of Belgium, Mark Twain wrote about the "incorruptible Kodak" as the "only witness that [the King] couldn't bribe" despite all his efforts to "ferret them out and suppress them." See Twain's *King Leopold's Soliloquy: A Defense of His Congo Rule* (Boston: P. R. Warren Co., 1905), 38. The camera could resist, as we see, in the hands of Škrovina, but it was also a tool of violence in the hands of the killers and accomplices. Josefine Block, a female perpetrator in Drohobych, Ukraine, beat, taunted, and mocked Jewish families with her camera as they were gathered in the marketplace before deportation to a gassing center in Poland. Another female accomplice, Vera Wolhauf, was also seen taking photos of Jews while they were being deported to Treblinka; see Wendy Lower, *Hitler's Furies: German Women in the Nazi Killing Fields* (Boston: Houghton Mifflin Harcourt, 2013).

"a world of fact": Aoife Duffy, "Bearing Witness to Atrocity Crimes: Photography and International Law," *Human Rights Quarterly* (2018): 777.

"transfer of the real": Piyel Halder, "The Evidencer's Eye: Representations of Truth in the Laws of Evidence," *Law and Critique* 2 (1991): 171–89.

177 *As readers and viewers:* Marianne Hirsch's work also stresses the agency of the photograph, but in the personal, mostly affective experience of memory shared among Holocaust survivors and victims and transmitted to their descendants. Hirsch, *The Generation of Postmemory,* and Hirsch, "Surviving Images: Holocaust Photographs and the Work of Postmemory," in *Visual Culture and the Holocaust,* ed. Zelizer, 215–46. Since Susan Sontag's provocative, indignant book *On Photography* was published, the debate over the ethics of the photographer has given way to nuanced theories, drawing from the ideas of Walter Benjamin and Roland Barthes and continuing with more recent studies by Georges Didi-Huberman, among others, illuminating the many facets of the image as a cultural and aesthetic object, as historical evidence, as an act of bearing witness, as a memory and artifact of trauma, and as an icon and anomaly. Didi-Huberman, *Images in Spite of All;* Heide Fehrenbach and Davide Rodogno, eds., *Humanitarian Photography: A History* (Cambridge,

UK: Cambridge University Press, 2015); Crane, "Choosing Not to Look";
Ariella Azoulay, *The Civil Contract with Photography* (Brooklyn, NY: Zone
Books, 2012); Susie Linfield, *The Cruel Radiance: Photography and Political
Violence* (Chicago: University of Chicago Press, 2010); David Shneer, *Grief:
The Biography of a Holocaust Photograph* (New York: Oxford University Press,
2020); Evans, Hoffmann, and Betts, eds., *The Ethics of Seeing.*

"We are witnessing": For Churchill's speech of August 24, 1941, see Rich-
ard Breitman, *Official Secrets: What the Nazis Planned, What the British and
Americans Knew* (New York: Hill and Wang, 1998), 93–94, and James Waller,
Confronting Evil: Engaging Our Responsibility to Prevent Genocide (New York:
Oxford University Press, 2019), 3–5.

ILLUSTRATION CREDITS

Security Services Archive, Historical Collection of the State Security Service (StB) Prague, archival no. H-770-3: German guards and Ukrainian militia shooting a Jewish family, Miropol, Ukraine, October 13, 1941 (page 3); The killers (page 7); The family (page 8); The forest (page 9); A local Ukrainian accessory (page 10); German guards and Ukrainian militia shooting a Jewish family, Miropol, Ukraine, October 13, 1941 (page 70); German guard surrounded by killers, shooting a Jewish woman, Miropol, Ukraine, October 13, 1941 (page 71, top); German guard shooting a Jewish woman at a second mass grave, Miropol, Ukraine, October 13, 1941 (page 71, bottom); Jewish victims inside the mass grave (page 72, top); Resisters killed on the path to the shooting site (page 72, bottom); The shoes (page 174).

German Federal Archives, Bundesarchiv Ludwigsburg: The crime report (page 38).

Courtesy of the Škrovina family: The photographer Lubomir Škrovina, seated in the center, Miropol, Ukraine, September 17, 1941 (page 82).

Courtesy of the author: Lubomir Škrovina's camera, Bratislava, September 2017 (page 91).

Courtesy of Yad Vashem, Jerusalem: The Sandler and Vaselyuk families, Miropol, Ukraine, 1941 (page 101); Forensic experts display the victims' bones, Miropol, Ukraine, October 1986 (page 134); Exhuming the mass graves, Miropol, Ukraine, October 1986 (page 135). Arrest photograph of former Ukrainian militiaman N. Rybak, 1986 (page 158, top); Arrest photograph of former Ukrainian militiaman D. Gnyatuk, 1986 (page 158, bottom); Former Ukrainian militiaman D. Gnyatuk reenacting what happened at the crime scene, Miropol, Ukraine, 1986 (page 163).

United States Holocaust Memorial Museum: Women searching through the shoes of the deported Jews, Szeged synagogue, by the photographer Bela Liebmann, 1945 (page 143).

INDEX

Page references in *italics* refer to photographs.